Astronomy

PRENTICE HALL Science Explorer

PEARSON

Boston, Massachusetts
Glenview, Illinois
Shoreview, Minnesota
Upper Saddle River, New Jersey

Astronomy

Book-Specific Resources

Student Edition
StudentExpress™ CD-ROM
Interactive Textbook Online
Teacher's Edition
All-in-One Teaching Resources
Color Transparencies
Guided Reading and Study Workbook
Student Edition in MP3 Audio
Discovery Channel School® Video
Consumable and Nonconsumable Materials Kits

Program Print Resources

Integrated Science Laboratory Manual
Computer Microscope Lab Manual
Inquiry Skills Activity Books
Progress Monitoring Assessments
Test Preparation Workbook
Test-Taking Tips With Transparencies
Teacher's ELL Handbook
Reading Strategies for Science Content

Differentiated Instruction Resources

Adapted Reading and Study Workbook
Adapted Tests
Differentiated Instruction Guide for Labs and Activities

Program Technology Resources

TeacherExpress™ CD-ROM
Interactive Textbooks Online
PresentationExpress™ CD-ROM
ExamView®, Test Generator CD-ROM
Lab zone™ Easy Planner CD-ROM
Probeware Lab Manual With CD-ROM
Computer Microscope and Lab Manual
Materials Ordering CD-ROM
Discovery Channel School® DVD Library
Lab Activity Video Library—DVD and VHS
Web Site at PearsonSchool.com

Spanish Print Resources

Spanish Student Edition
Spanish Guided Reading and Study Workbook
Spanish Teaching Guide With Tests

Acknowledgments appear on page 198, which constitutes an extension of this copyright page.

Cover
The Horsehead Nebula is part of a dark cosmic dust cloud in front of a bright red nebula of glowing gas (top). *Valles Marineris* seen from one of Mars's moons (bottom).

13-digit ISBN 978-0-13-365110-2
10-digit ISBN 0-13-365110-X
10 V063 12

Program Authors

Michael J. Padilla, Ph.D.
Associate Dean and Director
Eugene T. Moore School of Education
Clemson University
Clemson, South Carolina

Michael Padilla is a leader in middle school science education. He has served as an author and elected officer for the National Science Teachers Association and as a writer of the National Science Education Standards. As lead author of Science Explorer, Mike has inspired the team in developing a program that meets the needs of middle grades students, promotes science inquiry, and is aligned with the National Science Education Standards.

Ioannis Miaoulis, Ph.D.
President
Museum of Science
Boston, Massachusetts

Originally trained as a mechanical engineer, Ioannis Miaoulis is in the forefront of the national movement to increase technological literacy. As dean of the Tufts University School of Engineering, Dr. Miaoulis spearheaded the introduction of engineering into the Massachusetts curriculum. Currently he is working with school systems across the country to engage students in engineering activities and to foster discussions on the impact of science and technology on society.

Martha Cyr, Ph.D.
Director of K–12 Outreach
Worcester Polytechnic Institute
Worcester, Massachusetts

Martha Cyr is a noted expert in engineering outreach. She has over nine years of experience with programs and activities that emphasize the use of engineering principles, through hands-on projects, to excite and motivate students and teachers of mathematics and science in grades K–12. Her goal is to stimulate a continued interest in science and mathematics through engineering.

Book Author

Jay M. Pasachoff, Ph.D.
Professor of Astronomy
Williams College
Williamstown, Massachusetts

Contributing Writers

W. Russell Blake, Ph.D.
Planetarium Director
Plymouth Community
    Intermediate School
Plymouth, Massachusetts

Namoi Pasachoff, Ph.D.
Research Associate
Williams College
Williamstown, Massachusetts

Thomas R. Wellnitz
Science Instructor
The Paideia School
Atlanta, Georgia

Consultants

Reading Consultant

Nancy Romance, Ph.D.
Professor of Science
    Education
Florida Atlantic University
Fort Lauderdale, Florida

Mathematics Consultant

William Tate, Ph.D.
Professor of Education and
    Applied Statistics and
    Computation
Washington University
St. Louis, Missouri

Reviewers

Teacher Reviewers

David R. Blakely
Arlington High School
Arlington, Massachusetts

Jane E. Callery
Two Rivers Magnet Middle
School
East Hartford, Connecticut

Melissa Lynn Cook
Oakland Mills High School
Columbia, Maryland

James Fattic
Southside Middle School
Anderson, Indiana

Dan Gabel
Hoover Middle School
Rockville, Maryland

Wayne Goates
Eisenhower Middle School
Goddard, Kansas

Katherine Bobay Graser
Mint Hill Middle School
Charlotte, North Carolina

Darcy Hampton
Deal Junior High School
Washington, D.C.

Karen Kelly
Pierce Middle School
Waterford, Michigan

David Kelso
Manchester High School Central
Manchester, New Hampshire

Benigno Lopez, Jr.
Sleepy Hill Middle School
Lakeland, Florida

Angie L. Matamoros, Ph.D.
ALM Consulting, INC.
Weston, Florida

Tim McCollum
Charleston Middle School
Charleston, Illinois

Bruce A. Mellin
Brooks School
North Andover, Massachusetts

Ella Jay Parfitt
Southeast Middle School
Baltimore, Maryland

Evelyn A. Pizzarello
Louis M. Klein Middle School
Harrison, New York

Kathleen M. Poe
Fletcher Middle School
Jacksonville, Florida

Shirley Rose
Lewis and Clark Middle School
Tulsa, Oklahoma

Linda Sandersen
Greenfield Middle School
Greenfield, Wisconsin

Mary E. Solan
Southwest Middle School
Charlotte, North Carolina

Mary Stewart
University of Tulsa
Tulsa, Oklahoma

Paul Swenson
Billings West High School
Billings, Montana

Thomas Vaughn
Arlington High School
Arlington, Massachusetts

Susan C. Zibell
Central Elementary
Simsbury, Connecticut

Safety Reviewers

W. H. Breazeale, Ph.D.
Department of Chemistry
College of Charleston
Charleston, South Carolina

Ruth Hathaway, Ph.D.
Hathaway Consulting
Cape Girardeau, Missouri

Douglas Mandt, M.S.
Science Education Consultant
Edgewood, Washington

Activity Field Testers

Nicki Bibbo
Witchcraft Heights School
Salem, Massachusetts

Rose-Marie Botting
Broward County Schools
Fort Lauderdale, Florida

Colleen Campos
Laredo Middle School
Aurora, Colorado

Elizabeth Chait
W. L. Chenery Middle School
Belmont, Massachusetts

Holly Estes
Hale Middle School
Stow, Massachusetts

Laura Hapgood
Plymouth Community
Intermediate School
Plymouth, Massachusetts

Mary F. Lavin
Plymouth Community
Intermediate School
Plymouth, Massachusetts

James MacNeil, Ph.D.
Cambridge, Massachusetts

Lauren Magruder
St. Michael's Country
Day School
Newport, Rhode Island

Jeanne Maurand
Austin Preparatory School
Reading, Massachusetts

Joanne Jackson-Pelletier
Winman Junior High School
Warwick, Rhode Island

Warren Phillips
Plymouth Public Schools
Plymouth, Massachusetts

Carol Pirtle
Hale Middle School
Stow, Massachusetts

Kathleen M. Poe
Fletcher Middle School
Jacksonville, Florida

Cynthia B. Pope
Norfolk Public Schools
Norfolk, Virginia

Anne Scammell
Geneva Middle School
Geneva, New York

Karen Riley Sievers
Callanan Middle School
Des Moines, Iowa

David M. Smith
Eyer Middle School
Allentown, Pennsylvania

Gene Vitale
Parkland School
McHenry, Illinois

Contents

Astronomy

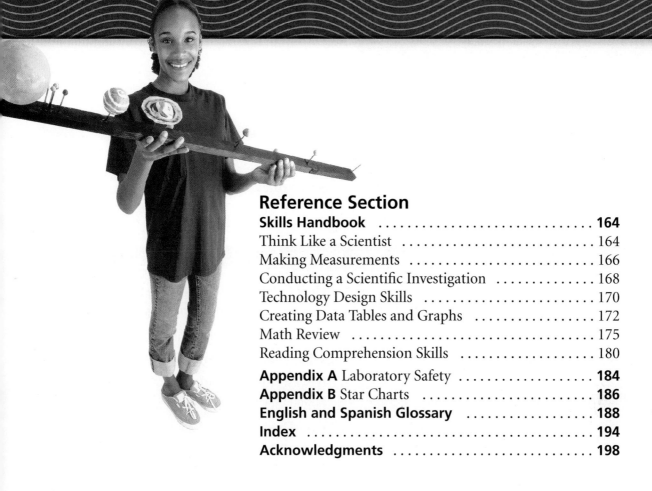

Reference Section

VIDEO

Enhance understanding through dynamic video.

Preview Get motivated with this introduction to the chapter content.

Field Trip Explore a real-world story related to the chapter content.

Assessment Review content and take an assessment.

Web Links

Get connected to exciting Web resources in every lesson.

SciLINKS NSTA Find Web links on topics relating to every section.

Active Art Interact with selected visuals from every chapter online.

Planet Diary® Explore news and natural phenomena through weekly reports.

Science News® Keep up to date with the latest science discoveries.

Experience the complete textbook online and on CD-ROM.

Activities Practice skills and learn content.

Videos Explore content and learn important lab skills.

Audio Support Hear key terms spoken and defined.

Self-Assessment Use instant feedback to help you track your progress.

Activities

Image of the sun ▶

A Solar Astronomer

Leonard Strachan always knew he wanted to be an astronomer. "The funny thing is: I thought I'd be a nighttime astronomer with a telescope. I'd go up on a mountain and study the stars at night."

But Leonard doesn't study the night sky. "I'm a daytime astronomer. I study the sun." And the instruments he uses are not on a mountaintop. They are on a satellite in space between Earth and the sun. The satellite's name is SOHO—the Solar and Heliospheric Observatory.

"The sun," Leonard says, "doesn't just shine as a steady yellow ball. It's always changing. Every so often the sun shoots out a huge cloud of gas particles into space. Within days the particles crash into Earth's upper atmosphere. They cause auroras: shimmering, glowing light shows in the sky. The particles interfere with radio waves. Pagers and cell phones can stop working. Even our electrical power can be affected. Telecommunications, weather satellites, and military operations are all affected by the space weather caused by the sun."

An instrument on SOHO, the Solar and Heliospheric Observatory (above), generated this image of the sun (top). SOHO is positioned in space between Earth and the sun.

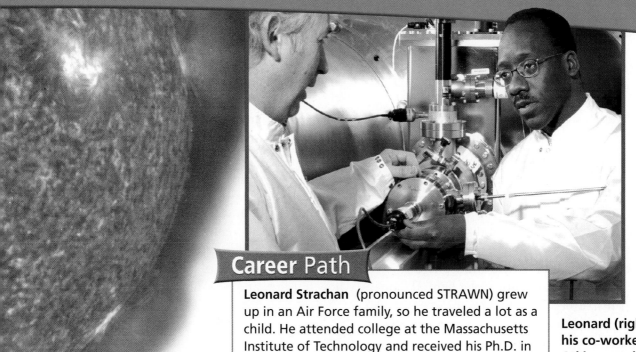

Career Path

Leonard Strachan (pronounced STRAWN) grew up in an Air Force family, so he traveled a lot as a child. He attended college at the Massachusetts Institute of Technology and received his Ph.D. in astronomy from Harvard University. Since 1991 he has been an Astrophysicist at the Harvard-Smithsonian Center for Astrophysics in Cambridge, Massachusetts. He enjoys giving talks at museums and schools as part of NASA's public outreach program.

Leonard (right) and his co-worker Nigel Atkins are shown here operating an ultraviolet lamp used for testing one of the instruments on SOHO.

Talking With **Dr. Leonard Strachan**

? How did you become interested in astronomy?

I was hooked from the very beginning. When I was in second grade in Washington, D.C., some high-school students gave a slide presentation on the stars. Later on, I started reading books on astronomy and science fiction. I loved thinking about what it would be like living on Mars or traveling to a black hole or moving at the speed of light. When I was in seventh grade, I asked my dad for an amateur telescope. I'd take it out every clear night and look at the stars.

? What do you study about the sun?

Most of my work involves learning about the solar corona and what causes the solar wind. The corona is the hot outer atmosphere of the sun. Just like Earth has an atmosphere, the sun, too, has an outer layer. But the sun is a ball of glowing gases with no solid surface inside. What we call the "surface" is just the layer where most of the visible light comes from. Most of the mass of the sun is inside that ball of light we can see. Above that is the corona, where it's super hot, about one or two million degrees Celsius.

The corona is so hot that most of the individual atoms in it are split apart. The heating of the corona may also force these particles to fly away from the sun. That stream of particles is called the solar wind. It can go as fast as 800 kilometers per second. It blows past Earth, past all the planets, out beyond the edge of the solar system.

Why can't you observe the corona from Earth?

The best way to study the sun is to look at all the light and energy it gives off, not just the visible light that our eyes can see. The photosphere, the surface layer of the sun, gives off mostly visible light. But the corona is hotter. Most of its light is invisible. We can only "see" invisible kinds of light, such as ultraviolet light and x-rays, with special equipment.

The problem is that Earth's atmosphere absorbs most of the sun's ultraviolet light. If you want your instruments to measure the sun's invisible light, you have to be in space, above the atmosphere.

So we go way beyond the atmosphere. That's where our SOHO satellite is. It's always between the sun and Earth so that it can observe the sun 24 hours a day. There are no eclipses and no atmosphere, and you can look at all wavelengths of light. That's the big advantage to being out there.

What instruments do you use?

The UVCS is an instrument which is both a coronagraph and a spectrometer. A coronagraph is needed to block out the bright disk of the sun so that the much fainter corona can be seen. A spectrometer spreads light out in a spectrum, a pattern of light and dark lines. Different elements in the sun, at different temperatures, have their own special pattern of lines. By looking at the patterns, we can tell what kind of particles are in the corona, how hot they are, even how fast they're going.

This all happens on SOHO?

Sure. We send commands up every day by radio to point the instrument to specific targets. That takes place at NASA's Goddard Space Flight Center in Maryland. We have three people there who "talk" to the satellite on a daily basis.

Projects like SOHO require people from all over the country, all over the world. In addition to Americans, we have Italians, a Russian, a Chinese, and a Palestinian. It's a really international project. We work and meet with each other all the time.

A model of the Ultraviolet Coronagraph Spectrometer (or UVCS) is shown here with Leonard. The UVCS is one of twelve instruments on the SOHO spacecraft.

This is a composite image made with two of the instruments on SOHO.

? How will you answer your questions?

I plan and analyze observations that can be used to prove whether our theories about the sun are correct. I also work with people who create the theories and others who build the instruments. The instruments are important because without them we would not have the much needed information that tells us what is happening right at the sun.

This work is fascinating. It's something I'd recommend to anybody who likes solving problems. They don't have to be grand problems, like figuring out how the universe began. You look at small things, and piece those small problems together. Eventually you build a bigger picture that helps us understand our universe.

? What are some unanswered questions?

One big question is: What makes the solar corona so hot? At first, it doesn't make sense. The central region of the sun is incredibly hot, about 30 million degrees Celsius. As you move away from the center, the sun's gases cool down so they are only about 6,000 degrees Celsius at the surface. But then, for reasons we don't fully understand, it suddenly rises back to millions of degrees in the corona, above the surface. It's as if your hand became warmer when you moved it away from a fire. You would expect it to get cooler when you move it away. With our UVCS instrument, we can look at the light from individual particles in the corona and maybe find out what's happening.

We want to understand what happens in the corona because the solar wind comes from there. We want to know how the particles in the corona speed up in the solar wind. And in the future, we would like to be able to predict the big explosions in the corona that can cause space weather. It is these explosions that kick out the gas clouds that can disrupt Earth's magnetic field.

Leonard shows a high school student how to find a planet.

Writing in Science

Career Link Leonard says he loved reading science fiction as a boy. He enjoyed imagining what it would be like to live on Mars or travel in space. This energized his desire to learn about science—like understanding how the conditions on Mars came to be. Write a paragraph in which you imagine what it would it be like to live on Mars. Include scientific information in your paragraph.

For: More on this career
Visit: PHSchool.com
Web Code: cfb-5000

Chapter 1

Earth, Moon, and Sun

The BIG Idea
Motion and Forces

 What effects are caused by the motions of Earth and the moon?

This time-lapse photo shows an eclipse of the moon as it rises over the Golden Gate Bridge in San Francisco.

Lab zone™ Chapter **Project**

Track the Moon

How does the moon move across the sky? How does its appearance change over the course of a month? In this project, you will observe how the position and apparent shape of the moon change over time.

Your Goal To observe the shape of the moon and its position in the sky every day for one month

To complete this project, you must

- observe the compass direction in which you see the moon, its phase, and its height above the horizon
- use your observations to explain the phases of the moon
- develop rules you can use to predict when and where you might see the moon each day

Plan It! Begin by preparing an observation log. You will record the date and time of each observation, the direction and height of the moon, a sketch of its shape, and notes about cloud cover and other conditions. Observe the moon every clear night, looking for patterns. Make a map of your observation site on which you will plot the direction of the moon. You can measure the moon's height in degrees above the horizon by making a fist and holding it at arm's length. One fist above the horizon is 10°, two fists are 20°, and so on. On at least one day, compare your observations of the moon an hour or two apart.

Earth in Space

Reading Preview

Key Concepts
- How does Earth move in space?
- What causes the cycle of seasons on Earth?

Key Terms
- astronomy • axis • rotation
- revolution • orbit • calendar
- solstice • equinox

Target Reading Skill
Using Prior Knowledge Your prior knowledge is what you already know before you read about a topic. Before you read, write what you know about seasons on Earth in a graphic organizer like the one below. As you read, write in what you learn.

What You Know
1. The sun's rays heat Earth.
2.

What You Learned
1.
2.

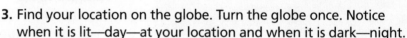

Lab zone Discover Activity

What Causes Day and Night?

1. Place a lamp with a bare bulb on a table to represent the sun. Put a globe at the end of the table about 1 meter away to represent Earth.
2. Turn the lamp on and darken the room. Which parts of the globe have light shining on them? Which parts are in shadow?
3. Find your location on the globe. Turn the globe once. Notice when it is lit—day—at your location and when it is dark—night.

Think It Over
Making Models What does one complete turn of the globe represent? In this model, how many seconds represent one day? How could you use the globe and bulb to represent a year?

Each year, ancient Egyptian farmers eagerly awaited the flood of the Nile River. For thousands of years, their planting was ruled by it. As soon as the Nile's floodwaters withdrew, the farmers had to be ready to plow and plant their fields along the river. Therefore, the Egyptians wanted to predict when the flood would occur. Around 3000 B.C., people noticed that the bright star Sirius first became visible in the early morning sky every year shortly before the flood began. The Egyptians used this knowledge to predict each year's flood. The ancient Egyptians were among the first people to study the stars. The study of the moon, stars, and other objects in space is called **astronomy.**

FIGURE 1
Ancient Egyptian Farmers
Egyptian farmers watched the sky in order to be prepared to plow and plant their fields.

How Earth Moves

Ancient astronomers studied the movements of the sun and the moon as they appeared to travel across the sky. It seemed to them as though Earth was standing still and the sun and moon were moving. Actually, the sun and moon seem to move across the sky each day because Earth is rotating on its axis. Earth also moves around the sun. **Earth moves through space in two major ways: rotation and revolution.**

Rotation The imaginary line that passes through Earth's center and the North and South poles is Earth's **axis.** The spinning of Earth on its axis is called **rotation.**

Earth's rotation causes day and night. As Earth rotates eastward, the sun appears to move westward across the sky. It is day on the side of Earth facing the sun. As Earth continues to turn to the east, the sun appears to set in the west. Sunlight can't reach the side of Earth facing away from the sun, so it is night there. It takes Earth about 24 hours to rotate once. As you know, each 24-hour cycle of day and night is called a day.

Revolution In addition to rotating on its axis, Earth travels around the sun. **Revolution** is the movement of one object around another. One complete revolution of Earth around the sun is called a year. Earth follows a path, or **orbit,** as it revolves around the sun. Earth's orbit is not quite circular. It is a slightly elongated circle, or ellipse.

FIGURE 2
Rotation
The rotation of Earth on its axis is similar to the movement of the figure skater as she spins.

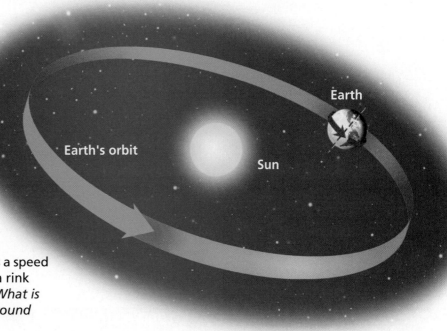

FIGURE 3
Revolution
Earth revolves around the sun just as a speed skater travels around the center of a rink during a race. **Applying Concepts** *What is one complete revolution of Earth around the sun called?*

Calendars People of many different cultures have struggled to establish calendars based on the length of time that Earth takes to revolve around the sun. A **calendar** is a system of organizing time that defines the beginning, length, and divisions of a year.

The ancient Egyptians created one of the first calendars. Egyptian astronomers counted the number of days between each first appearance of the star Sirius in the morning. In this way, they found that there are about 365 days in a year.

Dividing the year into smaller parts was also difficult. Early people used moon cycles to divide the year. The time from one full moon to the next is about $29\frac{1}{2}$ days. A year of 12 of these "moonths" adds up to only 354 days. The ancient Egyptian calendar had 12 months of 30 days each, with an extra 5 days at the end.

Science and **History**

Tracking the Cycle of the Year
For thousands of years, people have used observations of the sky to keep track of the time of year.

1500 B.C. British Isles
Ancient peoples complete Stonehenge, a monument with giant stones that mark the directions in which the sun rises and sets on the shortest and longest days of the year.

1300 B.C. China
Chinese astronomers make detailed observations of the sun, planets, and other objects they see in the night sky. Chinese astronomers calculated that the length of a year is $365\frac{1}{4}$ days.

80 B.C. Greece
Astronomers in Greece develop an instrument called the Antikythera Calculator. This instrument used a system of gears to show the movement of the sun, moon, planets, and stars.

1500 B.C.   **1000 B.C.**   **500 B.C.**

The Romans borrowed the Egyptian calendar of 365 days. But in fact, Earth orbits the sun in about $365\frac{1}{4}$ days. The Romans adjusted the Egyptian calendar by adding one day every four years. You know this fourth year as "leap year." During a leap year, February is given 29 days instead of its usual 28. Using a system of leap years helps to ensure that annual events, such as the beginning of summer, occur on the same date each year.

The Roman calendar was off by a little more than 11 minutes a year. Over the centuries, these minutes added up. By the 1500s, the beginning of spring was about ten days too early. To straighten things out, Pope Gregory XIII dropped ten days from the year 1582. He also made some other minor changes to the Roman system to form the calendar that we use today.

 **Reading Checkpoint**   **What is a leap year?**

Writing in Science

Writing Dialogue Research one of the accomplishments discussed in the timeline. Write a conversation, or dialogue, in which two people from the time and culture that made the discovery or structure discuss its importance in their lives. Examples might include their work or the timing of their celebrations.

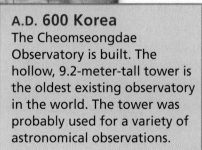

A.D. 900 Mexico
The Mayas study the movement of the sun, the moon, and the planet Venus. They had two different calendars, one with 365 days for everyday use and the other with 260 days for religious uses.

A.D. 1600 Turkey
Astronomers use a variety of astronomical instruments, including astrolabes, at an observatory in Istanbul. Astrolabes were used to predict the positions of stars and planets.

A.D. 600 Korea
The Cheomseongdae Observatory is built. The hollow, 9.2-meter-tall tower is the oldest existing observatory in the world. The tower was probably used for a variety of astronomical observations.

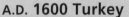

| A.D. 500 | A.D. 1000 | A.D. 1500 |

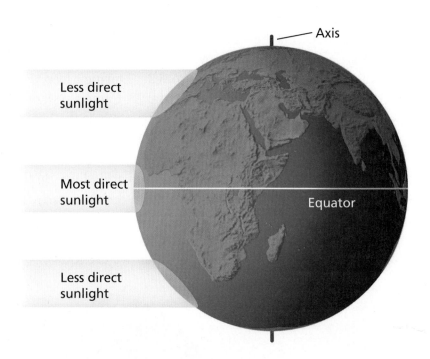

Axis

Less direct
sunlight

Most direct
sunlight

Equator

Less direct
sunlight

FIGURE 4
Sunlight Striking Earth's Surface
Near the equator, sunlight strikes
Earth's surface more directly and is
less spread out than near the poles.
Relating Cause and Effect *Why is it
usually colder near the poles than
near the equator?*

**Lab
zone** Try This **Activity**

Sun Shadows

The sun's shadow changes
predictably through the day.

1. On a sunny day, stand
   outside in the sun and use
   a compass to find north.

2. Have your partner place a
   craft stick about one meter
   to the north of where you
   are standing. Repeat for
   east, south, and west.

3. Insert a meter stick in the
   ground at the center of the
   craft sticks. Make sure the
   stick is straight up.

4. Predict how the sun's
   shadow will move
   throughout the day.

5. Record the direction and
   length of the sun's shadow
   at noon and at regular
   intervals during the day.

Predicting How did the
actual movement of the sun's
shadow compare with your
prediction? How do you think
the direction and length of
the sun's shadow at these
same times would change
over the next six months?

The Seasons on Earth

Most places outside the tropics and polar regions have four
distinct seasons: winter, spring, summer, and autumn. But
there are great differences in temperature from place to place.
For instance, it is generally warmer near the equator than near
the poles. Why is this so?

How Sunlight Hits Earth Figure 4 shows how sunlight
strikes Earth's surface. Notice that sunlight hits Earth's surface
most directly near the equator. Near the poles, sunlight arrives
at a steep angle. As a result, it is spread out over a greater area.
That is why it is warmer near the equator than near the poles.

Earth's Tilted Axis If Earth's axis were straight up and
down relative to its orbit, temperatures would remain fairly
constant year-round. There would be no seasons. **Earth has
seasons because its axis is tilted as it revolves around the sun.**

Notice in Figure 5 that Earth's axis is always tilted at an
angle of 23.5° from the vertical. As Earth revolves around the
sun, the north end of its axis is tilted away from the sun for part
of the year and toward the sun for part of the year.

Summer and winter are caused by Earth's tilt as it revolves
around the sun. The change in seasons is not caused by changes
in Earth's distance from the sun. In fact, Earth is farthest from
the sun when it is summer in the Northern Hemisphere.

 **Reading
Checkpoint** When is Earth farthest from the sun?

FIGURE 5

The Seasons

The yearly cycle of the seasons is caused by the tilt of Earth's axis as it revolves around the sun.

Go Online
active art

For: Seasons activity
Visit: PHSchool.com
Web Code: cfp-5012

June Solstice
The north end of Earth's axis is tilted toward the sun. It is summer in the Northern Hemisphere and winter in the Southern Hemisphere.

March Equinox

June Solstice

December Solstice

March and September Equinoxes
Neither end of Earth's axis is tilted toward the sun. Both hemispheres receive the same amount of energy.

September Equinox

December Solstice
The south end of Earth's axis is tilted toward the sun. It is summer in the Southern Hemisphere and winter in the Northern Hemisphere.

The height of the sun above the horizon varies with the season.
Interpreting Graphics *When is the sun at its maximum height in the Northern Hemisphere?*

S   N
E

June Solstice

S   N
E

March and September Equinoxes

S   N
E

December Solstice

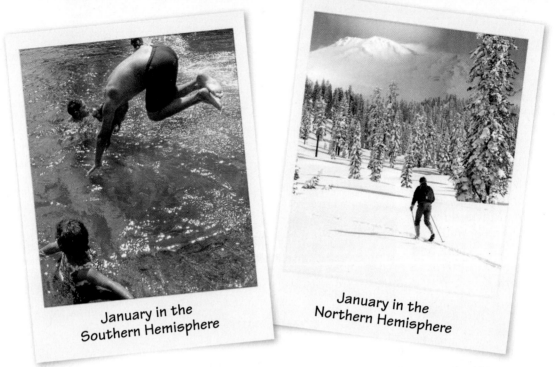

January in the Southern Hemisphere

January in the Northern Hemisphere

Solstices and Equinoxes

Summer in the Southern Hemisphere (left) occurs at the same time as winter in the Northern Hemisphere (right). Similarly, when it is spring in the Southern Hemisphere, it is fall in the Northern Hemisphere. **Interpreting Photographs** *In which direction was Earth's axis pointing at the time that each of the photographs was taken?*

Earth in June In June, the north end of Earth's axis is tilted toward the sun. In the Northern Hemisphere, the noon sun is high in the sky and there are more hours of daylight than darkness. The combination of direct rays and more hours of sunlight heats the surface more in June than at any other time of the year. It is summer in the Northern Hemisphere.

At the same time south of the equator, the sun's energy is spread over a larger area. The sun is low in the sky and days are shorter than nights. The combination of less direct rays and fewer hours of sunlight heats Earth's surface less than at any other time of the year. It is winter in the Southern Hemisphere.

Earth in December In December, people in the Southern Hemisphere receive the most direct sunlight, so it is summer there. At the same time, the sun's rays in the Northern Hemisphere are more slanted and there are fewer hours of daylight. So it is winter in the Northern Hemisphere.

Solstices The sun reaches its greatest distance north or south of the equator twice each year. Each of these days, when the sun is farthest north or south of the equator, is known as a **solstice** (SOHL stis). The day when the sun is farthest north of the equator is the summer solstice in the Northern Hemisphere. It is also the winter solstice in the Southern Hemisphere. This solstice occurs around June 21 each year. It is the longest day of the year in the Northern Hemisphere and the shortest day of the year in the Southern Hemisphere.

Similarly, around December 21, the sun is farthest south of the equator. This is the winter solstice in the Northern Hemisphere and the summer solstice in the Southern Hemisphere.

October in the
Southern Hemisphere

October in the
Northern Hemisphere

Equinoxes Halfway between the solstices, neither hemisphere is tilted toward or away from the sun. This occurs twice a year, when the noon sun is directly overhead at the equator. Each of these days is known as an **equinox,** which means "equal night." During an equinox, day and night are each about 12 hours long everywhere on Earth. The vernal (spring) equinox occurs around March 21 and marks the beginning of spring in the Northern Hemisphere. The autumnal equinox occurs around September 22. It marks the beginning of fall in the Northern Hemisphere.

 **Reading Checkpoint**   **What is an equinox?**

Section 1 Assessment

Target Reading Skill Using Prior Knowledge Review your graphic organizer and revise it based on what you just learned in this section. Use it to help answer Question 2.

Reviewing Key Concepts

1. **a. Identifying** What are the two major motions of Earth as it travels through space?
   b. Explaining Which motion causes day and night?
2. **a. Relating Cause and Effect** What causes the seasons?
   b. Comparing and Contrasting What are solstices and equinoxes? How are they related to the seasons?
   c. Predicting How would the seasons be different if Earth were not tilted on its axis?

Writing in Science

Descriptive Paragraph What seasons occur where you live? Write a detailed paragraph describing the changes that take place each season in your region. Explain how seasonal changes in temperature and hours of daylight relate to changes in Earth's position as it moves around the sun.

Reasons for the Seasons

Problem

How does the tilt of Earth's axis affect the light received by Earth as it revolves around the sun?

Skills Focus

making models, observing, inferring, predicting

Materials (per pair of students)

- books
- flashlight
- paper
- pencil
- protractor
- toothpick
- acetate sheet with thick grid lines drawn on it
- plastic foam ball marked with poles and equator

Procedure

1. Make a pile of books about 15 cm high.

2. Tape the acetate sheet to the head of the flashlight. Place the flashlight on the pile of books.

3. Carefully push a pencil into the South Pole of the plastic foam ball, which represents Earth.

4. Use the protractor to measure a 23.5° tilt of the axis of your Earth away from your "flashlight sun," as shown in the top diagram. This position represents winter in the Northern Hemisphere.

5. Hold the pencil so that Earth is steady at this 23.5° angle and about 15 cm from the flashlight head. Turn the flashlight on. Dim the room lights.

6. The squares on the acetate should show up on your model Earth. Move the ball closer if necessary or dim the room lights more. Observe and record the shape of the squares at the equator and at the poles.

7. Carefully stick the toothpick straight into your model Earth about halfway between the equator and the North Pole. Observe and record the length of the shadow.

8. Without changing the tilt, turn the pencil to rotate the model Earth once on its axis. Observe and record how the shadow of the toothpick changes.

9. Tilt your model Earth 23.5° toward the flashlight, as shown in the bottom diagram. This is summer in the Northern Hemisphere. Observe and record the shape of the squares at the equator and at the poles. Observe how the toothpick's shadow changes.

10. Rotate the model Earth and note the shadow pattern.

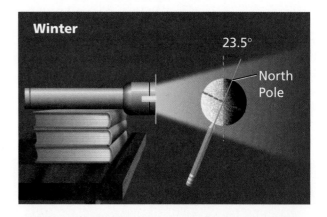

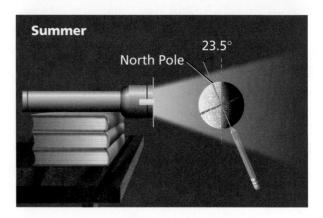

Analyze and Conclude

1. **Observing** When it is winter in the Northern Hemisphere, which areas on Earth get the most concentrated light? Which areas get the most concentrated light when it is summer in the Northern Hemisphere?

2. **Observing** Compare your observations of how the light hits the area halfway between the equator and the North Pole during winter (Step 6) and during summer (Step 9).

3. **Inferring** If the squares projected on the ball from the acetate become larger, what can you infer about the amount of heat distributed in each square?

4. **Inferring** According to your observations, which areas on Earth are consistently coolest? Which areas are consistently warmest? Why?

5. **Predicting** What time of year will the toothpick's shadow be longest? When will the shadow be shortest?

6. **Drawing Conclusions** How are the amounts of heat and light received in a square related to the angle of the sun's rays?

7. **Communicating** Use your observations of an Earth-sun model to write an explanation of what causes the seasons.

More to Explore

You can measure how directly light from the sun hits Earth's surface by making a shadow stick. You will need a stick or pole about 1 m long. With the help of your teacher, push the stick partway into the ground where it will not be disturbed. Make sure the stick stays vertical. At noon on the first day of every month, measure the length of the stick's shadow. The shorter the shadow, the higher the sun is in the sky and the more directly the sun's rays are hitting Earth. At what time of the year are the shadows longest? Shortest? How do your observations help explain the seasons?

Gravity and Motion

Reading Preview

Key Concepts
- What determines the strength of the force of gravity between two objects?
- What two factors combine to keep the moon and Earth in orbit?

Key Terms
- force
- gravity
- law of universal gravitation
- mass
- weight
- inertia
- Newton's first law of motion

Target Reading Skill
Asking Questions Before you read, preview the red headings. In a graphic organizer like the one below, ask a question for each heading. As you read, write answers to your questions.

Gravity

Question	Answer
What is gravity?	Gravity is . . .

Lab zone Discover **Activity**

Can You Remove the Bottom Penny?
1. Place 25 or so pennies in a stack on a table.
2. Write down your prediction of what will happen if you attempt to knock the bottom penny out of the stack.
3. Quickly slide a ruler along the surface of the table and strike the bottom penny. Observe what happens to the stack of pennies.
4. Repeat Step 3 several times, knocking more pennies from the bottom of the stack.

Think It Over
Developing Hypotheses Explain what happened to the stack of pennies as the bottom penny was knocked out of the stack.

Earth revolves around the sun in a nearly circular orbit. The moon orbits Earth in the same way. But what keeps Earth and the moon in orbit? Why don't they just fly off into space?

The first person to answer these questions was the English scientist Isaac Newton. Late in his life, Newton told a story of how watching an apple fall from a tree in 1666 had made him think about the moon's orbit. Newton realized that there must be a force acting between Earth and the moon that kept the moon in orbit. A **force** is a push or a pull. Most everyday forces require objects to be in contact. Newton realized that the force that holds the moon in orbit is different in that it acts over long distances between objects that are not in contact.

Gravity

Newton hypothesized that the force that pulls an apple to the ground also pulls the moon toward Earth, keeping it in orbit. This force, called **gravity,** attracts all objects toward each other. In Newton's day, most scientists thought that forces on Earth were different from those elsewhere in the universe. Although Newton did not discover gravity, he was the first person to realize that gravity occurs everywhere. Newton's **law of universal gravitation** states that every object in the universe attracts every other object.

The force of gravity is measured in units called newtons, named after Isaac Newton. **The strength of the force of gravity between two objects depends on two factors: the masses of the objects and the distance between them.**

Gravity, Mass, and Weight According to the law of universal gravitation, all of the objects around you, including Earth and even this book, are pulling on you, just as you are pulling on them. Why don't you notice a pull between you and the book? Because the strength of gravity depends in part on the masses of each of the objects. **Mass** is the amount of matter in an object.

Because Earth is so massive, it exerts a much greater force on you than this book does. Similarly, Earth exerts a gravitational force on the moon, large enough to keep the moon in orbit. The moon also exerts a gravitational force on Earth, as you will learn later in this chapter when you study the tides.

The force of gravity on an object is known as its **weight**. Unlike mass, which doesn't change, an object's weight can change depending on its location. For example, on the moon you would weigh about one sixth of your weight on Earth. This is because the moon is much less massive than Earth, so the pull of the moon's gravity on you would be far less than that of Earth's gravity.

Gravity and Distance The strength of gravity is affected by the distance between two objects as well as their masses. The force of gravity decreases rapidly as distance increases. For example, if the distance between two objects were doubled, the force of gravity between them would decrease to one fourth of its original value.

Reading Checkpoint **What is an object's weight?**

FIGURE 7
Gravity, Mass, and Distance
The strength of the force of gravity between two objects depends on their masses and the distance between them.
Inferring *How would the force of gravity change if the distance between the objects decreased?*

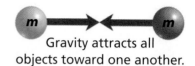

Gravity attracts all objects toward one another.

If mass increases, force also increases.

If distance increases, force decreases.

FIGURE 8
Earth Over the Moon
The force of gravity holds Earth and the moon together.

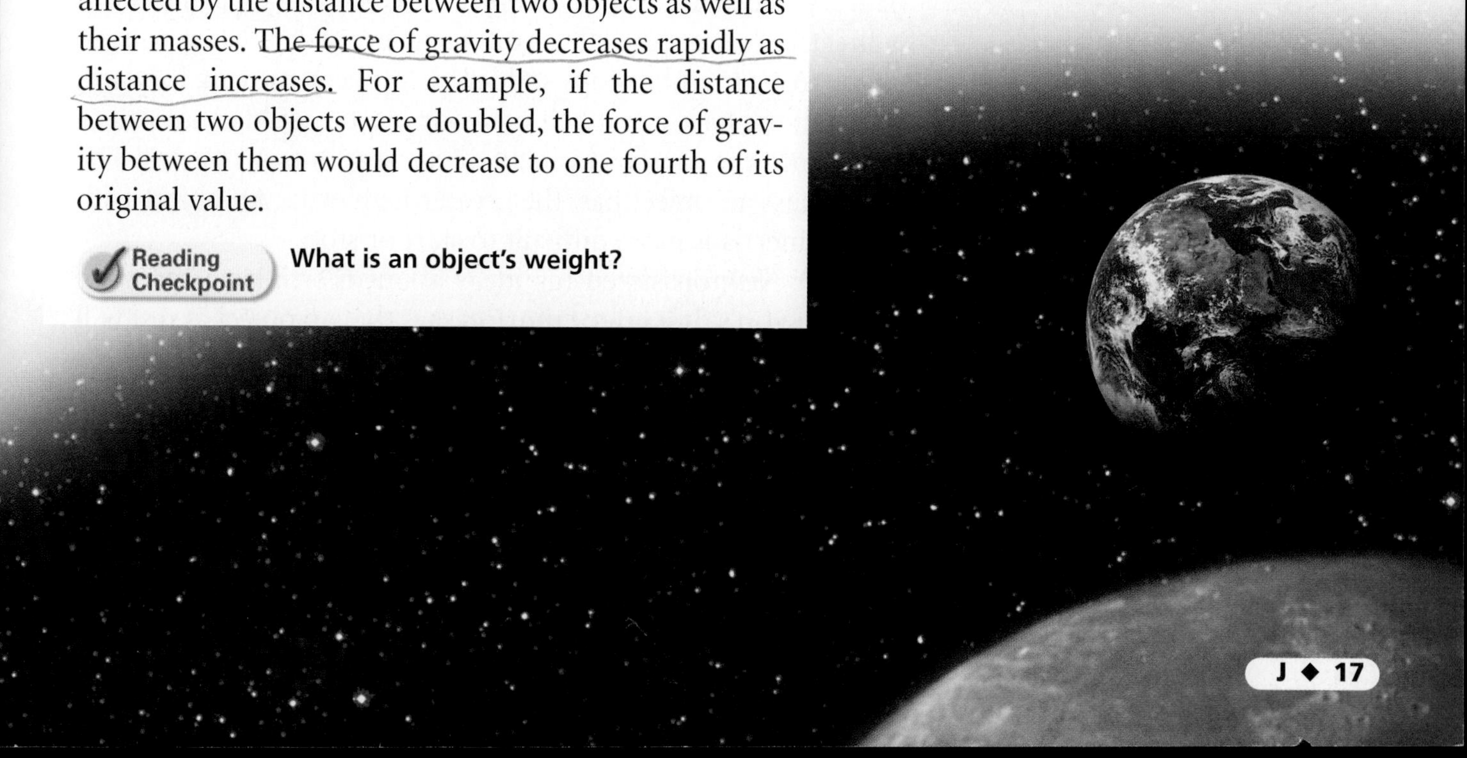

Gravity Versus Distance

As a rocket leaves a planet's surface, the force of gravity between the rocket and the planet changes. Use the graph at the right to answer the questions below.

1. **Reading Graphs** What two variables are being graphed? In what units is each variable measured?

2. **Reading Graphs** What is the force of gravity on the rocket at the planet's surface?

3. **Reading Graphs** What is the force of gravity on the rocket at a distance of two units (twice the planet's radius from its center)?

4. **Making Generalizations** In general, how does the force of gravity pulling on the rocket change as the distance between it and the planet increases?

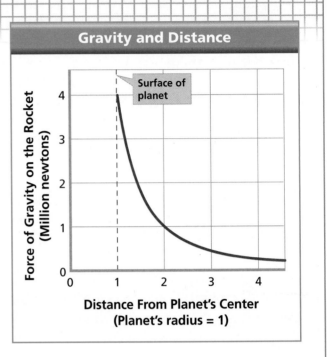

Gravity and Distance

Force of Gravity on the Rocket (Million newtons) vs. *Distance From Planet's Center (Planet's radius = 1)*

Surface of planet

Go Online

SciLINKS NSTA

For: Links on gravity
Visit: www.SciLinks.org
Web Code: scn-0612

Inertia and Orbital Motion

If the sun and Earth are constantly pulling on one another because of gravity, why doesn't Earth fall into the sun? Similarly, why doesn't the moon crash into Earth? The fact that such collisions have not occurred shows that there must be another factor at work. That factor is called inertia.

Inertia The tendency of an object to resist a change in motion is **inertia.** You feel the effects of inertia every day. When you are riding in a car and it stops suddenly, you keep moving forward. If you didn't have a seat belt on, your inertia could cause you to bump into the car's windshield or the seat in front of you. The more mass an object has, the greater its inertia. An object with greater inertia is more difficult to start or stop.

Isaac Newton stated his ideas about inertia as a scientific law. **Newton's first law of motion** says that an object at rest will stay at rest and an object in motion will stay in motion with a constant speed and direction unless acted on by a force.

Reading Checkpoint What is inertia?

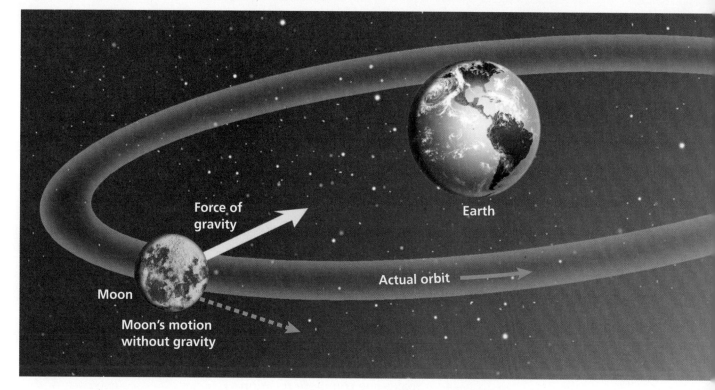

Force of gravity

Earth

Moon

Actual orbit

Moon's motion without gravity

Orbital Motion Why do Earth and the moon remain in their orbits? **Newton concluded that two factors—inertia and gravity—combine to keep Earth in orbit around the sun and the moon in orbit around Earth.**

As shown in Figure 9, Earth's gravity keeps pulling the moon toward it, preventing the moon from moving in a straight line. At the same time, the moon keeps moving ahead because of its inertia. If not for Earth's gravity, inertia would cause the moon to move off through space in a straight line. In the same way, Earth revolves around the sun because the sun's gravity pulls on it while Earth's inertia keeps it moving ahead.

FIGURE 9
Gravity and Inertia
A combination of gravity and inertia keeps the moon in orbit around Earth. If there were no gravity, inertia would cause the moon to travel in a straight line.
Interpreting Diagrams *What would happen to the moon if it were not moving in orbit?*

Section 2 Assessment

Target Reading Skill Asking Questions
Use your graphic organizer about the headings to help answer the questions below.

Reviewing Key Concepts

1. a. **Summarizing** What is the law of universal gravitation?
   b. **Reviewing** What two factors determine the force of gravity between two objects?
   c. **Predicting** Suppose the moon were closer to Earth. How would the force of gravity between Earth and the moon be different?
2. a. **Identifying** What two factors act together to keep Earth in orbit around the sun?

b. **Applying Concepts** Why doesn't Earth simply fall into the sun?
c. **Predicting** How would Earth move if the sun (including its gravity) suddenly disappeared? Explain your answer.

Writing in Science

Cause and Effect Paragraph Suppose you took a trip to the moon. Write a paragraph describing how and why your weight would change. Would your mass change too?

Phases, Eclipses, and Tides

Reading Preview

Key Concepts
- What causes the phases of the moon?
- What are solar and lunar eclipses?
- What causes the tides?

Key Terms
- phases
- eclipse
- solar eclipse
- umbra
- penumbra
- lunar eclipse
- tide
- spring tide
- neap tide

Target Reading Skill

Previewing Visuals Preview Figure 11. Then write two questions about the diagram of the phases of the moon in a graphic organizer like the one below. As you read, answer your questions.

Phases of the Moon

Q. Why does the moon have phases?
A.
Q.

Lab zone Discover **Activity**

How Does the Moon Move?

1. Place a quarter flat on your desk to represent Earth. Put a penny flat on your desk to represent the moon.
2. One side of the moon always faces Earth. Move the moon through one revolution around Earth, keeping Lincoln's face always looking at Earth. How many times did the penny make one complete rotation?

Think It Over
Inferring From the point of view of someone on Earth, does the moon seem to rotate? Explain your answer.

When you look up at the moon, you may see what looks like a face. Some people call this "the man in the moon." What you are really seeing is a pattern of light-colored and dark-colored areas on the moon's surface that just happens to look like a face. Oddly, this pattern never seems to move. That is, the same side of the moon, the "near side," always faces Earth. The "far side" of the moon always faces away from Earth. The reason has to do with how the moon moves in space.

Motions of the Moon

Like Earth, the moon moves through space in two ways. The moon revolves around Earth and also rotates on its own axis.

As the moon revolves around Earth, the relative positions of the moon, Earth, and sun change. **The changing relative positions of the moon, Earth, and sun cause the phases of the moon, eclipses, and tides.**

The moon rotates once on its axis in the same amount of time as it revolves around Earth. Thus, a "day" and a "year" on the moon are the same length. For this reason, the same side of the moon always faces Earth. The length of the moon's day is somewhat shorter than the 29.5 days between consecutive full moons. This is because as Earth revolves around the sun, the moon revolves around Earth.

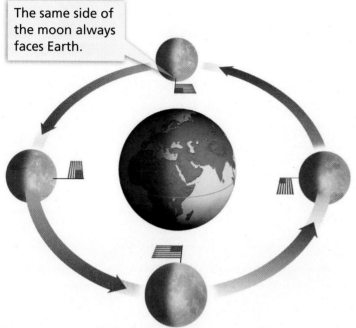

The same side of the moon always faces Earth.

FIGURE 10
The Moon in Motion
The moon rotates on its axis and revolves around Earth in the same amount of time. As a result, the near side of the moon (shown with a flag) always faces Earth. **Interpreting Diagrams** *Would Earth ever appear to set below the horizon for someone standing next to the flag on the moon? Explain.*

Phases of the Moon

On a clear night when the moon is full, the bright moonlight can keep you awake. But the moon does not produce the light you see. Instead, it reflects light from the sun. Imagine taking a flashlight into a dark room. If you were to shine the flashlight on a chair, you would see the chair because the light from your flashlight would bounce, or reflect, off the chair. In the same way that the chair wouldn't shine by itself, the moon doesn't give off light by itself. You can see the moon because it reflects the light of the sun.

When you see the moon in the sky, sometimes it appears round. Other times you see only a thin sliver, or crescent. The different shapes of the moon you see from Earth are called **phases.** The moon goes through its whole set of phases each time it makes a complete revolution around Earth.

Phases are caused by changes in the relative positions of the moon, Earth, and the sun. Because the sun lights the moon, half the moon is almost always in sunlight. However, since the moon revolves around Earth, you see the moon from different angles. The half of the moon that faces Earth is not always the half that is sunlit. **The phase of the moon you see depends on how much of the sunlit side of the moon faces Earth.**

The Moon Seen From Earth

1 New Moon
The sunlit side faces away from Earth.

2 Waxing Crescent
The portion of the moon you can see is waxing, or growing, into a crescent shape.

3 First Quarter
You can see half of the sunlit side of the moon.

4 Waxing Gibbous
The moon continues to wax. The visible shape of the moon is called gibbous.

FIGURE 11

Phases of the Moon

The photos at the top of the page show how the phases of the moon appear when you look up at the moon from Earth's surface. The circular diagram at the right shows how the Earth and moon would appear to an observer in space as the moon revolves around Earth.
Interpreting Diagrams *During what phases are the moon, Earth, and sun aligned in a straight line?*

Go Online
active art

For: Moon Phases and Eclipses activity
Visit: PHSchool.com
Web Code: cfp-5013

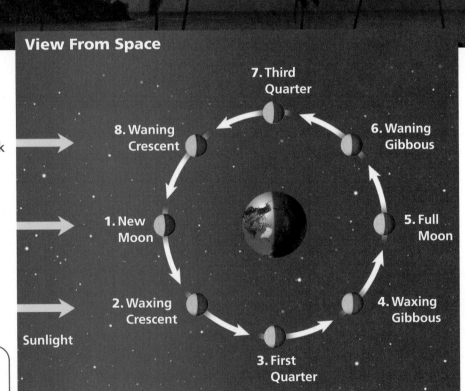

View From Space

7. Third Quarter

8. Waning Crescent

6. Waning Gibbous

1. New Moon

5. Full Moon

2. Waxing Crescent

4. Waxing Gibbous

Sunlight

3. First Quarter

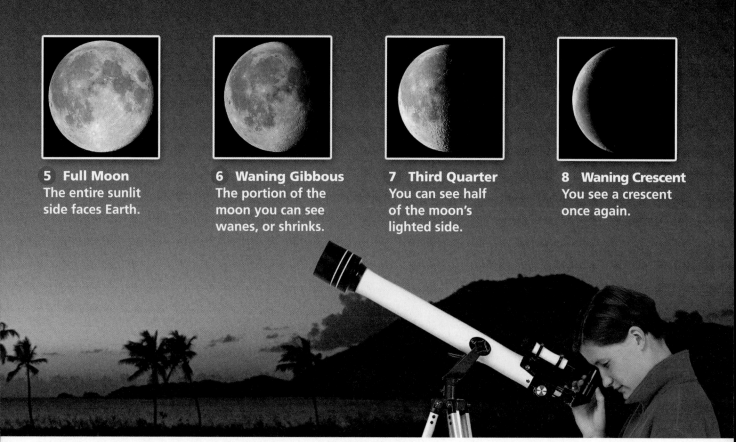

5 Full Moon
The entire sunlit side faces Earth.

6 Waning Gibbous
The portion of the moon you can see wanes, or shrinks.

7 Third Quarter
You can see half of the moon's lighted side.

8 Waning Crescent
You see a crescent once again.

To understand the phases of the moon, study Figure 11. During the new moon, the side of the moon facing Earth is not lit because the sun is behind the moon. As the moon revolves around Earth, you see more and more of the lighted side of the moon every day, until the side of the moon you see is fully lit. As the moon continues in its orbit, you see less and less of the lighted side. About 29.5 days after the last new moon, the cycle is complete, and a new moon occurs again.

 **What is a new moon?**

Eclipses

As Figure 12 shows, the moon's orbit around Earth is slightly tilted with respect to Earth's orbit around the sun. As a result, in most months the moon revolves around Earth without moving into Earth's shadow or the moon's shadow hitting Earth. **When the moon's shadow hits Earth or Earth's shadow hits the moon, an eclipse occurs.** When an object in space comes between the sun and a third object, it casts a shadow on that object, causing an **eclipse** (ih KLIPS) to take place. There are two types of eclipses: solar eclipses and lunar eclipses. (The words *solar* and *lunar* come from the Latin words for "sun" and "moon.")

FIGURE 12
The Moon's Orbit
The moon's orbit is tilted about 5 degrees relative to Earth's orbit around the sun.

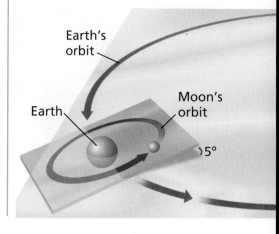

Earth's orbit

Moon's orbit

Earth

5°

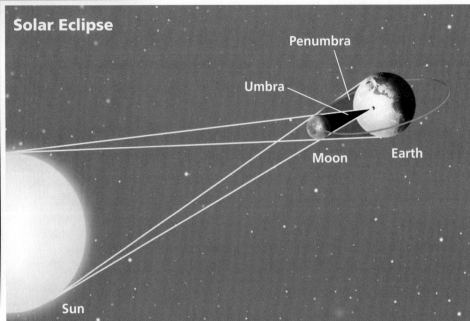

Solar Eclipse

Penumbra

Umbra

Moon

Earth

Sun

FIGURE 13
The outer layer of the sun's atmosphere, the solar corona, is visible surrounding the dark disk of the moon during a solar eclipse. During a solar eclipse, the moon blocks light from the sun, preventing sunlight from reaching parts of Earth's surface.

Lab zone Skills **Activity**

Making Models
Here is how you can draw a scale model of a solar eclipse. The moon's diameter is about one fourth Earth's diameter. The distance from Earth to the moon is about 30 times Earth's diameter. Make a scale drawing of the moon, Earth, and the distance between them. (*Hint:* Draw Earth 1 cm in diameter in one corner of the paper.) From the edges of the moon, draw and shade in a triangle just touching Earth to show the moon's umbra.

When Do Solar Eclipses Occur? During a new moon, the moon lies between Earth and the sun. But most months, as you have seen, the moon travels a little above or below the sun in the sky. **A solar eclipse occurs when the moon passes directly between Earth and the sun, blocking sunlight from Earth.** The moon's shadow then hits Earth, as shown in Figure 13. So a **solar eclipse** occurs when a new moon blocks your view of the sun.

Total Solar Eclipses The very darkest part of the moon's shadow, the **umbra** (UM bruh), is cone-shaped. From any point in the umbra, light from the sun is completely blocked by the moon. The moon's umbra happens to be long enough so that the point of the cone can just reach a small part of Earth's surface. Only the people within the umbra experience a total solar eclipse. During the short period of a total solar eclipse, the sky grows as dark as night, even in the middle of a clear day. The air gets cool and the sky becomes an eerie color. You can see the stars and the solar corona, which is the faint outer atmosphere of the sun.

Partial Solar Eclipses In Figure 13, you can see that the moon casts another part of its shadow that is less dark than the umbra. This larger part of the shadow is called the **penumbra** (peh NUM bruh). In the penumbra, part of the sun is visible from Earth. During a solar eclipse, people in the penumbra see only a partial eclipse. Since an extremely bright part of the sun still remains visible, it is not safe to look directly at the sun during a partial solar eclipse (just as you wouldn't look directly at the sun during a normal day).

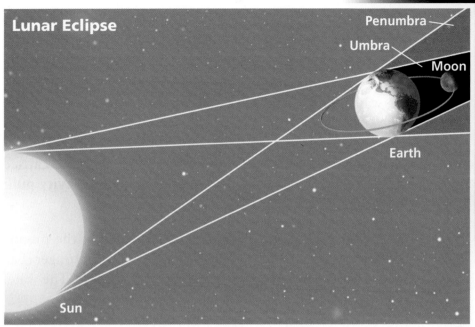

Lunar Eclipse

Penumbra

Umbra

Moon

Earth

Sun

When Do Lunar Eclipses Occur? During most months, the moon moves near Earth's shadow but not quite into it. A **lunar eclipse** occurs at a full moon when Earth is directly between the moon and the sun. You can see a lunar eclipse in Figure 14. **During a lunar eclipse, Earth blocks sunlight from reaching the moon.** The moon is then in Earth's shadow and looks dim from Earth. Lunar eclipses occur only when there is a full moon because the moon is closest to Earth's shadow at that time.

Total Lunar Eclipses Like the moon's shadow in a solar eclipse, Earth's shadow has an umbra and a penumbra. When the moon is in Earth's umbra, you see a total lunar eclipse. You can see the edge of Earth's shadow on the moon before and after a total lunar eclipse.

Unlike a total solar eclipse, a total lunar eclipse can be seen anywhere on Earth that the moon is visible. So you are more likely to see a total lunar eclipse than a total solar eclipse.

Partial Lunar Eclipses For most lunar eclipses, Earth, the moon, and the sun are not quite in line, and only a partial lunar eclipse results. A partial lunar eclipse occurs when the moon passes partly into the umbra of Earth's shadow. The edge of the umbra appears blurry, and you can watch it pass across the moon for two or three hours.

 **Reading Checkpoint** During which phase of the moon can lunar eclipses occur?

FIGURE 14
During a lunar eclipse, Earth blocks sunlight from reaching the moon's surface. The photo of the moon above was taken during a total lunar eclipse. The moon's reddish tint occurs because Earth's atmosphere bends some sunlight toward the moon.
Interpreting Diagrams *What is the difference between the umbra and the penumbra?*

For: Moon Phases and Eclipses activity
Visit: PHSchool.com
Web Code: cfp-5013

High Tide

Low Tide

FIGURE 15
High and Low Tides
In some locations, such as along this beach in Australia, there can be dramatic differences between the height of high and low tides.

Tides

Have you ever built a sand castle on an ocean beach? Was it washed away by rising water? This is an example of **tides,** the rise and fall of ocean water that occurs every 12.5 hours or so. The water rises for about six hours, then falls for about six hours, in a regular cycle.

The force of gravity pulls the moon and Earth (including the water on Earth's surface) toward each other. **Tides are caused mainly by differences in how much the moon's gravity pulls on different parts of Earth.**

The Tide Cycle Look at Figure 16. The force of the moon's gravity at point A, which is closer to the moon, is stronger than the force of the moon's gravity on Earth as a whole. The water flows toward point A, and a high tide forms.

The force of the moon's gravity at point C, which is on the far side of Earth from the moon, is weaker than the force of the moon's gravity on Earth as a whole. Earth is pulled toward the moon more strongly than the water at point C, so the water is "left behind." Water flows toward point C, and a high tide occurs there too. Between points A and C, water flows away from points B and D, causing low tides.

At any one time there are two places with high tides and two places with low tides on Earth. As Earth rotates, one high tide stays on the side of Earth facing the moon. The second high tide stays on the opposite side of Earth. Each location on Earth sweeps through those two high tides and two low tides every 25 hours or so.

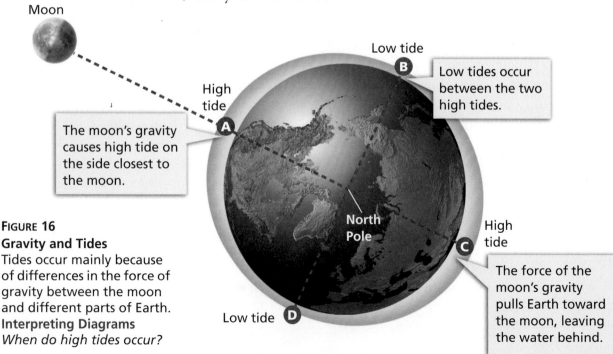

Moon

Low tide

B

Low tides occur between the two high tides.

High tide

A

The moon's gravity causes high tide on the side closest to the moon.

North Pole

High tide

C

The force of the moon's gravity pulls Earth toward the moon, leaving the water behind.

Low tide D

FIGURE 16
Gravity and Tides
Tides occur mainly because of differences in the force of gravity between the moon and different parts of Earth.
Interpreting Diagrams
When do high tides occur?

Spring Tides The sun's gravity also pulls on Earth's waters. As shown in the top diagram of Figure 17, the sun, moon, and Earth are nearly in a line during a new moon. The gravity of the sun and the moon pull in the same direction. Their combined forces produce a tide with the greatest difference between consecutive low and high tides, called a **spring tide**.

At full moon, the moon and the sun are on opposite sides of Earth. Since there are high tides on both sides of Earth, a spring tide is also produced. It doesn't matter in which order the sun, Earth, and moon line up. Spring tides occur twice a month, at new moon and at full moon.

Neap Tides During the moon's first-quarter and third-quarter phases, the line between Earth and the sun is at right angles to the line between Earth and the moon. The sun's pull is at right angles to the moon's pull. This arrangement produces a **neap tide**, a tide with the least difference between consecutive low and high tides. Neap tides occur twice a month.

 **What is a neap tide?**

FIGURE 17
Spring and Neap Tides
When Earth, the sun, and the moon are in a straight line (top), a spring tide occurs. When the moon is at a right angle to the sun (bottom), a neap tide occurs.

Spring Tide

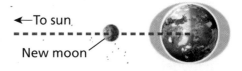
←To sun
New moon

Neap Tide

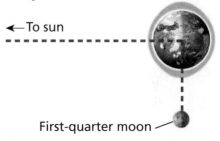
←To sun

First-quarter moon

Section 3 Assessment

Target Reading Skill Previewing Visuals Refer to your questions and answers about Figure 11 to help you answer Question 1 below.

Reviewing Key Concepts

1. a. Explaining What causes the moon to shine?
 b. Relating Cause and Effect Why does the moon appear to change shape during the course of a month?
 c. Interpreting Diagrams Use Figure 11 to explain why you can't see the moon at the time of a new moon.
2. a. Explaining What is an eclipse?
 b. Comparing and Contrasting How is a solar eclipse different from a lunar eclipse?
 c. Relating Cause and Effect Why isn't there a solar eclipse and a lunar eclipse each month?
3. a. Summarizing What causes the tides?
 b. Explaining Explain why most coastal regions have two high tides and two low tides each day.
 c. Comparing and Contrasting Compare the size of high and low tides in a spring tide and a neap tide. What causes the difference?

Lab zone **At-Home Activity**

Tracking the Tides Use a daily newspaper or the Internet to track the height of high and low tides at a location of your choice for at least two weeks. Make a graph of your data, with the date as the x-axis and tide height as the y-axis. Also find the dates of the new moon and full moon and add them to your graph. Show your completed graph to a relative and explain what the graph shows.

A "Moonth" of Phases

Problem

What causes the phases of the moon?

Skills Focus

making models, observing, drawing conclusions

Materials

- floor lamp with 150-watt bulb
- pencils
- plastic foam balls

Procedure

1. Place a lamp in the center of the room. Remove the lampshade.

2. Close the doors and shades to darken the room, and switch on the lamp.

3. Carefully stick the point of a pencil into the plastic foam ball so that the pencil can be used as a "handle."

4. Draw 8 circles on a sheet of paper. Number them 1–8.

5. Have your partner hold the plastic foam ball at arm's length in front and slightly above his or her head so that the ball is between him or her and the lamp. **CAUTION:** *Do not look directly at the bulb.*

6. The ball should be about 1 to 1.5 m away from the lamp. Adjust the distance between the ball and the lamp so that the light shines brightly on the ball.

7. Stand directly behind your partner and observe what part of the ball facing you is lit by the lamp. If light is visible on the ball, draw the shape of the lighted part of the ball in the first circle.

8. Have your partner turn 45° to the left while keeping the ball in front and at arm's length.

9. Repeat Step 7. Be sure you are standing directly behind your partner.

10. Repeat Steps 8 and 9 six more times until your partner is facing the lamp again. See the photograph for the 8 positions.

11. Change places and repeat Steps 4–10.

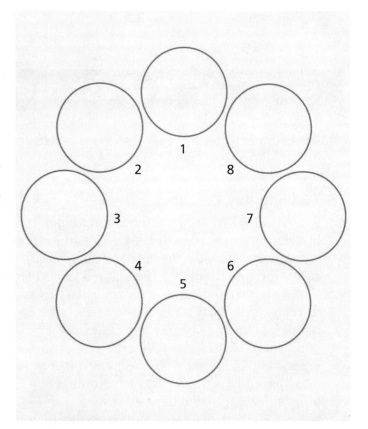

Analyze and Conclude

1. **Making Models** In your model, what represents Earth? The sun? The moon?

2. **Observing** Refer back to your 8 circles. How much of the lighted part of the ball did you see when facing the lamp?

3. **Classifying** Label your drawings with the names of the phases of the moon. Which drawing represents a full moon? A new moon? Which represents a waxing crescent? A waning crescent?

4. **Observing** How much of the lighted part of the ball did you see after each turn?

5. **Drawing Conclusions** Whether you could see it or not, how much of the ball's surface was always lit by the lamp? Was the darkness of the new moon caused by an eclipse? Explain your answer.

6. **Communicating** Write a brief analysis of this lab. How well did making a model help you understand the phases of the moon? What are some disadvantages of using models? What is another way to make a model to represent the various phases of the moon?

More to Explore

Design a model to show a lunar eclipse and a solar eclipse. What objects would you use for Earth, the sun, and the moon? Use the model to demonstrate why there isn't an eclipse every full moon and new moon.

45°

Earth's Moon

Reading Preview

Key Concepts
• What features are found on the moon's surface?
• What are some characteristics of the moon?
• How did the moon form?

Key Terms
• telescope • maria
• craters • meteoroids

Target Reading Skill
Identifying Main Ideas As you read "The Moon's Surface," write the main idea—the biggest or most important idea—in a graphic organizer like the one below. Then write three supporting details that further explain the main idea.

Main Idea

The moon's surface has a variety of features, such as . . .

Detail	Detail	Detail

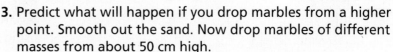
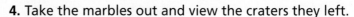

Lab zone Discover Activity

Why Do Craters Look Different From Each Other?

The moon's surface has pits in it, called craters.

1. Put on your goggles. Fill a large plastic basin to a depth of 2 cm with sand.
2. Drop marbles of different masses from about 20 cm high. Take the marbles out and view the craters they created.
3. Predict what will happen if you drop marbles from a higher point. Smooth out the sand. Now drop marbles of different masses from about 50 cm high.
4. Take the marbles out and view the craters they left.

Think It Over
Developing Hypotheses In which step do you think the marbles were moving faster when they hit the sand? If objects hitting the moon caused craters, how did the speeds of the objects affect the sizes of the craters? How did the masses of the objects affect the sizes of the craters?

For thousands of years, people could see shapes on the surface of the moon, but didn't know what caused them. The ancient Greeks thought that the moon was perfectly smooth. It was not until about 400 years ago that scientists could study the moon more closely.

In 1609, the Italian scientist Galileo Galilei heard about a **telescope,** a device built to observe distant objects by making them appear closer. Galileo soon made his own telescope by putting two lenses in a wooden tube. The lenses focused the light coming through the tube, making distant objects seem closer. When Galileo pointed his telescope at the moon, he was able to see much more detail than anyone had ever seen before. What Galileo saw astounded him. Instead of the perfect sphere imagined by the Greeks, he saw that the moon has an irregular surface with a variety of remarkable features.

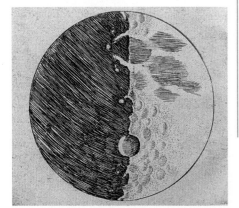

◀ Galileo used a telescope to help make this drawing of the moon.

The dark, flat areas on the moon's surface are called maria.

The light-colored features that cover much of the moon's surface are highlands.

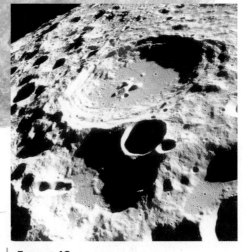

FIGURE 18
The Moon's Surface
The moon's surface is covered by craters, maria, and highlands. Craters on the moon formed from the impact of meteoroids. Most large craters are named after famous scientists or philosophers. **Observing** *What are the light regions in the top photograph called?*

The Moon's Surface

Recent photos of the moon show much more detail than Galileo could see with his telescope. **Features on the moon's surface include maria, craters, and highlands.**

Maria The moon's surface has dark, flat areas, which Galileo called **maria** (MAH ree uh), the Latin word for "seas." Galileo incorrectly thought that the maria were oceans. The maria are actually hardened rock formed from huge lava flows that occurred between 3 and 4 billion years ago.

Craters Galileo saw that the moon's surface is marked by large round pits called **craters.** Some craters are hundreds of kilometers across. For a long time, many scientists mistakenly thought that these craters had been made by volcanoes. Scientists now know that these craters were caused by the impacts of **meteoroids,** chunks of rock or dust from space.

The maria have few craters compared to surrounding areas. This means that most of the moon's craters formed from impacts early in its history, before the maria formed. On Earth, such ancient craters have disappeared. They were worn away over time by water, wind, and other forces. But since the moon has no liquid water or atmosphere, its surface has changed little for billions of years.

Highlands Galileo correctly inferred that some of the light-colored features he saw on the moon's surface were highlands, or mountains. The peaks of the lunar highlands and the rims of the craters cast dark shadows, which Galileo could see. The rugged lunar highlands cover much of the moon's surface.

 **Reading Checkpoint** What are maria?

Go Online
SCLINKS NSTA

For: Links on Earth's moon
Visit: www.SciLinks.org
Web Code: scn-0614

FIGURE 19
The Moon's Size
The diameter of the moon is a little less than the distance across the contiguous United States.
Calculating *What is the ratio of the moon's diameter to the distance between Earth and the moon?*

FIGURE 20
The Moon's Surface
This photo of a large boulder field and hills on the moon's surface was taken by one of the crew members of *Apollo 17*.

Characteristics of the Moon

Would you want to take a vacation on the moon? At an average distance of about 384,000 kilometers (about 30 times Earth's diameter), the moon is Earth's closest neighbor in space. Despite its proximity, the moon is very different from Earth. **The moon is dry and airless. Compared to Earth, the moon is small and has large variations in its surface temperature.** If you visited the moon, you would need to wear a bulky space suit to provide air to breathe, protect against sunburn, and to keep you at a comfortable temperature.

Size and Density The moon is 3,476 kilometers in diameter, a little less than the distance across the United States. This is about one-fourth Earth's diameter. However, the moon has only one-eightieth as much mass as Earth. Though Earth has a very dense core, its outer layers are less dense. The moon's average density is similar to the density of Earth's outer layers.

Temperature and Atmosphere On the moon's surface, temperatures range from a torrid 130°C in direct sunlight to a frigid −180°C at night. Temperatures on the moon vary so much because it has no atmosphere. The moon's surface gravity is so weak that gases can easily escape into space.

Water The moon has no liquid water. However, there is evidence that there may be large patches of ice near the moon's poles. Some areas are shielded from sunlight by crater walls. Temperatures in these regions are so low that ice there would remain frozen. If a colony were built on the moon in the future, any such water would be very valuable. It would be very expensive to transport large amounts of water to the moon from Earth.

✓ **Reading Checkpoint** Where on the moon is there evidence of the existence of ice?

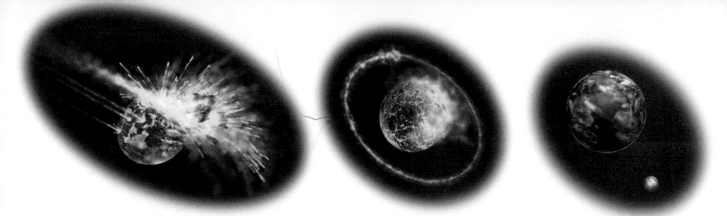

The Origin of the Moon

People have long wondered how the moon formed. Scientists have suggested many possible theories. For example, was the moon formed elsewhere in the solar system and captured by Earth's gravity as it came near? Was the moon formed near Earth at the same time that Earth formed? Scientists have found reasons to reject these ideas.

The theory of the moon's origin that seems to best fit the evidence is called the collision-ring theory. It is illustrated in Figure 21. About 4.5 billion years ago, when Earth was very young, the solar system was full of rocky debris. Some of this debris was the size of small planets. **Scientists theorize that a planet-sized object collided with Earth to form the moon.** Material from the object and Earth's outer layers was ejected into orbit around Earth, where it formed a ring. Gravity caused this material to combine to form the moon.

 **Reading Checkpoint** What theory best explains the moon's origin?

FIGURE 21
Formation of the Moon
According to the collision-ring theory, the moon formed early in Earth's history when a planet-sized object struck Earth. The resulting debris formed the moon.

Earth, Moon, and Sun
Video Preview
▶ Video Field Trip
Video Assessment

Section 4 Assessment

🎯 **Target Reading Skill** Identifying Main Ideas Use your graphic organizer to help you answer Question 1 below.

Reviewing Key Concepts

1. a. **Identifying** Name three major features of the moon's surface.
   b. **Explaining** How did the moon's craters form?
   c. **Relating Cause and Effect** Why is the moon's surface much more heavily cratered than Earth's surface?
2. a. **Describing** Describe the range of temperatures on the moon.
   b. **Comparing and Contrasting** Compare Earth and the moon in terms of size and surface gravity.

   c. **Relating Cause and Effect** What is the relationship between the moon's surface gravity, lack of an atmosphere, and temperature range?
3. a. **Describing** What was the solar system like when the moon formed?
   b. **Sequencing** Explain the various stages in the formation of the moon.

Lab zone At-Home **Activity**

Moonwatching With an adult, observe the moon a few days after the first-quarter phase. Make a sketch of the features you see. Label the maria, craters, and highlands.

The BIG Idea   **Motion and Forces** The motions of Earth and the moon and their position relative to the sun result in day and night, the seasons, phases of the moon, eclipses, and tides.

① Earth in Space

Key Concepts

- Earth moves through space in two major ways: rotation and revolution.
- Earth has seasons because its axis is tilted as it revolves around the sun.

Key Terms

- astronomy • rotation • orbit • solstice
- axis • revolution • calendar • equinox

② Gravity and Motion

Key Concepts

- The strength of the force of gravity between two objects depends on two factors: the masses of the objects and the distance between them.
- Newton concluded that two factors—inertia and gravity—combine to keep Earth in orbit around the sun and the moon in orbit around Earth.

Key Terms

force
gravity
law of universal gravitation
mass
weight
inertia
Newton's first law of motion

③ Phases, Eclipses, and Tides

Key Concepts

- The changing relative positions of the moon, Earth, and sun cause the phases of the moon, eclipses, and tides.
- The phase of the moon you see depends on how much of the sunlit side of the moon faces Earth.
- When the moon's shadow hits Earth or Earth's shadow hits the moon, an eclipse occurs.
- A solar eclipse occurs when the moon passes directly between Earth and the sun, blocking sunlight from Earth.
- During a lunar eclipse, Earth blocks sunlight from reaching the moon.
- Tides are caused mainly by differences in how much the moon's gravity pulls on different parts of Earth.

Key Terms

- phases • solar eclipse • penumbra • tide
- neap tide • eclipse • umbra • lunar eclipse
- spring tide

④ Earth's Moon

Key Concepts

- Features on the moon's surface include maria, craters, and highlands.
- The moon is dry and airless. Compared to Earth, the moon is small and has large variations in its surface temperature.
- Scientists theorize that a planet-sized object collided with Earth to form the moon.

Key Terms

telescope
maria
craters
meteoroids

Review and Assessment

Organizing Information

Concept Mapping Copy the concept map about how Earth moves in space onto a separate sheet of paper. Then complete it and add a title. (For more on Concept Mapping, see the Skills Handbook.)

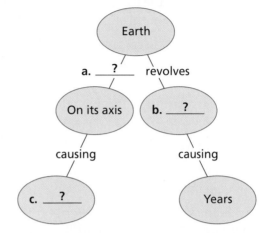

Earth

a. _____?_____   revolves

On its axis   b. __?__

causing   causing

c. __?__   Years

Reviewing Key Terms

Choose the letter of the best answer.

1. The movement of Earth around the sun once a year is called Earth's
   a. inertia.   **b.** rotation.
   c. revolution.   **d.** axis.

2. A day when the sun reaches its greatest distance north or south of the equator is called a(an)
   a. umbra.
   b. penumbra.
   c. equinox.
   d. solstice.

3. The tendency of an object to resist a change in motion is called
   a. gravity.
   b. inertia.
   c. force.
   d. the law of universal gravitation.

4. When Earth's shadow falls on the moon, the shadow causes a
   a. new moon.
   b. solar eclipse.
   c. full moon.
   d. lunar eclipse.

5. The craters on the moon were caused by
   a. tides.   **b.** volcanoes.
   c. meteoroids.   **d.** maria.

If the statement is true, write *true*. If it is false, change the underlined word or words to make the statement true.

6. Earth's spinning on its axis is called <u>rotation</u>.

7. The force that attracts all objects toward each other is called <u>inertia</u>.

8. The tilt of Earth's axis as Earth revolves around the sun causes <u>eclipses</u>.

9. The amount of matter in an object is its <u>weight</u>.

10. The greatest difference between low and high tides occurs during a <u>neap</u> tide.

Writing in Science

News Report Imagine that you are a reporter asked to write a story about the origin of the moon. Write an article explaining how the moon formed.

DISCOVERY CHANNEL SCHOOL

Earth, Moon, and Sun

Video Preview
Video Field Trip
▶ Video Assessment

Review and Assessment

Checking Concepts

11. Explain how the length of the day and year are related to Earth's movement through space.

12. Suppose you moved two objects farther apart. How would this affect the force of gravity between those objects?

13. Explain Newton's first law of motion in your own words.

14. Why does the moon have phases?

15. Why do more people see a total lunar eclipse than a total solar eclipse?

16. Why is there a high tide on the side of Earth closest to the moon? On the side of Earth farthest from the moon?

17. Does the diagram below show a spring tide or a neap tide? How do you know?

18. How did the invention of the telescope contribute to our knowledge of the moon's surface?

19. Why do temperatures vary so much on the moon?

20. Explain how scientists think the moon originated.

Thinking Critically

21. **Inferring** Mars's axis is tilted at about the same angle as Earth's axis. Do you think Mars has seasons? Explain your answer.

22. **Comparing and Contrasting** How are mass and weight different?

23. **Calculating** Suppose a person weighs 450 newtons (about 100 pounds) on Earth. How much would she weigh on the moon?

24. **Applying Concepts** At about what time does the full moon rise? Is it visible in the eastern sky or the western sky?

25. **Posing Questions** Suppose you were assigned to design a spacesuit for astronauts to wear on the moon. What characteristics of the moon would be important to consider in your design?

Applying Skills

Use the illustration below to answer Questions 26–28.

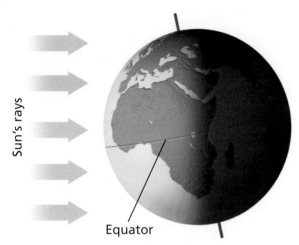

Sun's rays

Equator

26. **Interpreting Diagrams** On which hemisphere are the sun's rays falling most directly?

27. **Inferring** In the Northern Hemisphere, is it the summer solstice, winter solstice, or one of the equinoxes? How do you know?

28. **Predicting** Six months after this illustration, Earth will have revolved halfway around the sun. Draw a diagram that shows which end of Earth's axis will be tilted toward the sun.

Lab zone Chapter **Project**

Performance Assessment Present your observation log, map, and drawings of the moon. Some ways to graph your data include time of moonrise for each date; how often you saw the moon in each direction; or how often you saw the moon at a specific time. Display your graphs. Discuss any patterns that you discovered.

Standardized Test Prep

Choose the letter of the best answer.

1. You observe a thin crescent moon in the western sky during the early evening. About two weeks later, a full moon is visible in the eastern sky during the early evening. Which conclusion is best supported by these observations?

  A The moon revolves around Earth.

  B The moon rotates on its axis.

  C Earth revolves around the sun.

  D Earth's axis is tilted relative to the moon.

2. Only one side of the moon is visible from Earth because

  F the moon does not rotate on its axis.

  G the moon does not revolve around Earth.

  H the moon rotates faster than it revolves.

  J the moon revolves once and rotates once in the same period of time.

3. What type of eclipse occurs when Earth's umbra covers the moon?

  A a partial solar eclipse

  B a total solar eclipse

  C a partial lunar eclipse

  D a total lunar eclipse

4. The force of gravity depends on

  F mass and weight.

  G speed and distance.

  H mass and distance.

  J weight and speed.

The diagram below shows the relative positions of the sun, moon, and Earth. The numbers indicate specific locations of the moon in its orbit. Use the diagram to answer Questions 5 and 6.

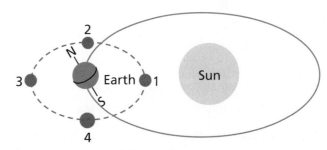

5. Which of the following can occur when the moon is at location 1?

  A only a lunar eclipse

  B only a solar eclipse

  C both a solar and a lunar eclipse

  D neither a solar nor a lunar eclipse

6. When the moon is at location 2, at most coastal locations there would be

  F only one high tide each day.

  G only one low tide each day.

  H two high tides and two low tides each day, with the most difference between high and low tide.

  J two high tides and two low tides each day, with the least difference between high and low tide.

Constructed Response

7. The sun rises on the east coast of the United States before it rises on the west coast of the United States. Explain why this happens.

Chapter 2

Exploring Space

The BIG Idea
Science and Technology

 How do scientists learn more about the other parts of the solar system?

Chapter Preview

An astronaut working on the International Space Station in orbit around Earth ▶

Lab zone™ Chapter **Project**

Design and Build a Space Exploration Vehicle

How do scientists study the other planets in our solar system? One way is to send a remotely operated vehicle to explore the surface, as was done by two Mars rovers in 2004. Such a vehicle must be designed to meet specific requirements, such as communicating with scientists on Earth and being able to operate in a variety of environments.

Your Goal To design, build, and test a vehicle for exploring the surface of a planet

You will

● identify the geological features that are found on the planets and moons of the solar system
● select a planet or moon, and brainstorm ways to build a vehicle that can move around its surface
● design and sketch a model of the vehicle
● build and test a model vehicle, and present your vehicle to the class
● follow the safety guidelines in Appendix A

Plan It! Begin by identifying the different types of planetary surfaces found in the solar system. Next, brainstorm how a vehicle could move over some of these surfaces. You may want to think about how all-terrain vehicles on Earth are designed. Consider how you would build a model of the vehicle, and what materials you will need. Then build and test your vehicle.

The Science of Rockets

Reading Preview

Key Concepts
- How were rockets developed?
- How does a rocket work?
- What is the main advantage of a multistage rocket?

Key Terms
- rocket • thrust • velocity
- orbital velocity • escape velocity

🔄 Target Reading Skill

Using Prior Knowledge Before you read, write what you know about rockets in a graphic organizer like the one below. As you read, write what you learn.

What You Know
1. Rockets were used to help transport astronauts to the moon.
2.

What You Learned
1.
2.

Lab zone Discover **Activity**

What Force Moves a Balloon?

1. Put on your goggles. Blow up a balloon and hold its neck closed with your fingers.
2. Point the far end of the balloon in a direction where there are no people. Put your free hand behind the balloon's neck, so you will be able to feel the force of the air from the balloon on your hand. Let go of the balloon. Observe what happens.
3. Repeat Steps 1 and 2 without your free hand behind the neck of the balloon.

Think It Over
Inferring What happened when you let go of the balloon? Which direction did the balloon move in comparison to the direction the air moved out of the balloon? What force do you think caused the balloon to move in that direction? Did the position of your free hand affect the balloon's movement?

People have dreamed of traveling through space for centuries. Although the moons and planets of our solar system are much closer than the stars, they are still very far away. How could someone travel such great distances through space?

In the 1860s, the science fiction writer Jules Verne envisioned a spacecraft shot to the moon out of a huge cannon. When people finally did travel to the moon, though, they used rockets rather than cannons. Although Verne was wrong about how humans would reach the moon, he did anticipate many aspects of the space program. By the late 1900s, rocket-powered spacecraft were able to travel to the moon and to many other places in the solar system.

FIGURE 1
Jules Verne's Spacecraft
Jules Verne imagined that a spacecraft and crew were shot to the moon by a cannon.

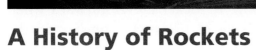

A History of Rockets

You've probably seen rockets at fireworks displays. As the rockets moved skyward, you may have noticed a fiery gas rushing out of the back. A **rocket** is a device that expels gas in one direction to move in the opposite direction. **Rocket technology originated in China hundreds of years ago and gradually spread to other parts of the world.** Rockets were developed for military use as well as for fireworks.

Origins of Rockets The first rockets were made in China in the 1100s. These early rockets were very simple—they were arrows coated with a flammable powder that were lighted and shot with bows. By about 1200, the Chinese were using gunpowder inside their rockets.

The British greatly improved rocketry in the early 1800s. British ships used rockets against American troops in the War of 1812. The *Star-Spangled Banner* contains the words "the rockets' red glare, the bombs bursting in air." These words describe a British rocket attack on Fort McHenry in Baltimore, Maryland.

Development of Modern Rockets Modern rockets were first developed in the early 1900s. They owe much of their development to a few scientists. One was the Russian physicist Konstantin Tsiolkovsky. In the early 1900s, Tsiolkovsky described in scientific terms how rockets work and proposed designs for advanced rockets. The American physicist Robert Goddard also designed rockets. Beginning around 1915, Goddard went a step further and built rockets to test his designs.

Rocket design made major advances during World War II. Military rockets were used to carry explosives. The Germans used a rocket called the V2 to destroy both military and civilian targets. The V2 was a large rocket that could travel about 300 kilometers. The designer of the V2, Wernher von Braun, came to the United States after the war was over. Von Braun used his experience to direct the development of many rockets used in the United States space program.

FIGURE 2
Chinese Rockets
According to a Chinese legend, around 1500 an official named Wan-Hoo tried to fly to the moon by tying a number of rockets to his chair. The rockets exploded with a tremendous roar. Once the smoke cleared, there was no trace of Wan-Hoo or his chair.

 **Reading Checkpoint** **Name three scientists who contributed to the development of modern rockets.**

Be a Rocket Scientist

You can build a rocket.

1. Use a plastic or paper cup as the rocket body. Cut out a paper nose cone. Tape it to the bottom of the cup.

2. Obtain an empty film canister with a lid that snaps on inside the canister. Go outside to do Steps 3–5.

3. Fill the canister about one-quarter full with water.

4. Put on your goggles. Now add half of a fizzing antacid tablet to the film canister and quickly snap on the lid.

5. Place the canister on the ground with the lid down. Place your rocket over the canister and stand back.

Observing

What action happened inside the film canister? What was the reaction of the rocket?

How Do Rockets Work?

A rocket can be as small as your finger or as large as a skyscraper. An essential feature of any rocket, though, is that it expels gas in one direction. **A rocket moves forward when gases shooting out the back of the rocket push it in the opposite direction.**

A rocket works in much the same way as a balloon that is propelled through the air by releasing gas. In most rockets, fuel is burned to make hot gas. The gas pushes outward in every direction, but it can leave the rocket only through openings at the back. The movement of gas out of these openings moves the rocket forward. Figure 3 shows how rockets move.

Action and Reaction Forces The movement of a rocket demonstrates a basic law of physics: For every force, or action, there is an equal and opposite force, or reaction. The force of the air moving out of a balloon is an action force. An equal force—the reaction force—pushes the balloon forward.

The reaction force that propels a rocket forward is called **thrust.** The amount of thrust depends on several factors, including the mass and speed of the gases propelled out of the rocket. The greater the thrust, the greater a rocket's velocity. **Velocity** is speed in a given direction.

Orbital and Escape Velocity In order to lift off the ground, a rocket must have more upward thrust than the downward force of gravity. Once a rocket is off the ground, it must reach a certain velocity in order to go into orbit. **Orbital velocity** is the velocity a rocket must achieve to establish an orbit around Earth. If the rocket moves slower than orbital velocity, Earth's gravity will cause it to fall back to the surface.

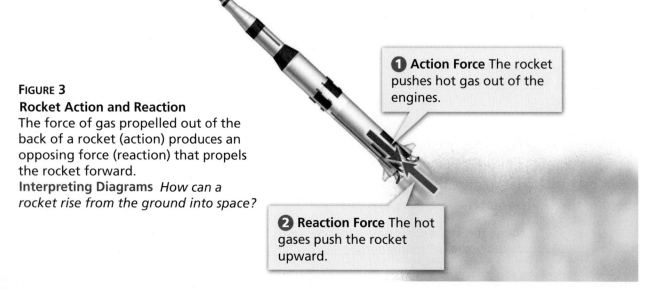

FIGURE 3

Rocket Action and Reaction
The force of gas propelled out of the back of a rocket (action) produces an opposing force (reaction) that propels the rocket forward.
Interpreting Diagrams *How can a rocket rise from the ground into space?*

❶ **Action Force** The rocket pushes hot gas out of the engines.

❷ **Reaction Force** The hot gases push the rocket upward.

Rocket Altitude

A rocket's altitude is how high it is above the ground. Use the graph at the right to answer the following questions about how a model rocket's altitude changes over time.

1. **Reading Graphs** What two variables are being graphed? In what unit is each measured?

2. **Reading Graphs** What was the rocket's altitude after 2 seconds? After 4 seconds?

3. **Reading Graphs** At what time did the rocket reach its greatest altitude?

4. **Inferring** Why do you think the rocket continued to rise after it ran out of fuel?

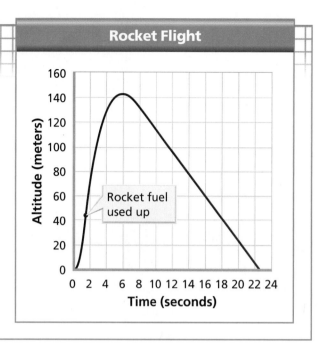

Rocket Flight

Rocket fuel used up

If the rocket has an even greater velocity, it can fly off into space. **Escape velocity** is the velocity a rocket must reach to fly beyond a planet's gravitational pull. The escape velocity a rocket needs to leave Earth is about 40,200 kilometers per hour. That's more than 11 kilometers every second!

Rocket Fuels Rockets create thrust by ejecting gas. Three types of fuel are used to power modern spacecraft: solid fuel, liquid fuel, and electrically charged particles of gas (ions). Solid-fuel and liquid-fuel rockets carry oxygen that allows the fuel to burn.

In a solid-fuel rocket, oxygen is mixed with the fuel, which is a dry explosive chemical. A fireworks rocket is a good example of a solid-fuel rocket. For such a simple rocket, a match can be used to ignite the fuel. Large solid-fuel rockets have a device called an igniter that can be triggered from a distance. Once a solid-fuel rocket is ignited, it burns until all the fuel is gone.

In a liquid-fuel rocket, both the oxygen and the fuel are in liquid form. They are stored in separate compartments. When the rocket fires, the fuel and oxygen are pumped into the same chamber and ignited. An advantage of liquid-fuel rockets is that the burning of fuel can be controlled by regulating how much liquid fuel and oxygen are mixed together.

Ion rockets do not burn chemical fuels. Rather, they expel gas ions out of their engines at very high speeds. Ion rockets generally create less thrust than solid-fuel or liquid-fuel rockets. But they are very fuel efficient.

FIGURE 4
Rocket Velocity
This artist's view shows a NASA rocket rising into space.

Reading Checkpoint What are the three types of rocket fuel?

J ◆ 43

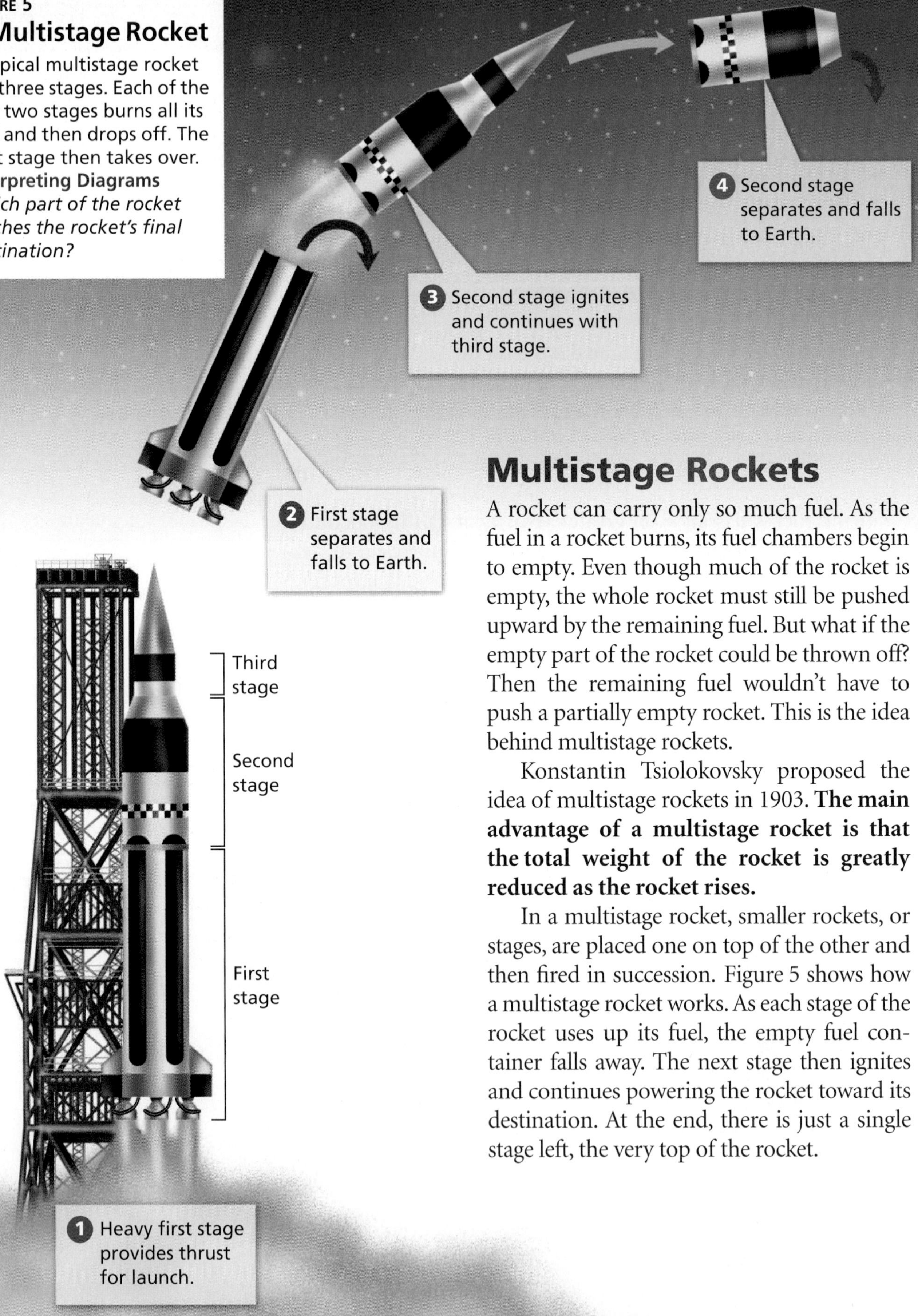

FIGURE 5

A Multistage Rocket

A typical multistage rocket has three stages. Each of the first two stages burns all its fuel and then drops off. The next stage then takes over.
Interpreting Diagrams
Which part of the rocket reaches the rocket's final destination?

4 Second stage separates and falls to Earth.

3 Second stage ignites and continues with third stage.

2 First stage separates and falls to Earth.

Third stage

Second stage

First stage

1 Heavy first stage provides thrust for launch.

Multistage Rockets

A rocket can carry only so much fuel. As the fuel in a rocket burns, its fuel chambers begin to empty. Even though much of the rocket is empty, the whole rocket must still be pushed upward by the remaining fuel. But what if the empty part of the rocket could be thrown off? Then the remaining fuel wouldn't have to push a partially empty rocket. This is the idea behind multistage rockets.

Konstantin Tsiolokovsky proposed the idea of multistage rockets in 1903. **The main advantage of a multistage rocket is that the total weight of the rocket is greatly reduced as the rocket rises.**

In a multistage rocket, smaller rockets, or stages, are placed one on top of the other and then fired in succession. Figure 5 shows how a multistage rocket works. As each stage of the rocket uses up its fuel, the empty fuel container falls away. The next stage then ignites and continues powering the rocket toward its destination. At the end, there is just a single stage left, the very top of the rocket.

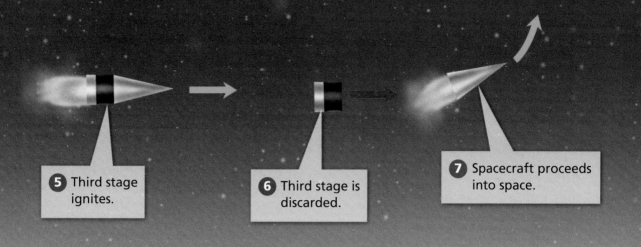

5 Third stage ignites.

6 Third stage is discarded.

7 Spacecraft proceeds into space.

Go Online
active art

For: Multistage Rocket activity
Visit: PHSchool.com
Web Code: cfp-5021

In the 1960s, the development of powerful multistage rockets such as the Saturn V made it possible to send spacecraft to the moon and the solar system beyond. The mighty Saturn V rocket stood 111 meters tall—higher than the length of a football field. It was by far the most powerful rocket ever built. Today, multistage rockets are used to launch a wide variety of satellites and space probes.

 **Reading Checkpoint** What is a multistage rocket?

Section **1** Assessment

Target Reading Skill Using Prior Knowledge
Review your graphic organizer and revise it based on what you just learned in the section.

Reviewing Key Concepts

1. a. Defining What is a rocket?
  b. Reviewing Where and when were rockets first developed?
  c. Summarizing For what purposes were rockets initially developed?
2. a. Explaining What is thrust?
  b. Explaining How do rockets create thrust?
  c. Interpreting Diagrams Use Figure 3 to explain how a rocket moves forward.
3. a. Describing Describe how a multistage rocket works.

  b. Comparing and Contrasting What is the main advantage of a multistage rocket compared to a single-stage rocket?
  c. Relating Cause and Effect Why can the third stage of a multistage rocket go faster than the first stage of the rocket, even though it has less fuel?

Writing in Science

Interview Suppose you were able to interview one of the scientists who helped to develop modern rockets. Choose one of the scientists identified in the section and write a series of questions that you would like to ask this person. Then use what you've learned to construct likely answers to these questions.

Design and Build a Water Rocket

Problem

Can you design and build a rocket propelled by water and compressed air?

Design Skills

observing, evaluating the design, redesigning

Materials

- large round balloon • tap water
- graduated cylinder • modeling clay
- 50 paper clips in a plastic bag
- empty 2-liter soda bottle • poster board
- scissors • hot glue gun or tape
- bucket, 5 gallon • stopwatch
- rocket launcher and tire pump (one per class)

Procedure   ⚠

PART 1 **Research and Investigate**

1. Copy the data table onto a separate sheet of paper.

Data Table	
Volume of Water (mL)	Motion of Balloon
No water	

2. In an outdoor area approved by your teacher, blow up a large round balloon. Hold the balloon so the opening is pointing down. Release the balloon and observe what occurs. **CAUTION:** *If you are allergic to latex, do not handle the balloon.*

3. Measure 50 mL of water with a graduated cylinder. Pour the water into the balloon. Blow it up to about the same size as the balloon in Step 2. Hold the opening down and release the balloon. Observe what happens.

4. Repeat Step 3 twice, varying the amount of water each time. Record your observations in the data table.

PART 2 **Design and Build**

5. You and a partner will design and build a water rocket using the materials provided or approved by your teacher. Your rocket must
   - be made from an empty 2-liter soda bottle
   - have fins and a removable nosecone
   - carry a load of 50 paper clips
   - use air only or a mixture of air and water as a propulsion system
   - be launched on the class rocket launcher
   - remain in the air for at least 5 seconds

6. Begin by thinking about how your rocket will work and how you would like it to look. Sketch your design and make a list of materials that you will need.

7. Rockets often have a set of fins to stabilize them in flight. Consider the best shape for fins, and decide how many fins your rocket needs. Use poster board to make your fins.

8. Decide how to safely and securely carry a load of 50 paper clips in your rocket.

9. Based on what you learned in Part 1, decide how much, if any, water to pour into your rocket.

10. After you obtain your teacher's approval, build your rocket.

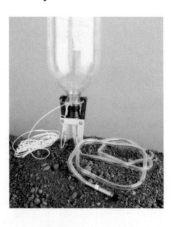

◀ **Rocket launcher**

PART 3 Evaluate and Redesign

11. Test your rocket by launching it on the rocket launcher provided by your teacher.
    CAUTION: *Make sure that the rocket is launched vertically in a safe, open area that is at least 30 m across. All observers should wear goggles and stay at least 8–10 m away from the rocket launcher. The rocket should be pumped to a pressure of no more than 50 pounds per square inch.*

12. Use a stopwatch to determine your rocket's flight time (how long it stays in the air.)

13. Record in a data table the results of your own launch and your classmates' launches.

14. Compare your design and results with those of your classmates.

Analyze and Conclude

1. **Observing** What did you observe about the motion of the balloon as more and more water was added?

2. **Drawing Conclusions** What purpose did adding water to the balloon serve?

3. **Designing a Solution** How did your results in Part 1 affect your decision about how much water, if any, to add to your rocket?

4. **Evaluating the Design** Did your rocket meet all the criteria listed in Step 5? Explain.

5. **Evaluating the Design** How did your rocket design compare to the rockets built by your classmates? Which rocket had the greatest flight time? What design features resulted in the most successful launches?

6. **Redesigning** Based on your launch results and your response to Question 5, explain how you could improve your rocket. How do you think these changes would help your rocket's performance?

7. **Evaluating the Impact on Society** Explain how an understanding of rocket propulsion has made space travel possible.

Communicate

Write a paragraph that describes how you designed and built your rocket. Explain how it worked. Include a labeled sketch of your design.

Go Online
PHSchool.com

For: Data sharing
Visit: PHSchool.com
Web Code: cfd-5021

The Space Program

Reading Preview

Key Concepts
- What was the space race?
- What were the major events in human exploration of the moon?

Key Term
- satellite

Target Reading Skill
Asking Questions Before you read, preview the red headings. In a graphic organizer like the one below, ask a question for each heading. As you read, write answers to your questions.

The Space Program

Question	Answer
What was the "space race"?	The "space race" was . . .

Discover **Activity**

Where on the Moon Did Astronauts Land?

1. Use a large map of the moon to find these locations: Sea of Tranquility, Ocean of Storms, Fra Mauro, Apennine Mountains, Descartes Highlands, and Valley of Taurus-Littrow.
2. American astronauts landed on and explored each of the locations you found. Using what you know about the moon and what you can see on the map, describe what you think astronauts saw at each place.

Think It Over
Inferring Did the names of the moon locations seem to fit with what you could see? Do you think the astronauts had to use boats to explore the Sea of Tranquility and the Ocean of Storms?

Sometimes competition results in great achievements. Maybe you've been motivated to try harder in a foot race when someone passed you by. Perhaps watching a friend accomplish a feat made you determined to do it, too. Competition resulted in one of the greatest achievements in history: In 1969 the first human set foot on the moon. This competition, though, was not between friends, but between the two most powerful nations in the world, the United States and the Soviet Union. Their rivalry in the exploration of space was called the "space race."

The Race for Space

The space race began in the 1950s. At that time, the Soviet Union was the greatest rival to the United States in politics and military power. The tensions between the two countries were so high that they were said to be in a "cold war." These tensions increased when the Soviets launched a satellite into space. **The space race began in 1957 when the Soviets launched the satellite *Sputnik I* into orbit. The United States responded by speeding up its own space program.**

◀ The first living creature sent into space was a dog named Laika. She orbited Earth aboard the Soviet spacecraft *Sputnik II* in November 1957.

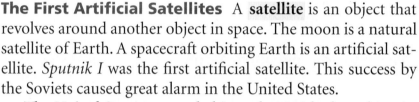

FIGURE 6
John Glenn
Friendship 7 lifted off from Cape Canaveral, Florida, in February 1962. It carried astronaut John Glenn, the first American to orbit Earth. The closeup photo shows Glenn climbing into the *Friendship 7* space capsule.
Observing *Where on the rocket was the space capsule located?*

The First Artificial Satellites A **satellite** is an object that revolves around another object in space. The moon is a natural satellite of Earth. A spacecraft orbiting Earth is an artificial satellite. *Sputnik I* was the first artificial satellite. This success by the Soviets caused great alarm in the United States.

The United States responded in early 1958 by launching its own satellite, *Explorer 1,* into orbit. Over the next few years, both the United States and the Soviet Union placed many more satellites into orbit around Earth.

Later in 1958, the United States established a government agency in charge of its space program, called the National Aeronautics and Space Administration (NASA). NASA brought together the talents of many scientists and engineers who worked together to solve the many difficult technical problems of space flight.

Humans in Space In 1961 the space race heated up even more when the Soviets launched the first human into space. Yuri Gagarin flew one orbit around Earth aboard *Vostok 1*. Less than a month later, astronaut Alan Shepard became the first American in space. His tiny spacecraft, called *Freedom 7*, was part of the U.S. Mercury space program. Other Soviet cosmonauts and American astronauts soon followed into space.

The first American to orbit Earth was John Glenn, who was launched into space in 1962 aboard *Friendship 7*. The spacecraft he traveled in was called a space capsule because it was like a small cap on the end of the rocket. The tiny capsule orbited Earth three times before returning to the surface.

 **Reading Checkpoint** Who was the first American in space?

Missions to the Moon

"I believe that this nation should commit itself to achieving the goal, before the decade is out, of landing a man on the moon and returning him safely to Earth." With these words from a May 1961 speech, President John F. Kennedy launched an enormous program of space exploration and scientific research. **The American effort to land astronauts on the moon was named the Apollo program.**

Exploring the Moon Between 1964 and 1972, the United States and the Soviet Union sent many unpiloted spacecraft to explore the moon. When a U.S. spacecraft called *Surveyor* landed on the moon, it didn't sink into the surface. This proved that the moon had a solid surface. Next, scientists searched for a suitable place to land humans on the moon.

The Moon Landings In July 1969, three American astronauts circled the moon aboard *Apollo 11*. Once in orbit, Neil Armstrong and Buzz Aldrin entered a tiny spacecraft called *Eagle*. On July 20, the *Eagle* descended toward a flat area on the moon's surface called the Sea of Tranquility. When Armstrong radioed that the *Eagle* had landed, cheers rang out at the NASA Space Center in Houston. A few hours later, Armstrong and Aldrin left the *Eagle* to explore the moon. When Armstrong first set foot on the surface, he said, "That's one small step for man, one giant leap for mankind." Armstrong meant to say, "That's one small step for *a* man," meaning himself, but in his excitement he never said the "a."

FIGURE 7
Apollo 11
On July 20, 1969, *Apollo 11* astronaut Neil Armstrong became the first person to walk on the moon. He took this photograph of Buzz Aldrin. The inset photo shows Armstrong's footprint on the lunar soil.

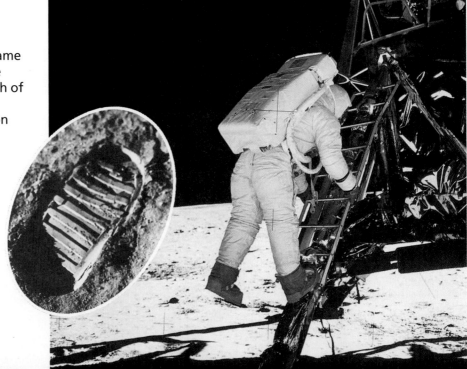

On the Moon's Surface Everything that the *Apollo 11* astronauts found was new and exciting. For about two hours, Armstrong and Aldrin explored the moon's surface, collecting samples to take back to Earth. They also planted an American flag.

Over the next three years, five more Apollo missions landed on the moon. In these later missions, astronauts were able to stay on the moon for days instead of hours. As shown in Figure 8, some astronauts even used a lunar rover, or buggy, to explore larger areas of the moon.

Moon Rocks and Moonquakes The astronauts collected nearly 400 kilograms of lunar samples, commonly called "moon rocks." When scientist analyzed these samples, they learned a great deal about the moon. For instance, they learned that the minerals that make up moon rocks are the same minerals that are found on Earth. However, in some moon rocks these minerals combine to form kinds of rocks that are not found on Earth. Scientists were also able to calculate the ages of the moon rocks. With that information, they could better estimate when different parts of the moon's surface formed.

One way that Apollo astronauts explored the structure of the moon was to purposely crash equipment onto the moon's surface. Instruments they left behind measured the "moonquake" waves that resulted. Using data collected from these artificial moonquakes, scientists determined that the moon may have a small core of molten rock at its center.

 **Reading Checkpoint** What did scientists learn from analyzing moon rocks?

FIGURE 8
Lunar Buggy
Astronauts on the later Apollo missions had a lunar buggy. **Inferring** *How could a lunar buggy help the astronauts to explore the moon's surface?*

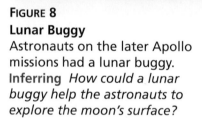
Go Online
PHSchool.com

For: More on lunar exploration
Visit: PHSchool.com
Web Code: cfd-5022

FIGURE 9
Lunar Base
A possible future base on the moon is shown in this painting.
Predicting *How might a lunar base be useful for the future human exploration of Mars?*

New Missions to the Moon The Apollo missions were a tremendous achievement. They yielded fascinating information and memorable images. Yet, the cost of those missions was high, and there were few immediate benefits beyond the knowledge gained about the moon. NASA moved on to other projects. For decades, the moon was largely ignored.

Recently, however, interest in the moon has revived. In 2003, the European Space Agency launched an unpiloted spacecraft to orbit the moon. Its main purpose was to collect data for a detailed map of the moon. Private businesses have funded similar research spacecraft.

Soon, humans may walk again on the moon. In 2004, the United States announced a plan to establish a permanent colony of people on the moon. From such a base, missions could be launched to carry people to Mars.

Section 2 Assessment

Target Reading Skills Asking Questions Use the answers to the questions you wrote about the headings to help you answer the questions below.

Reviewing Key Concepts

1. a. **Summarizing** What was the "space race"?
   b. **Identifying** What event began the space race?
   c. **Relating Cause and Effect** What role did competition play in the space race? Who were the competitors?
2. a. **Identifying** What was the Apollo program?
   b. **Sequencing** Place these events in the correct sequence: first humans on the moon, *Sputnik I,* first American in space, John Glenn orbits Earth, NASA formed, Yuri Gagarin orbits Earth.
   c. **Drawing Conclusions** Was the Apollo program successful in meeting President Kennedy's challenge?

Lab zone At-Home **Activity**

Landmarks in Space Flight
Interview someone who remembers the early space programs. Prepare your questions in advance, such as: What did you think when you heard that *Sputnik* was in orbit? How did you feel when the first Americans went into space? Did you watch any of the space flights on TV? You may want to record your interview and then write it out later.

Exploring Space Today

Reading Preview

Key Concepts
- What are the roles of space shuttles and space stations?
- What features do space probes have in common?

Key Terms
- space shuttle
- space station
- space probe
- rover

Target Reading Skill

Outlining As you read, make an outline about exploring space. Use the red headings for the main topics and the blue headings for the subtopics.

Exploring Space Today
I. Working in space
A. Space shuttles
B.
II. Space probes
A.

Discover **Activity**

What Do You Need to Survive in Space?

1. Make a list of everything that would be essential to your well-being if you were placed in a spacecraft in orbit around Earth.
2. Cross out everything on the list that you wouldn't be able to find while in orbit.
3. For each of the items you crossed out, suggest a way you could provide yourself with that essential item while in space.

Think It Over
Drawing Conclusions Is there anything necessary to your well-being that you wouldn't have to take with you into space? How hard would it be to provide everything you need for a journey into space?

Can you imagine living in space? When you're in orbit, you feel weightless, so there is no up or down. Astronaut Janet Kavandi knows how it feels. She spent eleven days aboard the Russian space station *Mir.* As she floated inside the central cabin, she could look into modules that extended outward in every direction.

"It was very amusing to look into one module and see people standing on the wall, working on an experiment. In the adjacent module, someone might be jogging on a treadmill on the ceiling. Beneath your feet, you might see someone having a meal. Above your head, you'd hear the thumping of a body coming toward you, and you'd have to move aside to let him pass."

Janet Kavandi aboard ▶
the space shuttle

FIGURE 10
The Space Shuttle
The Space Shuttle *Discovery* is launched into space by liquid–fuel powered engines as well as by a pair of reusable solid-fuel booster rockets.
Inferring What is one advantage of a reusable space vehicle?

External fuel tank

Solid fuel rocket booster

Shuttle orbiter

Working in Space

After the great success of the moon landings, the question for space exploration was, "What comes next?" Scientists and public officials decided that one goal should be to build space shuttles and space stations where astronauts can live and work.

Space Shuttles Before 1983, spacecraft could be used only once. In contrast, a space shuttle is like an airplane—it can fly, land, and then fly again. A **space shuttle** is a spacecraft that can carry a crew into space, return to Earth, and then be reused for the same purpose. A shuttle includes large rockets that launch it into orbit and then fall away. At the end of a mission, a shuttle returns to Earth by landing like an airplane. **NASA has used space shuttles to perform many important tasks. These include taking satellites into orbit, repairing damaged satellites, and carrying astronauts and equipment to and from space stations.**

During a shuttle mission, astronauts live in a pressurized crew cabin at the front of the shuttle. There, they can wear regular clothes and breathe without an oxygen tank. Behind the crew cabin is a large, open area called the payload bay. The payload bay is like the trailer end of a large truck that carries supplies to stores and factories. A shuttle payload bay might carry a satellite to be released into orbit or a scientific laboratory in which astronauts can perform experiments.

NASA has built six shuttles. Tragically, two—*Challenger* and *Columbia*—were destroyed during flights. After the *Columbia* disaster in 2003, there was much debate about whether to continue the shuttle program. One reason to keep flying space shuttles is to deliver astronauts and supplies to the International Space Station. NASA currently plans to retire the shuttle by 2010 and replace it with a new reusable spacecraft.

Space Stations A **space station** is a large artificial satellite on which people can live and work for long periods. **A space station provides a place where long-term observations and experiments can be carried out in space.** In the 1970s and 1980s, both the United States and the Soviet Union placed space stations in orbit. The Soviet space station *Mir* stayed in orbit for 15 years before it fell to Earth in 2001. Astronauts from many countries, including Janet Kavandi and other Americans, spent time aboard *Mir*.

In the 1980s, the United States and 15 other countries began planning the construction of the International Space Station. The first module, or section, of the station was placed into orbit in 1998. Since then, many other modules have been added. On board, astronauts and scientists from many countries are already carrying out experiments in various fields of science. They are also learning more about how humans adapt to space. Figure 11 shows how the space station will look when completed. It will be longer than a football field, and the living space will be about as large as the inside of the largest passenger jet.

The International Space Station has large batteries to guarantee that it always has power. Its main source of power, though, is its eight large arrays of solar panels. Together, the solar panels contain more than 250,000 solar cells, each capable of converting sunlight into electricity. At full power, the solar panels produce enough electricity to power about 55 houses on Earth.

Reading Checkpoint What is a space station?

Exploring Space

Video Preview
▶ Video Field Trip
Video Assessment

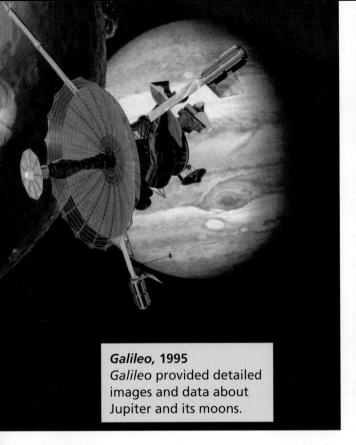

Lunar Prospector, **1998**
Lunar Prospector found evidence of water ice and identified other minerals on the moon's surface.

Galileo, **1995**
Galileo provided detailed images and data about Jupiter and its moons.

FIGURE 12

Space Probes

These are artist's views of the *Galileo, Lunar Prospector, Mars Exploration Rover,* and *Cassini* space probes.
Comparing and Contrasting *What advantage does a rover have compared to a probe that remains in orbit?*

Go Online

SC*LINKS* NSTA

For: Links on space exploration
Visit: www.SciLinks.org
Web Code: scn-0623

Space Probes

Since space exploration began in the 1950s, only 24 people have traveled as far as the moon—and no one has traveled farther. Yet, during this period space scientists have gathered great amounts of information about other parts of the solar system. This data was collected by space probes. A **space probe** is a spacecraft that carries scientific instruments that can collect data, but has no human crew.

How Do Probes Work? Each space probe is designed for a specific mission. Some probes are designed to land on a certain planet. Other probes are designed to fly by and collect data about more than one planet. Thus, each probe is unique. Still, all probes have some features in common. **Each space probe has a power system to produce electricity, a communication system to send and receive signals, and scientific instruments to collect data and perform experiments.**

The scientific instruments that a probe contains depend on the probe's mission. Some probes are equipped to photograph and analyze the atmosphere of a planet. Other probes are equipped to land on a planet and analyze the materials on its surface. Some probes have small robots called **rovers** that move around on the surface. A rover typically has instruments that collect and analyze soil and rock samples.

Mars Rovers, 2004–Present
Two rovers, *Opportunity* and *Spirit,* explored Mars's surface and found evidence of ancient water.

Cassini, 2004–2008
Cassini is exploring Saturn's moons. It launched a smaller probe, *Huygens,* to explore Titan, Saturn's largest moon.

Exploring With Space Probes Probes have now visited or passed near to all of the planets. They have also explored many moons, asteroids, and comets. The information gathered by probes has given scientists tremendous new insights about the environments on the different planets. These probes have helped to solve many of the mysteries of the solar system.

 Reading Checkpoint **What is a rover?**

Section 3 Assessment

Target Reading Skill Outlining Use the information in your outline about exploring space to answer the questions below.

Reviewing Key Concepts

1. a. **Describing** What is the space shuttle? What is its main advantage?
   b. **Defining** What is a space station?
   c. **Comparing and Contrasting** What are the roles of space shuttles and space stations in the space program?
2. a. **Summarizing** What is a space probe?
   b. **Listing** List three features that are common to all space probes.
   c. **Making Judgments** What do you think are some advantages and disadvantages of a space probe compared to a piloted spacecraft?

Writing in Science

News Report As a newspaper reporter, you are covering the launch of a new space probe. Write a brief news story, including details on the probe's mission and how the probe works. What planet will it explore? What question will it try to answer?

Using Space Science on Earth

Reading Preview

Key Concepts
- How are the conditions in space different from those on Earth?
- How has space technology benefited modern society?
- What are some uses of satellites orbiting Earth?

Key Terms
- vacuum • microgravity
- space spinoff
- remote sensing
- geostationary orbit

Target Reading Skill
Identifying Main Ideas As you read the Space Spinoffs section, write the main idea in a graphic organizer like the one below. Then write three supporting details that give examples of the main idea.

Main Idea

The space program has produced many spinoffs in areas such as . . .

Detail	Detail	Detail

Discover Activity

Which Tool Would Be More Useful in Space?
1. Observe your teacher using two types of drills.
2. Pick up each drill and examine how it works.
3. Repeat Step 2 for a space pen and a regular pen.

Think It Over
Drawing Conclusions What is the main difference between the two drills? The pens? Which drill would be more useful to have while constructing the International Space Station? Why? How would a space pen be useful in space?

You've probably used a joystick to play a video game. A joystick is a great way to control images on a screen. It's easy to use because it is designed to fit the hand just right. Joystick controllers have many uses besides video games. They're so well engineered that people with disabilities can use them to operate a wheelchair.

The joystick was invented for controlling airplanes. It was later improved by NASA for the space program. Apollo astronauts used a joystick to operate a lunar rover on the moon. From the surface of the moon to video games on Earth—it's not such a stretch. Many materials and devices have made a similar transition from use in space to everyday use by people on Earth.

FIGURE 13
Joystick Controls
The joysticks used for some wheelchairs were originally improved for the space program.

The Challenges of Space

Astronauts who travel into space face conditions that are very different from those on Earth. **Conditions in space that differ from those on Earth include near vacuum, extreme temperatures, and microgravity.** Many types of engineers and scientists have worked together to respond to the challenges of space.

Vacuum Space is nearly a vacuum. A **vacuum** is a place that is empty of all matter. Except for a few stray atoms and molecules, most of space is empty. Since there is no air in space, there is no oxygen for astronauts to breathe. To protect astronauts, spacecraft must be airtight.

Because there is no air, there is nothing to hold the sun's heat. In direct sunlight, the surface of a spacecraft heats up to high temperatures. But in shadow, temperatures fall to very low levels. Spacecraft must be well insulated to protect astronauts against the extreme temperatures outside.

Microgravity Astronauts in orbit experience a feeling of weightlessness, or **microgravity**. Their mass is the same as it was on Earth, but on a scale their weight would register as zero. Although they are in microgravity, they are still under the influence of Earth's gravity. In fact, Earth's gravity is holding them in orbit. Astronauts in orbit feel weightless because they are falling through space with their spacecraft. They don't fall to Earth because their inertia keeps them moving forward.

Space engineers must create systems and devices that are capable of working in microgravity. For example, drink containers must be designed so that their contents do not simply float off. Long periods in microgravity can cause health problems. Scientists are trying to discover how to reduce the effects of microgravity on people.

FIGURE 14
Microgravity
This astronaut appears to be floating in space, but he is actually falling through space at the same rate as the nearby spacecraft.
Inferring *Why doesn't the astronaut fall directly down toward Earth?*

Reading Checkpoint What is microgravity?

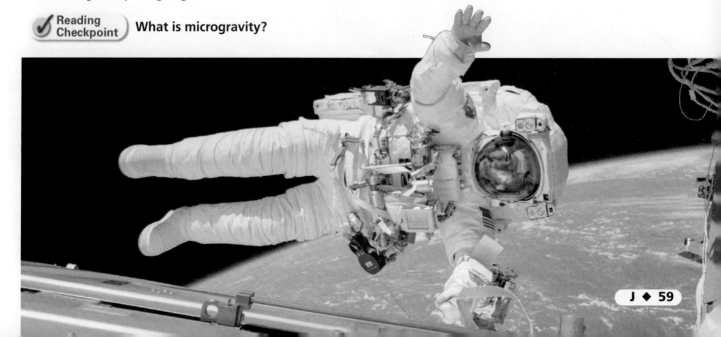

Go Online

SciLINKS NSTA

For: Links on satellite technology
Visit: www.SciLinks.org
Web Code: scn-0624

FIGURE 15

Spinoffs From the Space Program

Many technologies that were developed for the space program have proved useful on Earth as well. A few of these technologies are shown here.
Applying Concepts *What advantage is there to fog-free vision in space? On Earth?*

Space Spinoffs

The scientists and engineers who have worked on the space program have developed thousands of new materials and devices for use in space. Many of these items have proved useful on Earth, as well. An item that has uses on Earth but was originally developed for use in space is called a **space spinoff.** Often such spinoffs are modified somewhat for use on Earth.

The space program has developed thousands of products that affect many aspects of modern society, including consumer products, new materials, medical devices, and communications satellites. Figure 15 shows a few familiar examples.

Consumer Products Space spinoffs include many devices that are used in consumer products. The joystick controller is one example. The bar codes on every product you buy at a grocery store are another space spinoff. Similar bar codes were developed by NASA to keep an accurate inventory of the many parts used in spacecraft.

Cordless power tools were also originally developed for astronauts. There's no place to "plug in" a tool when repairing a satellite in space. Cordless, rechargeable tools met the need for work in space. Now they're very popular here on Earth. Other examples of consumer product spinoffs from the space program include scratch-resistant lenses, freeze-dried foods, shock-absorbing helmets, and smoke detectors.

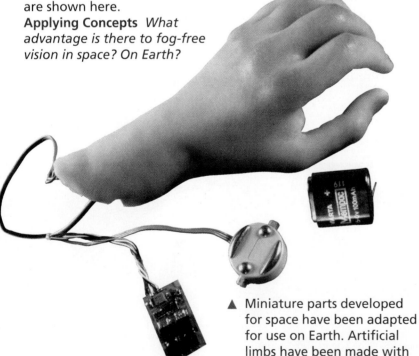

▲ Miniature parts developed for space have been adapted for use on Earth. Artificial limbs have been made with controls as small as coins.

▼ A metal alloy of nickel and titanium used in dental braces was originally developed for space equipment such as antennas.

New Materials A variety of materials were first developed by chemists and engineers for use in spacecraft. For example, flexible metal eyeglass frames are made with memory metals—metals that "remember" their former shapes when bent. The composite materials used in modern tennis rackets and golf clubs were developed to make spacecraft components lightweight yet strong. The athletic shoes you wear might contain a shock-absorbing material developed for astronauts' moon boots. A clear, ceramic material used for invisible dental braces was the result of research to make tough materials for spacecraft.

Highly efficient insulating materials were developed to protect spacecraft against radiation in space. These insulating materials are now being used in houses, cars, and trucks. Fire-resistant material developed for spacesuits is used in fireproof clothing and firefighter's suits.

Medical Devices Medical science has benefited greatly from the technology of the space program. Medical spinoffs include devices that use lasers to clean clogged arteries and pacemakers for hearts. These pacemakers use longer-life batteries originally developed for space power systems. Most hospitals use computer-aided imaging techniques developed for use on the moon during the Apollo program.

Reading Checkpoint Why did NASA develop cordless power tools?

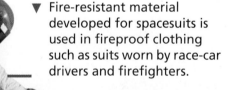

▼ Fire-resistant material developed for spacesuits is used in fireproof clothing such as suits worn by race-car drivers and firefighters.

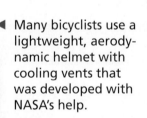

◄ Many bicyclists use a lightweight, aerody-namic helmet with cooling vents that was developed with NASA's help.

◄ The design of the Apollo helmet, which gave the astronauts fog-free sight, has been adapted for use in ski goggles.

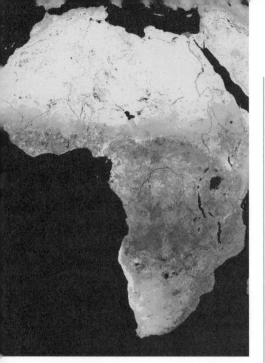

FIGURE 16
Remote Sensing
This satellite image shows patterns of vegetation in Africa. It is a false-color image, meaning that the colors have been adjusted to make certain features more obvious.
Inferring *What do you think the yellow areas in the image represent?*

Satellites

When a World Cup soccer final is played, almost the entire world can watch! Today, hundreds of satellites are in orbit around Earth, relaying television signals from one part of the planet to another. Satellites also relay telephone signals and computer data. **Satellites are used for communications and for collecting weather data and other scientific data.**

Observation satellites are used for many purposes, including tracking weather systems, mapping Earth's surface, and observing changes in Earth's environment. Observation satellites collect data using **remote sensing,** which is the collection of information about Earth and other objects in space without being in direct contact. Modern computers take the data collected by satellites and produce images for various purposes. For example, Figure 16 shows vegetation patterns in Africa. Satellite data might also be used to analyze the amount of rainfall over a wide area, or they might be used to discover where oil deposits lie underground.

Satellites are placed in different orbits depending on their purpose. Most communications satellites are placed in a geostationary orbit. In a **geostationary orbit,** a satellite orbits Earth at the same rate as Earth rotates and thus stays over the same place on Earth all the time. Read the *Technology and Society* feature on pages 64–65 to learn more about communications satellites.

 **Reading Checkpoint** **What is remote sensing?**

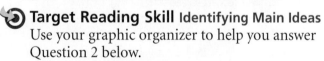

Section 4 Assessment

🎯 **Target Reading Skill Identifying Main Ideas**
Use your graphic organizer to help you answer Question 2 below.

Reviewing Key Concepts

1. **a. Listing** Name three ways that conditions in space are different from conditions on Earth.
   b. Relating Cause and Effect How have engineers designed spacecraft to operate in the special conditions of space?
2. **a. Defining** What is a space spinoff?
   b. Summarizing How has medical science benefited from the space program?
   c. Comparing and Contrasting Choose one space spinoff and compare how it is used in space and on Earth.

3. **a. Listing** Name three uses of satellites that affect everyday life.
   b. Inferring What advantage would there be to placing a satellite in geostationary orbit?
   c. Designing Experiments How could a scientist use satellites to determine whether a rain forest was becoming smaller over time?

Lab zone **At-Home Activity**

Spinoffs at Home Look back at the various space spinoffs discussed in the chapter. Then, with a family member, make a list of space spinoffs in your home.

Space Spinoffs

Problem

Which blanket protects better against heat loss?

Skills Focus

graphing, drawing conclusions

Materials

- 1 foil blanket piece • 1 cloth blanket piece
- 3 thermometers • 1 beaker, 600 mL • ice
- 3 identical small test tubes • hot water
- 3 identical large test tubes • cotton balls
- cellophane tape or rubber bands • tap water

Procedure

1. On a separate sheet of paper, copy the data table below to record your observations.

2. Wrap the outside of one small test tube with the foil blanket piece. Wrap a second small test tube with the cloth blanket piece. Use tape or rubber bands to secure the blankets. Leave the third small test tube unwrapped.

3. Fill each of the three small test tubes half full with hot water. Be sure to use the same volume of water in each test tube. Insert a thermometer into each small test tube. Use cotton to "seal" the top of the small test tube and to hold the thermometer in place. Then, insert each small test tube into a large test tube.

4. Put ice in the beaker and fill the beaker two-thirds of the way with water.

5. Put the large test tubes into the ice water. Do not let water enter the test tubes. Record the starting temperatures of all three thermometers.

6. Allow the test tubes to sit in the ice water bath for about 10 minutes. Every minute note the temperature of each thermometer and record the results in your data table.

Analyze and Conclude

1. **Graphing** Graph the temperature over time for each of the thermometers.

2. **Calculating** Calculate the difference between the starting and ending temperatures of each thermometer. Which thermometer was best protected against heat loss?

3. **Controlling Variables** What was the purpose of the third, unwrapped small test tube?

4. **Drawing Conclusions** Which type of blanket protects better against heat loss? Explain.

5. **Communicating** Write an advertisement for the blanket that proved to be the best insulator. In the ad, describe the test procedures you used to justify your claim. Also explain why this blanket would benefit consumers.

Design an Experiment

The activity you just completed tested how well different materials protected against the loss of heat. Design an experiment that would test how well the same blankets would protect against an increase in heat. Obtain your teacher's approval before conducting your experiment.

Data Table			
Time (minutes)	Temperature (°C)		
	Foil-Wrapped Thermometer	Cloth-Wrapped Thermometer	Unwrapped Thermometer
0			
1			

Communications Satellites

What do watching TV, talking on a cellular phone, and sending e-mails have in common? Satellites orbiting Earth make these types of communication possible. Using microwaves, communications satellites receive and transmit radio, telephone, TV, computer data, and other signals. This technology has changed the way people around the globe communicate.

Orbiting Satellites

Communications satellites orbit Earth at different speeds and different altitudes. One type—geostationary satellites—are especially useful for long-distance communication because they orbit Earth at the same rate as Earth rotates. As a result, these satellites remain over fixed points on Earth. Geostationary satellites orbit at an altitude of about 35,880 km. Today there are more than 150 geostationary satellites located in a band around the Equator.

Bus
The bus is the satellite framework. It holds and protects the computer, the engine, and other equipment. Batteries in the bus store the energy that's used to power the satellite.

Kick Motor
The kick motor maintains the orbit of the satellite.

Receiving Antenna
This antenna receives signals sent from Earth and converts them to messages that the onboard computer understands.

Ground Station
These stations receive and transmit signals.

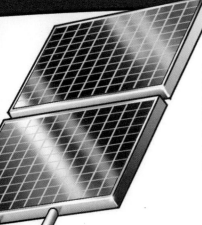

Solar Panels
Solar cells in the solar panels convert sunlight into electricity. Batteries store the energy that's used to power the satellite.

The Cost of Going Global

Communications satellites can relay signals, allowing the immediate exchange of information worldwide. Like all technology, though, there are trade-offs to using satellites. Earth's atmosphere can interfere with signals, causing problems such as static and time delays. Satellites cost hundreds of millions of dollars to build and even more to launch into space. When they are no longer useful, many burn up in space or become space junk.

Transmitting Antenna
This antenna changes data into signals that can be sent to Earth.

Cellular phone signals are sent by communications satellites.

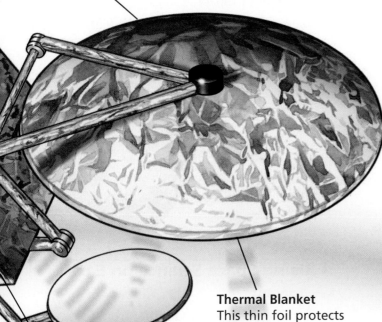

Thermal Blanket
This thin foil protects the satellite from extreme temperatures.

Onboard Computer
A computer controls and monitors all parts of the satellite.

Ground Station

Weigh the Impact

1. Identify the Need
How have communications satellites changed people's lives?

2. Research
Research the uses of communications satellites over the last 20 years. List their influences on society.

3. Write
In several paragraphs, describe ways in which you and your family use this satellite technology in your daily lives.

Go Online
PHSchool.com

For: More on communications satellites
Visit: PHSchool.com
Web Code: cfh-5020

1 The Science of Rockets

Key Concepts

- Rocket technology originated in China hundreds of years ago and gradually spread to other parts of the world.

- A rocket moves forward when gases shooting out the back of the rocket push it in the opposite direction.

- The main advantage of a multistage rocket is that the total weight of the rocket is greatly reduced as the rocket rises.

Key Terms

rocket
thrust
velocity
orbital velocity
escape velocity

2 The Space Program

Key Concepts

- The space race began in 1957 when the Soviets launched the satellite *Sputnik I* into orbit. The United States responded by speeding up its own space program.

- The American effort to land astronauts on the moon was named the Apollo program.

Key Term

satellite

3 Exploring Space Today

Key Concepts

- NASA has used space shuttles to perform many important tasks. These include taking satellites into orbit, repairing damaged satellites, and carrying astronauts and equipment to and from space stations.

- A space station provides a place where long-term observations and experiments can be carried out in space.

- Space probes contain a power system to produce electricity, a communication system to send and receive signals, and scientific instruments to collect data and perform experiments.

Key Terms

space shuttle
space station
space probe
rover

4 Using Space Science on Earth

Key Concepts

- Conditions in space that differ from those on Earth include the near vacuum, temperature extremes, and microgravity.

- The space program has developed thousands of products that affect many aspects of modern society, including consumer products, new materials, medical devices, and communications satellites.

- Satellites are used for communications and for collecting weather data and other scientific data.

Key Terms

vacuum
microgravity
space spinoff
remote sensing
geostationary orbit

Review and Assessment

Organizing Information

Comparing and Contrasting Copy the graphic organizer onto a separate sheet of paper. Then complete it and add a title. (For more on Comparing and Contrasting, see the Skills Handbook.)

Astronaut	Year	Spacecraft	Accomplishment
Yuri Gagarin	1961	a. ___?___	First human in space
Alan Shepard	b. ___?___	Freedom 7	c. ___?___
d. ___?___	1962	Friendship 7	e. ___?___
Neil Armstrong	f. ___?___	g. ___?___	First human to walk on the moon

Reviewing Key Terms

Choose the letter of the best answer.

1. A device that expels gas in one direction to move in the opposite direction is a
   a. rocket.   **b.** space probe.
   c. space station.   **d.** rover.

2. To fly beyond a planet's gravitational pull, a spacecraft must reach
   a. velocity.
   b. orbital velocity.
   c. escape velocity.
   d. geostationary orbit.

3. Any object that revolves around another object in space is called a
   a. vacuum.
   b. space station.
   c. satellite.
   d. rocket.

4. A spacecraft that can carry a crew into space, return to Earth, and then be reused for the same purpose is a
   a. rover.
   b. space shuttle.
   c. space station.
   d. space probe.

5. Acquiring information about Earth and other objects in space without being in direct contact with these worlds is called
   a. microgravity.
   b. spinoff.
   c. thrust.
   d. remote sensing.

If the statement is true, write *true*. If it is false, change the underlined word or words to make the statement true.

6. The reaction force that propels a rocket forward is called <u>microgravity</u>.

7. The velocity a rocket must reach to establish an orbit in space is <u>escape velocity.</u>

8. A large artificial satellite on which people can live for long periods is a <u>space station</u>.

9. An item that has uses on Earth, but was originally developed for use in space is called a <u>space shuttle</u>.

10. A satellite in <u>geostationary orbit</u> stays over the same place on Earth all the time.

Writing in Science

Descriptive Paragraph Imagine that you are a scientist planning the first human expedition to Mars. In a detailed paragraph, list some of the major challenges that such a mission would face and provide possible solutions. Think about the physical stresses of space travel and how the crew's basic needs will be met.

Discovery CHANNEL **SCHOOL**™

Exploring Space
Video Preview
Video Field Trip
▶ Video Assessment

Review and Assessment

Checking Concepts

11. What are three types of rocket fuels?

12. What did Neil Armstrong say when he first set foot on the moon?

13. Describe some tasks carried out by the crew of the space shuttle.

14. What is the purpose of a space station?

15. Name a space spinoff in each of the following categories: medical devices, materials, and consumer products.

Thinking Critically

16. **Applying Concepts** The diagram below shows a rocket lifting off. What does each of the arrows represent?

17. **Classifying** A jet airplane usually uses liquid fuel that is burned with oxygen from the atmosphere. A jet engine expels hot gases to the rear, and the airplane moves forward. Is a jet a type of rocket? Explain.

18. **Relating Cause and Effect** When the Soviet Union launched *Sputnik I* into orbit in 1957, educators in the United States decided to improve math and science education in U.S. schools. Why do you think educators made that decision?

19. **Making Judgments** Do you think that the benefits of the Apollo program outweighed the program's costs? Explain.

20. **Comparing and Contrasting** How is orbital velocity different from escape velocity?

21. **Making Generalizations** How could the International Space Station help with further exploration of the solar system?

Applying Skills

Use the graph below to answer Questions 22–24.

The graph shows the amounts of time needed for satellites at different altitudes above Earth's surface to complete one orbit.

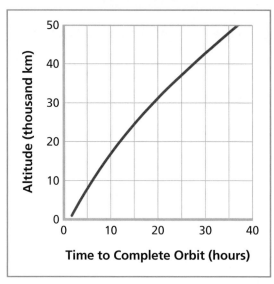

22. **Interpreting Diagrams** How long will a satellite orbiting at an altitude of 50,000 km take to complete one orbit?

23. **Applying Concepts** A geostationary satellite orbits Earth once every 24 hours. At what altitude does such a satellite orbit?

24. **Making Generalizations** What is the relationship between satellite altitude and the time needed to complete one orbit?

▶ Lab zone Chapter **Project**

Performance Assessment Before testing your vehicle, list your design goals and criteria. Describe some of the challenges you faced. What could you change to improve your model?

Standardized Test Prep

Choose the letter of the answer that best answers the question or completes the statement.

1. Which of the following developments was most directly responsible for the creation of rockets that were capable to going to the moon?

   A gunpowder   B explosives
   C single-stage   D multistage rockets
      rockets

2. What force must a rocket overcome to be launched into space?

   F thrust   G gravity
   H orbital velocity   J escape velocity

3. During the space race, the former Soviet Union was the first to accomplish all of the following except
   A launching the first satellite into orbit.
   B sending the first living creature into space.
   C sending the first human into space.
   D landing the first human on the moon.

4. A satellite in geostationary orbit revolves around Earth once each
   F hour.   G week.
   H month.   J day.

The diagram below shows a rocket and the direction of four forces. Use the diagram and your knowledge of rockets to answer Question 5.

5. Which of the lettered forces shown in the diagram represents an equal and opposite force to the thrust of the rocket?
   A Force A   B Force B
   C Force C   D Force D

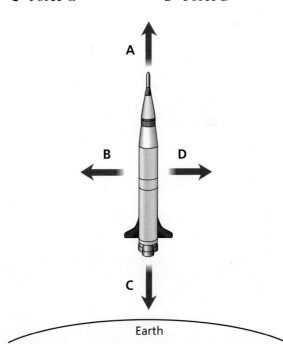

Earth

Constructed Response

6. Space probes have been used to explore all the planets, but not yet Pluto. Describe three types of information that a probe orbiting Pluto could gather about it.

Chapter

3

The Solar System

The BIG Idea
Structure of the Solar System

 Q What types of objects are found in the solar system?

This illustration shows the planets ▶ in orbit around the sun.

Lab zone™ Chapter **Project**

Build a Model of the Solar System

The solar system is a vast region containing the sun, planets, and many other objects. To help you understand the huge distances involved, you will design three different scale models of the solar system.

Your Goal To design scale models of the solar system

To complete this project, you will

- design a model to show the planets' distances from the sun
- design a model to show the planets' sizes compared to the sun
- test different scales to see if you can use the same scale for both size and distance in one model

Plan It! Begin by previewing the planet tables in this chapter. With a group of classmates, brainstorm how to build your models. Then design two models—one to show distances and one to show diameters. Next, design a third model that uses the same scale for both size and distance. Try several different scales to find which works best. Prepare a data table to record your calculations.

Observing the Solar System

Reading Preview

Key Concepts
- What are the geocentric and heliocentric systems?
- How did Copernicus, Galileo, and Kepler contribute to our knowledge of the solar system?
- What objects make up the solar system?

Key Terms
- geocentric • heliocentric
- ellipse

Target Reading Skill

Previewing Visuals Preview Figure 2 and Figure 3. Then write two questions that you have about the diagrams in a graphic organizer. As you read, answer your questions.

Models of the Universe

Q. What is a geocentric model?
A.
Q.

FIGURE 1
Star Trails
This photo was made by exposing the camera film for several hours. Each star appears as part of a circle, and all the stars seem to revolve around the North Star.

Lab zone Discover **Activity**

What Is at the Center?

1. Stand about 2 meters from a partner who is holding a flashlight. Have your partner shine the flashlight in your direction. Tell your partner not to move the flashlight.
2. Continue facing your partner, but move sideways in a circle, staying about 2 meters away from your partner.
3. Record your observations about your ability to see the light.
4. Repeat the activity, but this time remain stationary and continually face one direction. Have your partner continue to hold the flashlight toward you and move sideways around you, remaining about 2 meters from you.
5. Record your observations about your ability to see the light.

Think It Over
Drawing Conclusions Compare your two sets of observations. If you represent Earth and your partner represents the sun, is it possible, just from your observations, to tell whether Earth or the sun is in the center of the solar system?

Have you ever gazed up at the sky on a starry night? If you watch for several hours, the stars seem to move across the sky. The sky seems to be rotating right over your head. In fact, from the Northern Hemisphere, the sky appears to rotate completely around the North Star once every 24 hours.

Now think about what you see every day. During the day, the sun appears to move across the sky. From here on Earth, it seems as if Earth is stationary and that the sun, moon, and stars are moving around Earth. But is the sky really moving above you? Centuries ago, before there were space shuttles or even telescopes, there was no easy way to find out.

Earth at the Center

When the ancient Greeks watched the stars move across the sky, they noticed that the patterns of the stars didn't change. Although the stars seemed to move, they stayed in the same position relative to one another. These patterns of stars, called constellations, kept the same shapes from night to night and from year to year.

Greek Observations As the Greeks observed the sky, they noticed something surprising. Several points of light seemed to wander slowly among the stars. The Greeks called these objects *planets,* from the Greek word meaning "wanderers." The Greeks made careful observations of the motions of the planets that they could see. You know these planets by the names the ancient Romans later gave them: Mercury, Venus, Mars, Jupiter, and Saturn.

Most early Greek astronomers believed the universe to be perfect, with Earth at the center. The Greeks thought that Earth is inside a rotating dome they called the celestial sphere. Since *geo* is the Greek word for "Earth," an Earth-centered model is known as a **geocentric** (jee oh SEN trik) system. **In a geocentric system, Earth is at the center of the revolving planets and stars.**

Ptolemy's Model About A.D. 140, the Greek astronomer Ptolemy (TAHL uh mee) further developed the geocentric model. Like the earlier Greeks, Ptolemy thought that Earth is at the center of a system of planets and stars. In Ptolemy's model, however, the planets move on small circles that move on bigger circles.

Even though Ptolemy's geocentric model was incorrect, it explained the motions observed in the sky fairly accurately. As a result, the geocentric model of the universe was widely accepted for nearly 1,500 years after Ptolemy.

✓ **Reading Checkpoint** What is a geocentric system?

FIGURE 2
Geocentric System
In a geocentric system, the planets and stars are thought to revolve around a stationary Earth. In the 1500s, an astronomy book published the illustration of Ptolemy's geocentric system shown below.
Interpreting Diagrams *Where is Earth located in each illustration?*

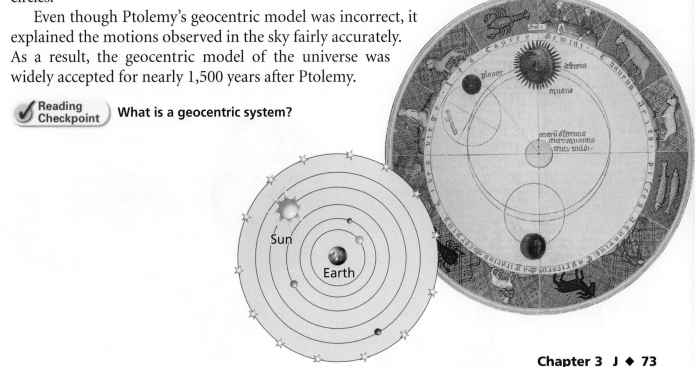

Sun at the Center

Not everybody believed in the geocentric system. An ancient Greek scientist developed another explanation for the motion of the planets. This sun-centered model is called a **heliocentric** (hee lee oh SEN trik) system. *Helios* is Greek for "sun." **In a heliocentric system, Earth and the other planets revolve around the sun.** This model was not well received in ancient times, however, because people could not accept that Earth is not at the center of the universe.

The Copernican Revolution In 1543, the Polish astronomer Nicolaus Copernicus further developed the heliocentric model. **Copernicus was able to work out the arrangement of the known planets and how they move around the sun.** Copernicus's theory would eventually revolutionize the science of astronomy. But at first, many people were unwilling to accept his theory. They needed more evidence to be convinced.

In the 1500s and early 1600s, most people still believed in the geocentric model. However, evidence collected by the Italian scientist Galileo Galilei gradually convinced others that the heliocentric model was correct.

Galileo's Evidence **Galileo used the newly invented telescope to make discoveries that supported the heliocentric model.** For example, in 1610, Galileo used a telescope to discover four moons revolving around Jupiter. The motion of these moons proved that not everything in the sky revolves around Earth.

FIGURE 3
Heliocentric System
In a heliocentric system, Earth and the other planets revolve around the sun. The illustration by Andreas Cellarius (top) was made in the 1660s.
Interpreting Diagrams *In a heliocentric model, what revolves around Earth?*

FIGURE 4
Major Figures in the History of Astronomy

Nicolaus Copernicus
1473–1543

Galileo Galilei
1564–1642

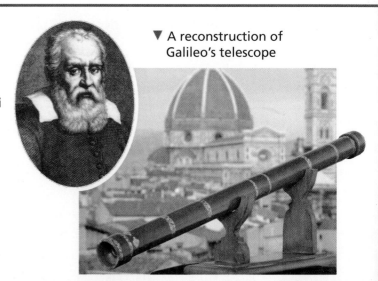

▼ A reconstruction of Galileo's telescope

Galileo's observations of Venus also supported the heliocentric system. Galileo knew that Venus is always seen near the sun. He discovered that Venus goes through a series of phases similar to those of Earth's moon. But Venus would not have a full set of phases if it circled around Earth. Therefore, Galileo reasoned, the geocentric model must be incorrect.

Tycho Brahe's Observations Copernicus correctly placed the sun at the center of the planets. But he incorrectly assumed that the planets travel in orbits that are perfect circles. Copernicus had based his ideas on observations made by the ancient Greeks.

In the late 1500s, the Danish astronomer Tycho Brahe (TEE koh BRAH uh) and his assistants made much more accurate observations. For more than 20 years, they carefully observed and recorded the positions of the planets. Surprisingly, these observations were made without using a telescope. Telescopes had not yet been invented!

Kepler's Calculations Tycho Brahe died in 1601. His assistant, Johannes Kepler, went to work analyzing the observations. Kepler began by trying to figure out the shape of Mars's orbit. At first, he assumed that the orbit was circular. But his calculations did not fit the observations. Kepler eventually found that Mars's orbit was a slightly flattened circle, or ellipse. An **ellipse** is an oval shape, which may be elongated or nearly circular.

After years of detailed calculations, Kepler reached a remarkable conclusion about the motion of the planets. **Kepler found that the orbit of each planet is an ellipse.** Kepler had used the evidence gathered by Tycho Brahe to disprove the long-held belief that the planets move in perfect circles.

Reading Checkpoint What is an ellipse?

Lab zone Try This **Activity**

A Loopy Ellipse
You can draw an ellipse.

1. ✂ Carefully stick two pushpins about 10 cm apart through a sheet of white paper on top of corrugated cardboard. One pushpin represents the sun.
2. Tie the ends of a 30-cm piece of string together. Place the string around the pushpins.
3. Keeping the string tight, move a pencil around inside the string.
4. Now place the pushpins 5 cm apart. Repeat Step 3.

Predicting How does changing the distance between the pushpins affect the ellipse's shape? What shape would you draw if you used only one pushpin? Is the "sun" at the center of the ellipse?

Tycho Brahe
1546–1601

Johannes Kepler
1571–1630

◀ Brahe's observatory on an island between Denmark and Sweden

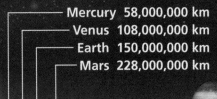
Mercury 58,000,000 km
Venus 108,000,000 km
Earth 150,000,000 km
Mars 228,000,000 km

Jupiter
779,000,000 km

Saturn
1,434,000,000 km

FIGURE 5

The Sun and Planets
This illustration shows the average distances of the planets from the sun. The solar system also includes smaller objects, such as Pluto. These distances are drawn to scale, but the sizes of the planets are not drawn to the same scale.
Observing *Which planet is closest to the sun?*

Modern Discoveries

Today, people talk about the "solar system" rather than the "Earth system." This shows that people accept the idea that Earth and the other planets revolve around the sun.

Since Galileo's time, our knowledge of the solar system has increased dramatically. Galileo knew the same planets that the ancient Greeks had known—Mercury, Venus, Earth, Mars, Jupiter, and Saturn. Since Galileo's time, astronomers have discovered two more planets—Uranus and Neptune, as well as Pluto, which is no longer considered to be a planet. Astronomers have also identified many other objects in the solar system, such as comets and asteroids. **Today we know that the solar system consists of the sun, the planets and their moons, and several kinds of smaller objects that revolve around the sun.**

Math Analyzing Data

Planet Speed Versus Distance
Johannes Kepler discovered a relationship between the speed of a planet and its distance from the sun. Use the graph to help discover what Kepler learned.

1. **Reading Graphs** According to the graph, what is Earth's average speed?

2. **Interpreting Data** Which is closer to the sun, Mercury or Mars? Which moves faster?

3. **Drawing Conclusions** What is the general relationship between a planet's speed and its average distance from the sun?

4. **Predicting** The planet Uranus is about 2,900 million km from the sun. Predict whether its speed is greater or less than Jupiter's speed. Explain your answer.

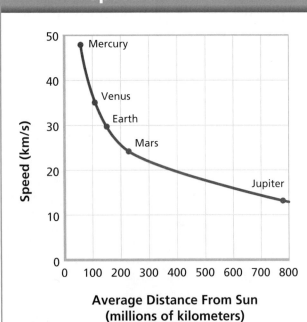

Speed of Planets

| Uranus | Neptune | Pluto |
| 2,873,000,000 km | 4,495,000,000 km | 5,870,000,000 km |

Galileo used a telescope to observe the solar system from Earth's surface. Astronomers today still use telescopes located on Earth, but they have also placed telescopes in space to gain a better view of the universe beyond Earth. Scientists have also sent astronauts to the moon and launched numerous space probes to explore the far reaches of the solar system. Our understanding of the solar system continues to grow every day. Who knows what new discoveries will be made in your lifetime!

Go Online
active art

For: Solar System activity
Visit: PHSchool.com
Web Code: cfp-5031

Reading Checkpoint Which six planets were known to the ancient Greeks?

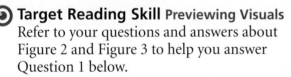

Section 1 Assessment

Target Reading Skill Previewing Visuals Refer to your questions and answers about Figure 2 and Figure 3 to help you answer Question 1 below.

Reviewing Key Concepts

1. a. **Explaining** What are the geocentric and heliocentric systems?
   b. **Comparing and Contrasting** How was Copernicus's model of the universe different from Ptolemy's model?
   c. **Drawing Conclusions** What discoveries by Galileo support the heliocentric model?
   d. **Applying Concepts** People often say the sun rises in the east, crosses the sky, and sets in the west. Is this literally true? Explain.

2. a. **Interpreting Data** How did Kepler use Tycho Brahe's data?
   b. **Describing** What did Kepler discover about the shapes of the planets' orbits?
   c. **Inferring** How did Tycho Brahe and Kepler employ the scientific method?

3. a. **Describing** What objects make up the solar system?
   b. **Listing** What are the planets, in order of increasing distance from the sun?
   c. **Interpreting Diagrams** Use Figure 5 to find the planet with the closest orbit to Earth.

Writing in Science

Dialogue Write an imaginary conversation between Ptolemy and Galileo about the merits of the geocentric and heliocentric systems. Which system would each scientist favor? What evidence could each offer to support his view? Do you think that one scientist could convince the other to change his mind? Use quotation marks around the comments of each scientist.

2 The Sun

Reading Preview

Key Concepts
- What are the three layers of the sun's interior?
- What are the three layers of the sun's atmosphere?
- What features form on or above the sun's surface?

Key Terms
- core
- nuclear fusion
- radiation zone
- convection zone
- photosphere
- chromosphere
- corona
- solar wind
- sunspot
- prominence
- solar flare

Target Reading Skill
Outlining As you read, make an outline about the sun that you can use for review. Use the red headings for main topics and the blue headings for subtopics.

The Sun
I. The sun's interior
A. The core
B.
C.
II. The sun's atmosphere
A. The photosphere

Lab zone Discover Activity

How Can You Safely Observe the Sun?

1. Clamp a pair of binoculars to a ring stand as shown in the photo.
2. Cut a hole in a 20-cm by 28-cm sheet of thin cardboard so that it will fit over the binoculars, as shown in the photo. The cardboard should cover one lens, but allow light through the other lens. Tape the cardboard on securely.
3. Use the binoculars to project an image of the sun onto a sheet of white paper. The cardboard will shade the white paper. Change the focus and move the paper back and forth until you get a sharp image.
   CAUTION: *Never look directly at the sun. You will hurt your eyes if you do. Do not look up through the binoculars.*

Think It Over
Observing Draw what you see on the paper. What do you see on the surface of the sun?

Suppose you are aboard a spaceship approaching the solar system from afar. Your first impression of the solar system might be that it consists of a single star with a few tiny objects orbiting around it. Your first impression wouldn't be that far off. In fact, the sun accounts for 99.8 percent of the solar system's total mass. As a result of its huge mass, the sun exerts a powerful gravitational force throughout the solar system. Although this force decreases rapidly with distance, it is strong enough to hold all the planets and other distant objects in orbit.

FIGURE 6
Active Sun
The sun is a huge, hot ball of glowing gas.

The Sun's Interior

Unlike Earth, the sun does not have a solid surface. Rather, the sun is a ball of glowing gas through and through. About three fourths of the sun's mass is hydrogen and one fourth is helium. There are also small amounts of other elements. Like Earth, the sun has an interior and an atmosphere. **The sun's interior consists of the core, the radiation zone, and the convection zone.**

Go Online
PLANET DIARY

For: More on the sun
Visit: PHSchool.com
Web Code: cfd-5032

The Core The sun produces an enormous amount of energy in its **core,** or central region. This energy is not produced by burning fuel. Rather, the sun's energy comes from nuclear fusion. In the process of **nuclear fusion,** hydrogen atoms join together to form helium. Nuclear fusion occurs only under conditions of extremely high temperature and pressure. The temperature inside the sun's core reaches about 15 million degrees Celsius, high enough for nuclear fusion to take place.

The total mass of the helium produced by nuclear fusion is slightly less than the total mass of the hydrogen that goes into it. What happens to this mass? It is changed into energy. This energy slowly moves outward from the core, eventually escaping into space.

The Radiation Zone The energy produced in the sun's core moves outward through the middle layer of the sun's interior, the radiation zone. The **radiation zone** is a region of very tightly packed gas where energy is transferred mainly in the form of electromagnetic radiation. Because the radiation zone is so dense, energy can take more than 100,000 years to move through it.

The Convection Zone The **convection zone** is the outermost layer of the sun's interior. Hot gases rise from the bottom of the convection zone and gradually cool as they approach the top. Cooler gases sink, forming loops of gas that move energy toward the sun's surface.

Reading Checkpoint   **What is nuclear fusion?**

FIGURE 7
The Sun's Corona
During a total solar eclipse, you can see light from the corona, the outer layer of the sun's atmosphere around the dark disk of the moon.

Lab zone **Try This Activity**

Viewing Sunspots
You can observe changes in the number of sunspots.

1. Make a data table to record the number of sunspots you see each day.

2. Decide on a time to study sunspots each day.

3. View the sun's image in the way described in the Discover activity in this section. **CAUTION:** *Never look directly at the sun. You will hurt your eyes if you do.*

4. Make and record your observations.

Interpreting Data How much did the number of sunspots change from day to day?

The Sun's Atmosphere

The sun's atmosphere includes the photosphere, the chromosphere, and the corona. Each layer has unique properties.

The Photosphere The inner layer of the sun's atmosphere is called the **photosphere** (FOH tuh sfeer). The Greek word *photos* means "light," so *photosphere* means the sphere that gives off visible light. The sun does not have a solid surface, but the gases of the photosphere are thick enough to be visible. When you look at an image of the sun, you are looking at the photosphere. It is considered to be the sun's surface layer.

The Chromosphere During a total solar eclipse, the moon blocks light from the photosphere. The photosphere no longer produces the glare that keeps you from seeing the sun's faint, outer layers. At the start and end of a total eclipse, a reddish glow is visible just around the photosphere. This glow comes from the middle layer of the sun's atmosphere, the **chromosphere** (KROH muh sfeer). The Greek word *chroma* means "color," so the chromosphere is the "color sphere."

The Corona During a total solar eclipse an even fainter layer of the sun becomes visible, as you can see in Figure 7. This outer layer, which looks like a white halo around the sun, is called the **corona,** which means "crown" in Latin. The corona extends into space for millions of kilometers. It gradually thins into streams of electrically charged particles called the **solar wind.**

 **Reading Checkpoint** During what event could you see the sun's corona?

Features on the Sun

For hundreds of years, scientists have used telescopes to study the sun. They have spotted a variety of features on the sun's surface. **Features on or just above the sun's surface include sunspots, prominences, and solar flares.**

Sunspots Early observers noticed dark spots on the sun's surface. These became known as sunspots. Sunspots look small. But in fact, they can be larger than Earth. **Sunspots** are areas of gas on the sun's surface that are cooler than the gases around them. Cooler gases don't give off as much light as hotter gases, which is why sunspots look darker than the rest of the photosphere. Sunspots seem to move across the sun's surface, showing that the sun rotates on its axis, just as Earth does. The number of sunspots on the sun varies over a period of about 11 years.

FIGURE 8

The Layers of the Sun

The sun has an interior and an atmosphere, each of which consists of several layers. The diameter of the sun (not including the chromosphere and the corona) is about 1.4 million kilometers. *Interpreting Diagrams Name the layers of the sun's interior, beginning at its center.*

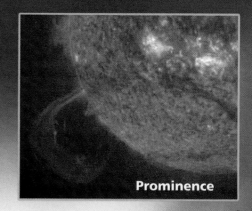

Prominence

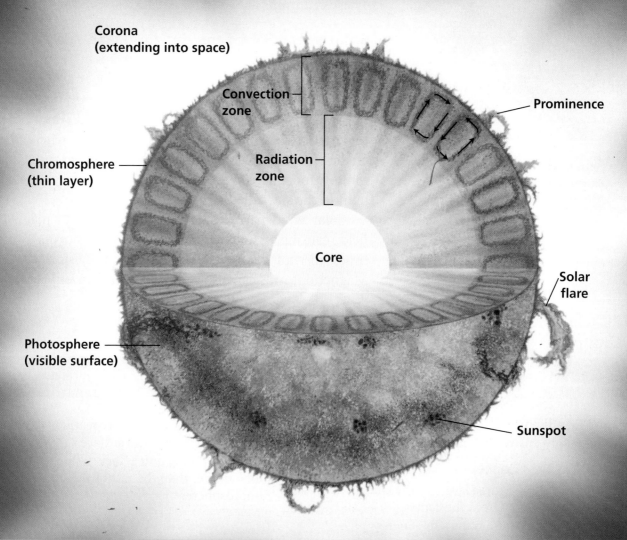

Corona (extending into space)

Convection zone

Chromosphere (thin layer)

Radiation zone

Core

Photosphere (visible surface)

Prominence

Solar flare

Sunspot

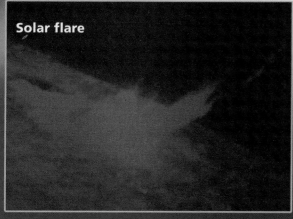

Solar flare

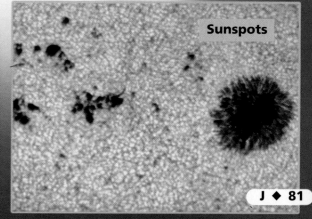

Sunspots

Prominences Sunspots usually occur in groups. Huge, reddish loops of gas called **prominences** often link different parts of sunspot regions. When a group of sunspots is near the edge of the sun as seen from Earth, these loops can be seen extending over the edge of the sun.

Solar Flares Sometimes the loops in sunspot regions suddenly connect, releasing large amounts of magnetic energy. The energy heats gas on the sun to millions of degrees Celsius, causing the gas to erupt into space. These eruptions are called **solar flares.**

Solar Wind Solar flares can greatly increase the solar wind from the corona, resulting in an increase in the number of particles reaching Earth's upper atmosphere. Normally, Earth's atmosphere and magnetic field block these particles. However, near the North and South poles, the particles can enter Earth's atmosphere, where they create powerful electric currents that cause gas molecules in the atmosphere to glow. The result is rippling sheets of light in the sky called auroras.

Solar wind particles can also affect Earth's magnetic field, causing magnetic storms. Magnetic storms sometimes disrupt radio, telephone, and television signals. Magnetic storms can also cause electrical power problems.

FIGURE 9
Auroras
Auroras such as this can occur near Earth's poles when particles of the solar wind strike gas molecules in Earth's upper atmosphere.

✓ **Reading Checkpoint** What is a prominence?

Section 2 Assessment

🎯 **Target Reading Skill** Outlining Use your outline to help answer the questions below.

Reviewing Key Concepts

1. **a. Listing** List the three layers of the sun's interior, starting from the center.
   b. Explaining Where is the sun's energy produced?
   c. Comparing and Contrasting Compare how energy moves through the radiation zone and the convection zone.
2. **a. Listing** What three layers make up the sun's atmosphere?
   b. Identifying Which of the sun's layers produces its visible light?
   c. Relating Cause and Effect Why is it usually impossible to see the sun's corona from Earth?

3. **a. Describing** Describe three features found on or just above the sun's surface.
   b. Relating Cause and Effect Why do sunspots look darker than the rest of the sun's photosphere?

Lab zone At-Home **Activity**

Sun Symbols As the source of heat and light, the sun is an important symbol in many cultures. With family members, look around your home and neighborhood for illustrations of the sun on signs, flags, clothing, and in artwork. Which parts of the sun's atmosphere do the illustrations show?

Stormy Sunspots

Problem

How are magnetic storms on Earth related to sunspot activity?

Skills Focus

graphing, interpreting data

Materials

• graph paper
• ruler

Procedure

1. Use the data in the table of Annual Sunspot Numbers to make a line graph of sunspot activity between 1972 and 2002.

2. On the graph, label the *x*-axis "Year." Use a scale with 2-year intervals, from 1972 to 2002.

3. Label the *y*-axis "Sunspot Number." Use a scale of 0 through 160 in intervals of 10.

4. Graph a point for the Sunspot Number for each year.

5. Complete your graph by drawing lines to connect the points.

Analyze and Conclude

1. **Graphing** Based on your graph, which years had the highest Sunspot Number? The lowest Sunspot Number?

2. **Interpreting Data** How often does the cycle of maximum and minimum activity repeat?

3. **Interpreting Data** When was the most recent maximum sunspot activity? The most recent minimum sunspot activity?

4. **Inferring** Compare your sunspot graph with the magnetic storms graph. What relationship can you infer between periods of high sunspot activity and magnetic storms? Explain.

	Annual Sunspot Numbers		
Year	Sunspot Number	Year	Sunspot Number
1972	68.9	1988	100.2
1974	34.5	1990	142.6
1976	12.6	1992	94.3
1978	92.5	1994	29.9
1980	154.6	1996	8.6
1982	115.9	1998	64.3
1984	45.9	2000	119.6
1986	13.4	2002	104.0

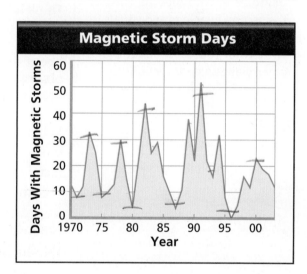

5. **Communicating** Suppose you are an engineer working for an electric power company. Write a brief summary of your analysis of sunspot data. Explain the relationship between sunspot number and electrical disturbances on Earth.

More to Explore

Using the pattern of sunspot activity you found, predict the number of peaks you would expect in the next 30 years. Around which years would you expect the peaks to occur?

The Inner Planets

Reading Preview

Key Concepts
- What characteristics do the inner planets have in common?
- What are the main characteristics that distinguish each of the inner planets?

Key Terms
- terrestrial planets
- greenhouse effect

Target Reading Skill

Using Prior Knowledge Look at the section headings and visuals to see what this section is about. Then write what you know about the inner planets in a graphic organizer like the one below. As you read, write what you learn.

What You Know
1. Most of Earth is covered with water.
2.

What You Learned
1.
2.

Lab zone Discover Activity

How Does Mars Look From Earth?

1. Work in pairs. On a sheet of paper, draw a circle 20 cm across to represent Mars. Draw about 100 small lines, each about 1 cm long, at random places inside the circle.

2. Have your partner look at your drawing of Mars from the other side of the room. Your partner should draw what he or she sees.

3. Compare your original drawing with what your partner drew. Then look at your own drawing from across the room.

Think It Over

Observing Did your partner draw any connecting lines that were not actually on your drawing? What can you conclude about the accuracy of descriptions of other planets based on observations from Earth?

Where could you find a planet whose atmosphere has almost entirely leaked away into space? How about a planet whose surface is hot enough to melt lead? And how about a planet with volcanoes higher than any on Earth? Finally, where could you find a planet with oceans of water brimming with fish and other life? These are descriptions of the four planets closest to the sun, known as the inner planets.

Earth and the three other inner planets—Mercury, Venus, and Mars—are more similar to each other than they are to the five outer planets. **The four inner planets are small and dense and have rocky surfaces.** The inner planets are often called the **terrestrial planets,** from the Latin word *terra,* which means "Earth." Figure 10 summarizes data about the inner planets.

Earth

As you can see in Figure 11, Earth has three main layers—a crust, a mantle, and a core. The crust includes the solid, rocky surface. Under the crust is the mantle, a layer of hot molten rock. When volcanoes erupt, this hot material rises to the surface. Earth has a dense core made of mainly iron and nickel. The outer core is liquid, but the inner core is solid.

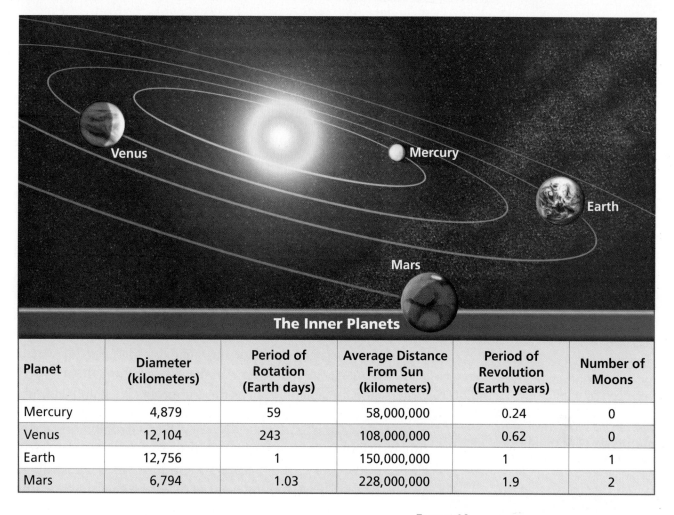

The Inner Planets

Planet	Diameter (kilometers)	Period of Rotation (Earth days)	Average Distance From Sun (kilometers)	Period of Revolution (Earth years)	Number of Moons
Mercury	4,879	59	58,000,000	0.24	0
Venus	12,104	243	108,000,000	0.62	0
Earth	12,756	1	150,000,000	1	1
Mars	6,794	1.03	228,000,000	1.9	2

Water Earth is unique in our solar system in having liquid water at its surface. In fact, most of Earth's surface, about 70 percent, is covered with water. Perhaps our planet should be called "Water" instead of "Earth"! Earth has a suitable temperature range for water to exist as a liquid, gas, or solid. Water is also important in shaping Earth's surface, wearing it down and changing its appearance over time.

Atmosphere Earth has enough gravity to hold on to most gases. These gases make up Earth's atmosphere, which extends more than 100 kilometers above its surface. Other planets in the solar system have atmospheres too, but only Earth has an atmosphere that is rich in oxygen. The oxygen you need to live makes up about 20 percent of Earth's atmosphere. Nearly all the rest is nitrogen, with small amounts of other gases such as argon and carbon dioxide. The atmosphere also includes varying amounts of water in the form of a gas. Water in a gaseous form is called water vapor.

Reading Checkpoint What two gases make up most of Earth's atmosphere?

FIGURE 10
The inner planets take up only a small part of the solar system. Note that sizes and distances are not drawn to scale.

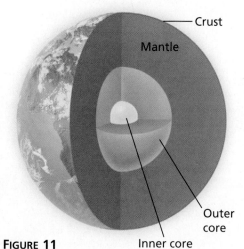
— Crust
Mantle
Outer core
Inner core

FIGURE 11
Earth's Layers
Earth has a solid, rocky surface.
Interpreting Diagrams *What are Earth's three main layers?*

Size of Mercury
compared to Earth

FIGURE 12
Mercury
This image of Mercury was
produced by combining a series of
smaller images made by the
Mariner 10 space probe.
Interpreting Photographs *How is
Mercury's surface different from
Earth's?*

Mercury

**Mercury is the smallest terrestrial planet and the planet
closest to the sun.** Mercury is not much larger than Earth's
moon and has no moons of its own. The interior of Mercury is
probably made up mainly of the dense metal iron.

Exploring Mercury Because Mercury is so close to the sun, it
is hard to see from Earth. Much of what astronomers know about
Mercury's surface came from a single probe, *Mariner 10*. It flew
by Mercury three times in 1974 and 1975. Two new missions to
Mercury are planned. The first of these, called *MESSENGER*, is
scheduled to go into orbit around Mercury in 2009.

Mariner 10's photographs show that Mercury has many flat
plains and craters on its surface. The large number of craters
shows that Mercury's surface has changed little for billions of
years. Many of Mercury's craters have been named for artists,
writers, and musicians, such as the composers Bach and Mozart.

Mercury's Atmosphere Mercury has virtually no atmosphere. Mercury's high daytime temperatures cause gas particles to move very fast. Because Mercury's mass is small, its
gravity is weak. Fast-moving gas particles can easily escape into
space. However, astronomers have detected small amounts of
sodium and other gases around Mercury.

Mercury is a planet of extremes, with a greater temperature
range than any other planet in the solar system. It is so close to
the sun that during the day, the side facing the sun reaches
temperatures of 430°C. Because Mercury has almost no atmosphere, at night its heat escapes into space. Then its temperature drops below −170°C.

Reading
Checkpoint) **Compare daytime and nighttime temperatures on
Mercury.**

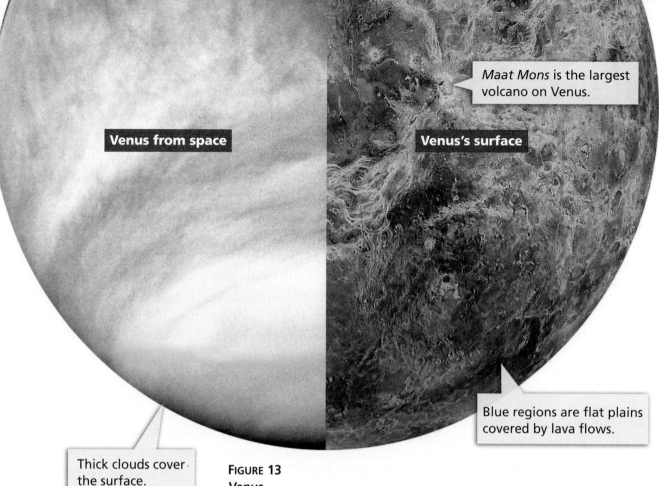

Maat Mons is the largest volcano on Venus.

Venus from space

Venus's surface

Thick clouds cover the surface.

Blue regions are flat plains covered by lava flows.

FIGURE 13
Venus
This figure combines images of Venus taken from space with a camera (left) and radar (right). The camera image shows Venus's thick atmosphere. Radar is able to penetrate Venus's clouds to reveal the surface. Both images are false color.

Venus

You can sometimes see Venus in the west just after sunset. When Venus is visible in that part of the sky, it is known as the "evening star," though of course it really isn't a star at all. At other times, Venus rises before the sun in the morning. Then it is known as the "morning star."

Venus is so similar in size and mass to Earth that it is sometimes called "Earth's twin." **Venus's density and internal structure are similar to Earth's. But, in other ways, Venus and Earth are very different.**

Venus's Rotation Venus takes about 7.5 Earth months to revolve around the sun. It takes about 8 months for Venus to rotate once on its axis. Thus, Venus rotates so slowly that its day is longer than its year! Oddly, Venus rotates from east to west, the opposite direction from most other planets and moons. Astronomers hypothesize that this unusual rotation was caused by a very large object that struck Venus billions of years ago. Such a collision could have caused Venus to change its direction of rotation. Another hypothesis is that Venus's thick atmosphere could have somehow altered its rotation.

Size of Venus compared to Earth

Go Online

For: Links on the planets
Visit: www.SciLinks.org
Web Code: scn-0633

Try This Activity

Greenhouse Effect
How can you measure the effect of a closed container on temperature?

1.  Carefully place a thermometer into each of two glass jars. Cover one jar with cellophane. Place both jars either in direct sunlight or under a strong light source.

2. Observe the temperature of both thermometers when you start. Check the temperatures every 5 minutes for a total of 20 minutes. Record your results in a data table.

Inferring Compare how the temperature changed in the uncovered jar and the covered jar. What do you think is the reason for any difference in the temperatures of the two jars? Which jar is a better model of Venus's atmosphere?

Venus's Atmosphere Venus's atmosphere is so thick that it is always cloudy there. From Earth or space, astronomers can see only a smooth cloud cover over Venus. The clouds are made mostly of droplets of sulfuric acid.

If you could stand on Venus's surface, you would quickly be crushed by the weight of its atmosphere. The pressure of Venus's atmosphere is 90 times greater than the pressure of Earth's atmosphere. You couldn't breathe on Venus because its atmosphere is mostly carbon dioxide.

Because Venus is closer to the sun than Earth is, it receives more solar energy than Earth does. Much of this radiation is reflected by Venus's atmosphere. However, some radiation reaches the surface and is later given off as heat. The carbon dioxide in Venus's atmosphere traps heat so well that Venus has the hottest surface of any planet. At 460°C, its average surface temperature is hot enough to melt lead. This trapping of heat by the atmosphere is called the **greenhouse effect**.

Exploring Venus Many space probes have visited Venus. The first probe to land on the surface and send back data, *Venera 7*, landed in 1970. It survived for only a few minutes because of the high temperature and pressure. Later probes were more durable and sent images and data back to Earth.

The *Magellan* probe reached Venus in 1990, carrying radar instruments. Radar works through clouds, so *Magellan* was able to map nearly the entire surface. The *Magellan* data confirmed that Venus is covered with rock. Venus's surface has many volcanoes and broad plains formed by lava flows.

Reading Checkpoint What are Venus's clouds made of?

FIGURE 14
Maat Mons
Scientists used radar data to develop this computer image of the giant volcano *Maat Mons*. The height of the mountains is exaggerated to make them stand out.

Mars

Mars is called the "red planet." When you see it in the sky, it has a slightly reddish tinge. This reddish color is due to the breakdown of iron-rich rocks, which creates a rusty dust that covers much of Mars's surface.

Mars's Atmosphere The atmosphere of Mars is more than 95 percent carbon dioxide. It is similar in composition to Venus's atmosphere, but much thinner. You could walk around on Mars, but you would have to wear an airtight suit and carry your own oxygen, like a scuba diver. Mars has few clouds, and they are very thin compared to clouds on Earth. Mars's transparent atmosphere allows people on Earth to view its surface with a telescope. Temperatures on the surface range from −140°C to 20°C.

Water on Mars In 1877, an Italian astronomer named Giovanni Schiaparelli (sky ah puh REL ee) announced that he had seen long, straight lines on Mars. He called them *canale*, or channels. In the 1890s and early 1900s, Percival Lowell, an American astronomer, convinced many people that these lines were canals that had been built by intelligent Martians to carry water. Astronomers now know that Lowell was mistaken. There are no canals on Mars.

Images of Mars taken from space do show a variety of features that look as if they were made by ancient streams, lakes, or floods. There are huge canyons and features that look like the remains of ancient coastlines. **Scientists think that a large amount of liquid water flowed on Mars's surface in the distant past.** Scientists infer that Mars must have been much warmer and had a thicker atmosphere at that time.

At present, liquid water cannot exist for long on Mars's surface. Mars's atmosphere is so thin that any liquid water would quickly turn into a gas. So where is Mars's water now? Some of it is located in the planet's two polar ice caps, which contain frozen water and carbon dioxide. A small amount also exists as water vapor in Mars's atmosphere. Some water vapor has probably escaped into space. But scientists think that a large amount of water may still be frozen underground.

Size of Mars compared to Earth

FIGURE 15
Mars
Because of its thin atmosphere and its distance from the sun, Mars is quite cold. Mars has ice caps at both poles. **Inferring** *Why is it easy to see Mars's surface from space?*

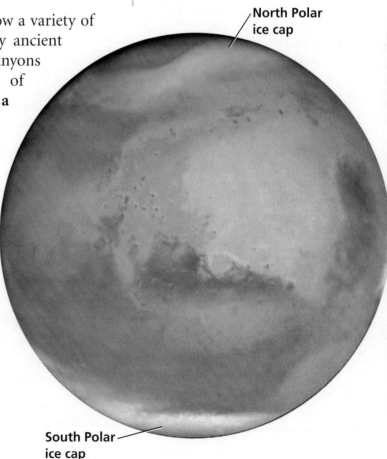

North Polar ice cap

South Polar ice cap

The Solar System

Video Preview
▶ Video Field Trip
Video Assessment

Lab zone Try This Activity

Remote Control

How hard is it to explore another planet by remote control?

1. Tape a piece of paper over the front of a pair of goggles. Have your partner put them on.

2. Walk behind your partner and direct him or her to another part of the room. **CAUTION:** *Do not give directions that would cause your partner to walk into a wall or a corner, trip on an obstacle, or bump into anything.*

3. Trade places and repeat Steps 1 and 2.

Drawing Conclusions Which verbal directions worked best? How quickly could you move? How is this activity similar to the way engineers have moved rovers on Mars? How fast do you think such a rover could move?

Seasons on Mars Because Mars has a tilted axis, it has seasons just as Earth does. During the Martian winter, an ice cap grows larger as a layer of frozen carbon dioxide covers it. Because the northern and southern hemispheres have opposite seasons, one ice cap grows while the other one shrinks.

As the seasons change on the dusty surface of Mars, windstorms arise and blow the dust around. Since the dust is blown off some regions, these regions look darker. A hundred years ago, some people thought these regions looked darker because plants were growing there. Astronomers now realize that the darker color is often just the result of windstorms.

Exploring Mars Many space probes have visited Mars. The first ones seemed to show that Mars is barren and covered with craters like the moon. Recently, two new probes landed on Mars's surface. NASA's *Spirit* and *Opportunity* rovers explored opposite sides of the planet. They examined a variety of rocks and soil samples. At both locations, the rovers found strong evidence that liquid water was once present. The European Space Agency's *Mars Express* probe orbited overhead, finding clear evidence of frozen water (ice). However, the *Mars Express* lander failed.

Volcanoes on Mars Some regions of Mars have giant volcanoes. Astronomers see signs that lava flowed from the volcanoes in the past, but the volcanoes are no longer active. *Olympus Mons* on Mars is the largest volcano in the solar system. It covers a region as large as the state of Missouri and is nearly three times as tall as Mount Everest, the tallest mountain on Earth!

FIGURE 16
Mars's Surface
As the large photo shows, the surface of Mars is rugged and rocky. Mars has many large volcanoes. The volcano *Olympus Mons* (inset) rises about 27 km from the surface. It is the largest volcano in the solar system.

Mars's Moons Mars has two very small moons. Phobos, the larger moon, is only 27 kilometers in diameter, about the distance a car can travel on the highway in 20 minutes. Deimos is even smaller, only 15 kilometers in diameter. Like Earth's moon, Phobos and Deimos are covered with craters. Phobos, which is much closer to Mars than Deimos is, is slowly spiraling down toward Mars. Astronomers predict that Phobos will smash into Mars in about 40 million years.

 **Reading Checkpoint** **How many moons does Mars have? What are their names?**

Section 3 Assessment

Target Reading Skill Using Prior Knowledge Review your graphic organizer about the inner planets and revise it based on what you just learned in the section.

Reviewing Key Concepts

1. a. **Listing** List the four inner planets in order of size, from smallest to largest.
   b. **Comparing and Contrasting** How are the four inner planets similar to one another?
2. a. **Describing** Describe an important characteristic of each inner planet.
   b. **Comparing and Contrasting** Compare the atmospheres of the four inner planets.
   c. **Relating Cause and Effect** Venus is much farther from the sun than Mercury is. Yet average temperatures on Venus's surface are much higher than those on Mercury. Explain why.

Writing in Science

Travel Brochure Select one of the inner planets other than Earth. Design a travel brochure for your selected planet, including basic facts and descriptions of places of interest. Also include a few sketches or photos to go along with your text.

Space Exploration— Is It Worth the Cost?

Imagine that your spacecraft has just landed on the moon or on Mars. You've spent years planning for this moment. Canyons, craters, plains, and distant mountains stretch out before you. Perhaps a group of scientists has already begun construction of a permanent outpost. You check your spacesuit and prepare to step out onto the rocky surface.

Is such a trip likely? Would it be worthwhile? How much is space flight really worth to human society? Scientists and public officials have already started to debate such questions. Space exploration can help us learn more about the universe. But exploration can be risky and expensive. Sending people into space costs billions of dollars and risks the lives of astronauts. How can we balance the costs and benefits of space exploration?

▼ **Moon Landing**
A rocket is preparing to dock with a lander on the moon's surface in this imaginative artwork.

The Issues

Should Humans Travel Into Space?

Many Americans think that Neil Armstrong's walk on the moon in 1969 was one of the great moments in history. Learning how to keep people alive in space has led to improvements in everyday life. Safer equipment for firefighters, easier ways to package frozen food, and effective heart monitors have all come from space program research.

What Are the Alternatives?

Space exploration can involve a project to establish a colony on the moon or Mars. It also can involve a more limited use of scientific instruments near Earth, such as the Hubble Space Telescope. Instead of sending people, we could send space probes like *Cassini* to other planets.

◄ Lunar Outpost
A mining operation on the moon is shown in this imaginative artwork. Such a facility may someday harvest oxygen from the moon's soil.

◄ Lunar Module
This artwork shows a futuristic vehicle that may one day be used to explore the moon and Mars. The vehicle serves as a combination lander, rover, and habitat for astronauts.

Is Human Space Exploration Worth the Cost?

Scientists who favor human travel into space say that only people can collect certain kinds of information. They argue that the technologies developed for human space exploration will have many applications on Earth. But no one knows if research in space really provides information more quickly than research that can be done on Earth. Many critics of human space exploration think that other needs are more important. One United States senator said, "Every time you put money into the space station, there is a dime that won't be available for our children's education or for medical research."

You Decide

1. Identify the Problem
In your own words, list the various costs and benefits of space exploration.

2. Analyze the Options
Make a chart of three different approaches to space exploration: sending humans to the moon or another planet, doing only Earth-based research, and one other option. What are the benefits and drawbacks of each of these approaches?

3. Find a Solution
Imagine that you are a member of Congress who has to vote on a new budget. There is a fixed amount of money to spend, so you have to decide which needs are most important. Make a list of your top ten priorities. Explain your decisions.

For: More on space exploration
Visit: PHSchool.com
Web Code: cfh-5030

The Outer Planets

Reading Preview

Key Concepts
- What characteristics do the gas giants have in common?
- What characteristics distinguish each of the outer planets?

Key Terms
- gas giant • ring

⊙ Target Reading Skill
Identifying Main Ideas As you read the *Gas Giants and Pluto* section, write the main idea—the biggest or most important idea—in a graphic organizer like the one below. Then write three supporting details that further explain the main idea.

Main Idea

The four gas giants are similar in . . .

Detail	Detail	Detail

Lab zone · Discover **Activity**

How Big Are the Planets?
The table shows the diameters of the outer planets compared to Earth. For example, Jupiter's diameter is about 11 times Earth's diameter.

1. Measure the diameter of a quarter in millimeters. Trace the quarter to represent Earth.
2. If Earth were the size of a quarter, calculate how large Jupiter would be. Now draw a circle to represent Jupiter.
3. Repeat Step 2 for each of the other planets in the table.

Think It Over
Classifying List the outer planets in order from largest to smallest. What is the largest outer planet?

Planet	Diameter (Earth = 1)
Earth	1.0
Jupiter	11.2
Saturn	9.4
Uranus	4.0
Neptune	3.9

Imagine you are in a spaceship approaching Jupiter. You'll quickly discover that Jupiter is very different from the terrestrial planets. The most obvious difference is Jupiter's great size. Jupiter is so large that more than 1,300 Earths could fit within it!

As your spaceship enters Jupiter's atmosphere, you encounter thick, colorful bands of clouds. Next, you sink into a denser and denser mixture of hydrogen and helium gas. Eventually, if the enormous pressure of the atmosphere does not crush your ship, you'll reach an incredibly deep "ocean" of liquid hydrogen and helium. But where exactly is Jupiter's surface? Surprisingly, there isn't a solid surface. Like the other giant planets, Jupiter has no real surface, just a solid core buried deep within the planet.

◀ An illustration of the space probe *Galileo* approaching the cloud-covered atmosphere of Jupiter.

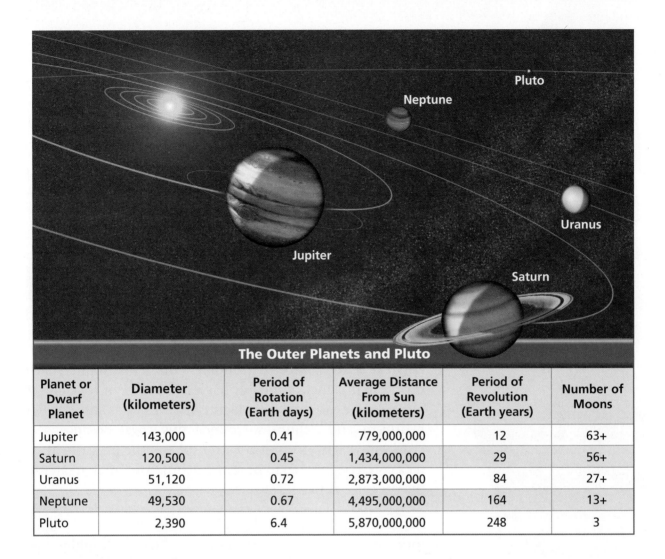

The Outer Planets and Pluto

Planet or Dwarf Planet	Diameter (kilometers)	Period of Rotation (Earth days)	Average Distance From Sun (kilometers)	Period of Revolution (Earth years)	Number of Moons
Jupiter	143,000	0.41	779,000,000	12	63+
Saturn	120,500	0.45	1,434,000,000	29	56+
Uranus	51,120	0.72	2,873,000,000	84	27+
Neptune	49,530	0.67	4,495,000,000	164	13+
Pluto	2,390	6.4	5,870,000,000	248	3

Gas Giants and Pluto

Jupiter and the other planets farthest from the sun are called the outer planets. **The four outer planets—Jupiter, Saturn, Uranus, and Neptune—are much larger and more massive than Earth, and they do not have solid surfaces.** Because these four planets are all so large, they are often called the **gas giants.** Figure 17 provides information about these planets. It also includes Pluto, which is now classified as a dwarf planet.

Like the sun, the gas giants are composed mainly of hydrogen and helium. Because they are so massive, the gas giants exert a much stronger gravitational force than the terrestrial planets. Gravity keeps the giant planets' gases from escaping, so they have thick atmospheres. Despite the name "gas giant," much of the hydrogen and helium is actually in liquid form because of the enormous pressure inside the planets. The outer layers of the gas giants are extremely cold because of their great distance from the sun. Temperatures increase greatly within the planets.

All the gas giants have many moons. In addition, each of the gas giants is surrounded by a set of rings. A **ring** is a thin disk of small particles of ice and rock.

FIGURE 17
The outer planets are much farther apart than the inner planets. Pluto is now considered to be a dwarf planet. Note that planet sizes and distances are not drawn to scale. **Observing** *Which outer planet has the most moons?*

For: More on the planets
Visit: PHSchool.com
Web Code: ced-5034

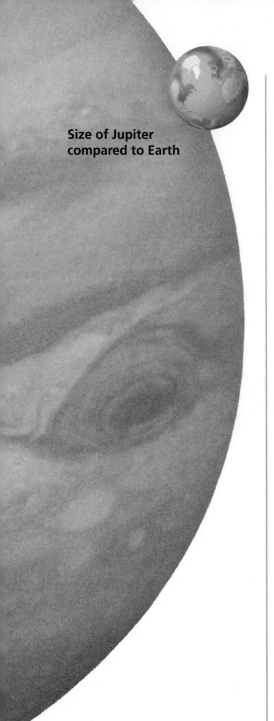

Size of Jupiter compared to Earth

Jupiter

Jupiter is the largest and most massive planet. Jupiter's enormous mass dwarfs the other planets. In fact, its mass is about $2\frac{1}{2}$ times that of all the other planets combined!

Jupiter's Atmosphere Like all of the gas giants, Jupiter has a thick atmosphere made up mainly of hydrogen and helium. An especially interesting feature of Jupiter's atmosphere is its Great Red Spot, a storm that is larger than Earth! The storm's swirling winds blow hundreds of kilometers per hour, similar to a hurricane. But hurricanes on Earth weaken quickly as they pass over land. On Jupiter, there is no land to weaken the huge storm. The Great Red Spot, which was first observed in the mid-1600s, shows no signs of going away soon.

Jupiter's Structure Astronomers think that Jupiter, like the other giant planets, probably has a dense core of rock and iron at its center. As shown in Figure 18, a thick mantle of liquid hydrogen and helium surrounds this core. Because of the crushing weight of Jupiter's atmosphere, the pressure at Jupiter's core is estimated to be about 30 million times greater than the pressure at Earth's surface.

Jupiter's Moons Recall that Galileo discovered Jupiter's four largest moons. These moons, which are highlighted in Figure 19, are named Io (EYE oh), Europa, Ganymede, and Callisto. All four are larger than Earth's own moon. However, they are very different from one another. Since Galileo's time, astronomers have discovered dozens of additional moons orbiting Jupiter. Many of these are small moons that have been found in the last few years thanks to improved technology.

 Reading Checkpoint What is Jupiter's atmosphere composed of?

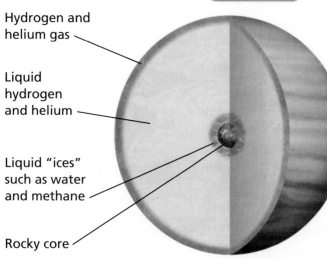

Hydrogen and helium gas

Liquid hydrogen and helium

Liquid "ices" such as water and methane

Rocky core

FIGURE 18
Jupiter's Structure
Jupiter is composed mainly of the elements hydrogen and helium. Although Jupiter is often called a "gas giant," much of it is actually liquid.
Comparing and Contrasting *How does the structure of Jupiter differ from that of a terrestrial planet?*

FIGURE 19

Jupiter's Moons

The astronomer Galileo discovered Jupiter's four largest moons. These images are not shown to scale.
Interpreting Photographs *Which is the largest of Jupiter's moons?*

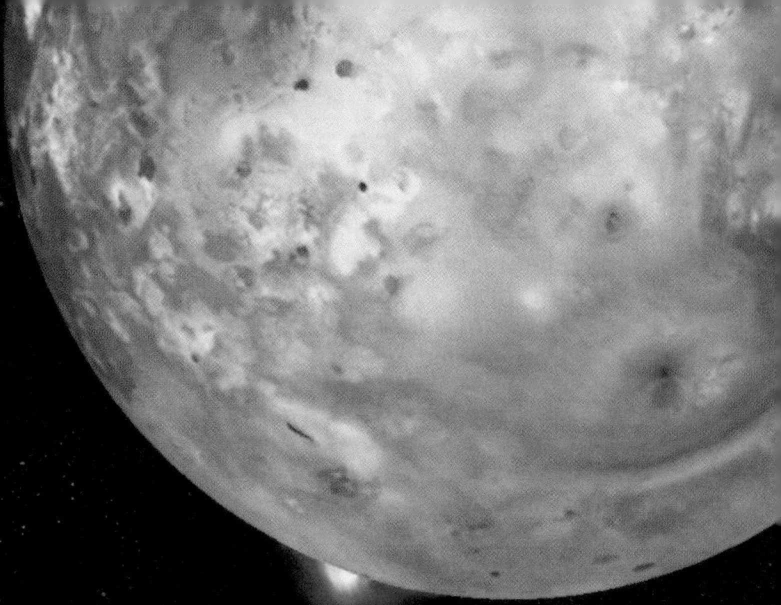

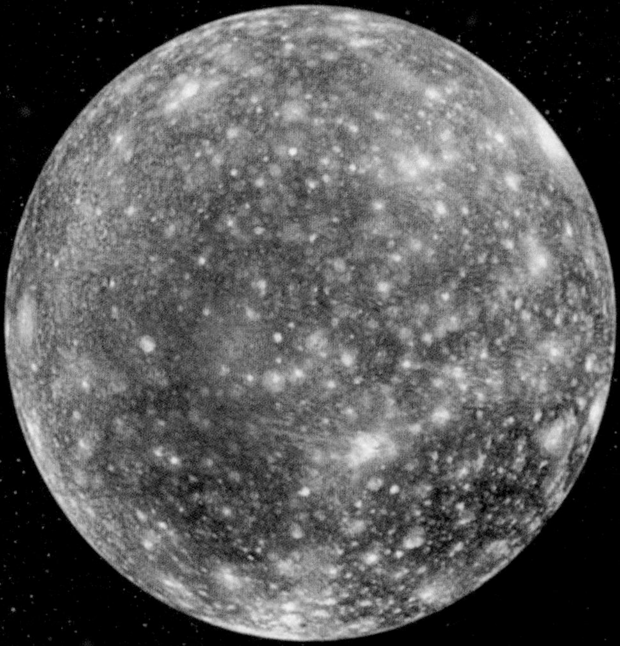

▲ Io's surface is covered with large, active volcanoes. An eruption of sulfur lava can be seen near the bottom of this photo. Sulfur gives Io its unusual colors.

Callisto's surface is icy and covered with craters. ▼

Ganymede is the largest moon in the solar system. It is larger than either Mercury or Pluto. ▼

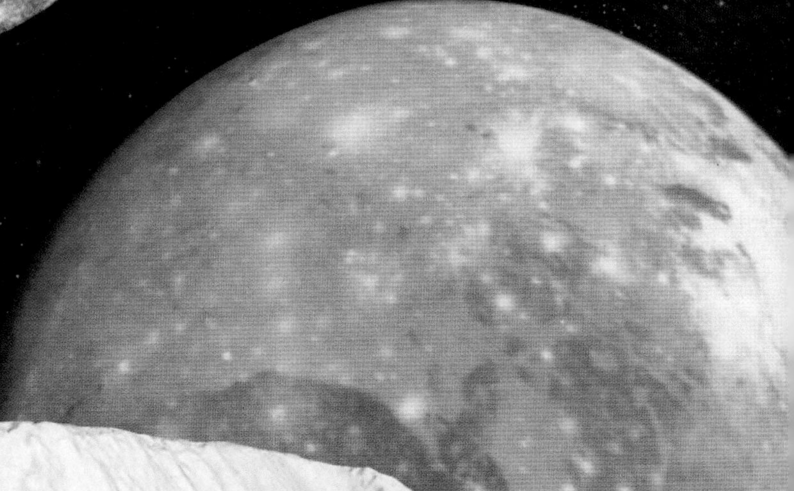

Europa ▼

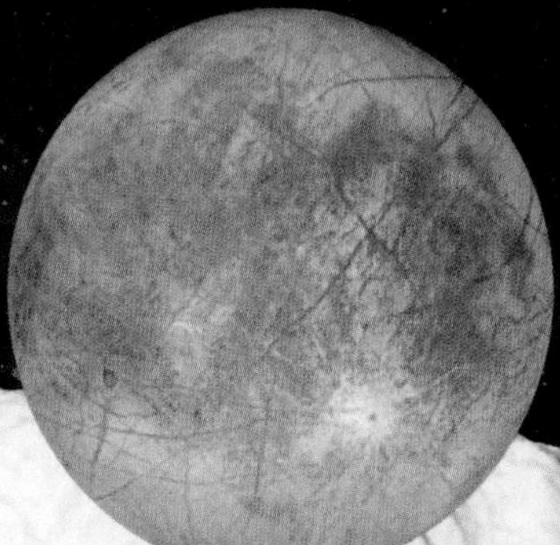

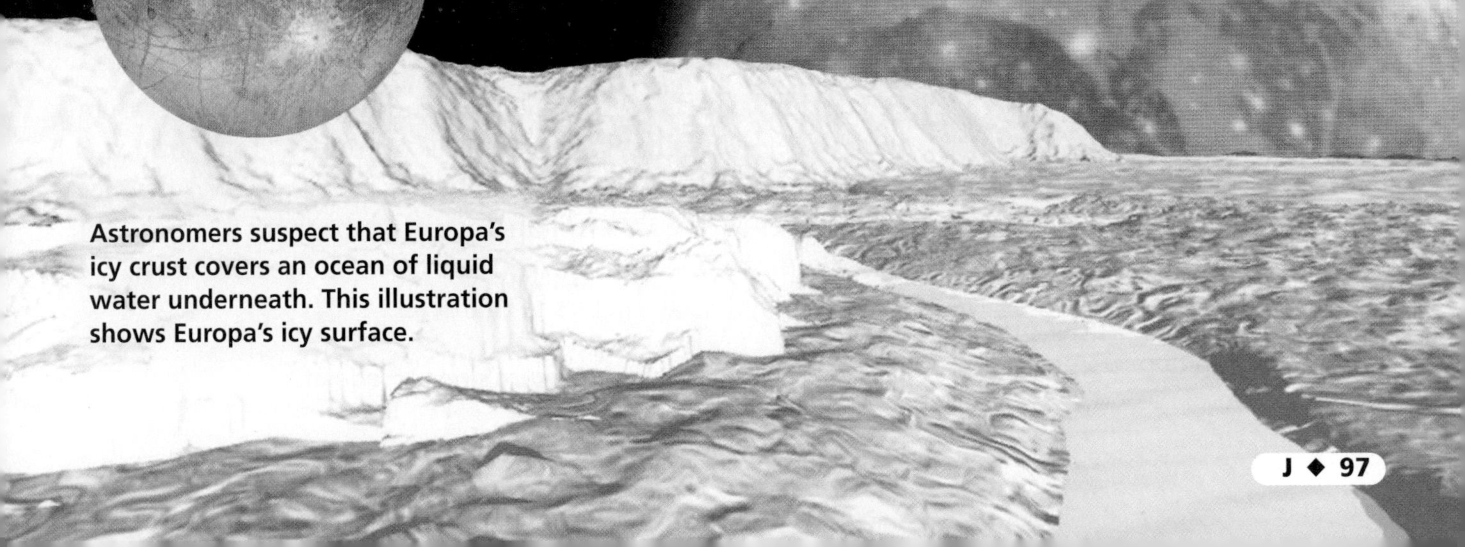

Astronomers suspect that Europa's icy crust covers an ocean of liquid water underneath. This illustration shows Europa's icy surface.

FIGURE 20
Exploring Saturn
The *Cassini* probe is exploring Saturn and its moons.
Observing *Why might it be hard to see Saturn's rings when their edges are facing Earth?*

Size of Saturn compared to Earth

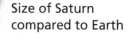

Making Models

1. Use a plastic foam sphere 8 cm in diameter to represent Saturn.

2. Use an overhead transparency to represent Saturn's rings. Cut a circle 18 cm in diameter out of the transparency. Cut a hole 9 cm in diameter out of the center of the circle.

3. Stick five toothpicks into Saturn, spaced equally around its equator. Put the transparency on the toothpicks and tape it to them. Sprinkle baking soda on the transparency.

4. Use a peppercorn to represent Titan. Place the peppercorn 72 cm away from Saturn on the same plane as the rings.

5. What do the particles of baking soda represent?

Saturn

The second-largest planet in the solar system is Saturn. The *Voyager* probes showed that Saturn, like Jupiter, has a thick atmosphere made up mainly of hydrogen and helium. Saturn's atmosphere also contains clouds and storms, but they are less dramatic than those on Jupiter. Saturn is the only planet whose average density is less than that of water.

Saturn's Rings When Galileo first looked at Saturn with a telescope, he could see something sticking out on the sides. But he didn't know what it was. A few decades later, an astronomer using a better telescope discovered that Saturn had rings around it. These rings are made of chunks of ice and rock, each traveling in its own orbit around Saturn.

Saturn has the most spectacular rings of any planet. From Earth, it looks as though Saturn has only a few rings and that they are divided from each other by narrow, dark regions. The *Voyager* spacecraft discovered that each of these obvious rings is divided into many thinner rings. Saturn's rings are broad and thin, like a compact disc.

Saturn's Moons Saturn's largest moon, Titan, is larger than the planet Mercury. Titan was discovered in 1665 but was known only as a point of light until the *Voyager* probes flew by. The probes showed that Titan has an atmosphere so thick that little light can pass through it. Four other moons of Saturn are each over 1,000 kilometers in diameter.

 **Reading Checkpoint** What are Saturn's rings made of?

Size of Uranus compared to Earth

Uranus

Although the gas giant Uranus (YOOR uh nus) is about four times the diameter of Earth, it is still much smaller than Jupiter and Saturn. Uranus is twice as far from the sun as Saturn, so it is much colder. Uranus looks blue-green because of traces of methane in its atmosphere. Like the other gas giants, Uranus is surrounded by a group of thin, flat rings, although they are much darker than Saturn's rings.

Discovery of Uranus In 1781, Uranus became the first new planet discovered since ancient times. Astronomer William Herschel, in England, found a fuzzy object in the sky that did not look like a star. At first he thought it might be a comet, but it soon proved to be a planet beyond Saturn. The discovery made Herschel famous and started an era of active solar system study.

Exploring Uranus About 200 years after Herschel's discovery, *Voyager 2* arrived at Uranus and sent back close-up views of that planet. Images from *Voyager 2* show only a few clouds on Uranus's surface. But even these few clouds allowed astronomers to calculate that Uranus rotates in about 17 hours.

Uranus's axis of rotation is tilted at an angle of about 90 degrees from the vertical. Viewed from Earth, Uranus is rotating from top to bottom instead of from side to side, the way most of the other planets do. Uranus's rings and moons rotate around this tilted axis. Astronomers think that billions of years ago Uranus was hit by an object that knocked it on its side.

Uranus's Moons Photographs from *Voyager 2* show that Uranus's five largest moons have icy, cratered surfaces. The craters show that rocks from space have hit the moons. Uranus's moons also have lava flows on their surfaces, suggesting that material has erupted from inside each moon. *Voyager 2* images revealed 10 moons that had never been seen before. Recently, astronomers discovered several more moons, for a total of at least 27.

 **Reading Checkpoint** Who discovered Uranus?

FIGURE 21
Uranus
The false color image of Uranus below was taken by the Hubble Space Telescope. Unlike most other planets, Uranus rotates from top to bottom rather than side to side. **Inferring** *How must Uranus's seasons be unusual?*

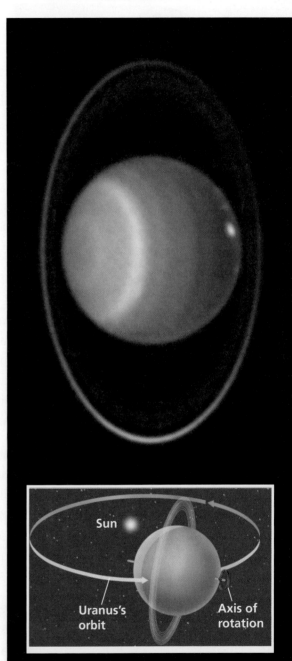

Sun

Uranus's orbit

Axis of rotation

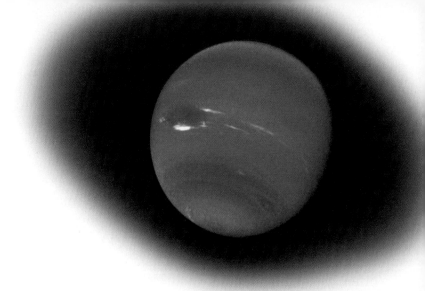

FIGURE 22
Neptune
The Great Dark Spot was a giant storm in Neptune's atmosphere. White clouds, probably made of methane ice crystals, can also be seen in the photo.

Size of Neptune compared to Earth

Math Skills

Circumference

To calculate the circumference of a circle, use this formula:

$$C = 2\pi r$$

In the formula, $\pi \approx 3.14$, and r is the circle's radius, which is the distance from the center of the circle to its edge. The same formula can be used to calculate the circumference of planets, which are nearly spherical.

Neptune's radius at its equator is about 24,800 km. Calculate its circumference.

$C = 2\pi r$

$\quad = 2.00 \times 3.14 \times 24,800$ km

$\quad = 156,000$ km

Practice Problem Saturn's radius is 60,250 km. What is its circumference?

Neptune

Neptune is even farther from the sun than Uranus. In some ways, Uranus and Neptune look like twins. They are similar in size and color. **Neptune is a cold, blue planet. Its atmosphere contains visible clouds.** Scientists think that Neptune, shown in Figure 22, is slowly shrinking, causing its interior to heat up. As this energy rises toward Neptune's surface, it produces clouds and storms in the planet's atmosphere.

Discovery of Neptune Neptune was discovered as a result of a mathematical prediction. Astronomers noted that Uranus was not quite following the orbit predicted for it. They hypothesized that the gravity of an unseen planet was affecting Uranus's orbit. By 1846, mathematicians in England and France had calculated the orbit of this unseen planet. Shortly thereafter, an observer saw an unknown object in the predicted area of the sky. It was the new planet, now called Neptune.

Exploring Neptune In 1989, *Voyager 2* flew by Neptune and photographed a Great Dark Spot about the size of Earth. Like the Great Red Spot on Jupiter, the Great Dark Spot was probably a giant storm. But the storm didn't last long. Images taken five years later showed that the Great Dark Spot was gone. Other, smaller spots and regions of clouds on Neptune also seem to come and go.

Neptune's Moons Astronomers have discovered at least 13 moons orbiting Neptune. The largest moon is Triton, which has a thin atmosphere. The *Voyager* images show that the region near Triton's south pole is covered by nitrogen ice.

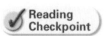 **Reading Checkpoint** Before they could see Neptune, what evidence led scientists to conclude that it existed?

Size of Pluto
compared to Earth

Pluto

Pluto is very different from the gas giants. **Pluto has a solid surface and is much smaller and denser than the outer planets.** In fact, Pluto is smaller than Earth's moon.

Pluto has three known moons. The largest of these, Charon, is more than half of Pluto's size.

Pluto's Orbit Pluto is so far from the sun that it revolves around the sun only once every 248 Earth years. Pluto's orbit is very elliptical, bringing it closer to the sun than Neptune on part of its orbit.

Dwarf Planets Until recently, Pluto was considered to be the ninth planet in our solar system. Pluto was always thought to be something of an oddball because of its small size and unusual orbit. Then, in recent years, astronomers discovered many icy objects beyond Neptune's orbit. Some of these were fairly similar to Pluto in size and makeup. Following the discovery of a body that is even larger and farther from the sun than Pluto, astronomers decided to create a new class of objects called "dwarf planets." A dwarf planet, like a planet, is round and orbits the sun. But unlike a planet, a dwarf planet has not cleared out the neighborhood around its orbit. Astronomers classified Pluto and two other bodies as dwarf planets.

FIGURE 23
Pluto and Charon
The illustration above shows Pluto (lower right) and its moon Charon. Charon is more than half the size of Pluto.

 Reading Checkpoint **How is Pluto now classified?**

Section 3 Assessment

Target Reading Skill Identifying Main Ideas Use your graphic organizer about the structure of the gas giants to help you answer Question 1 below.

Reviewing Key Concepts

1. a. **Describing** How are the gas giants similar to one another?
   b. **Explaining** Why do all of the gas giants have thick atmospheres?
   c. **Listing** List the outer planets in order of size, from smallest to largest.
   d. **Comparing and Contrasting** Compare the structure of a typical terrestrial planet with that of a gas giant.

2. a. **Describing** Describe an important characteristic of each outer planet that helps to distinguish it from the other outer planets.
   b. **Comparing and Contrasting** How is Pluto different from the gas giants?
   c. **Classifying** Why did astronomers reclassify Pluto as a dwarf planet?

Math Practice

3. **Circumference** Jupiter's radius is about 71,490 km. What is its circumference?

Speeding Around the Sun

Problem

How does a planet's distance from the sun affect its period of revolution?

Skills Focus

making models, developing hypotheses, designing experiments

Materials

- string, 1.5 m   • plastic tube, 6 cm
- meter stick   • weight or several washers
- one-hole rubber stopper
- stopwatch or watch with second hand

Procedure

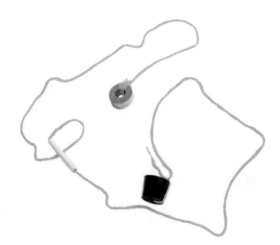

PART 1   Modeling Planetary Revolution

1. Copy the data table onto a sheet of paper.

Data Table				
Distance (cm)	Period of Revolution			
	Trial 1	Trial 2	Trial 3	Average
20				
40				
60				

2. Make a model of a planet orbiting the sun by threading the string through the rubber stopper hole. Tie the end of the string to the main part of the string. Pull tightly to make sure that the knot will not become untied.

3. Thread the other end of the string through the plastic tube and tie a weight to that end. Have your teacher check both knots.

4. Pull the string so the stopper is 20 cm away from the plastic tube. Hold the plastic tube in your hand above your head. Keeping the length of string constant, swing the rubber stopper in a circle above your head just fast enough to keep the stopper moving. The circle represents a planet's orbit, and the length of string from the rubber stopper to the plastic tube represents the distance from the sun. **CAUTION:** *Stand away from other students. Make sure the swinging stopper will not hit students or objects. Do not let go of the string.*

5. Have your lab partner time how long it takes for the rubber stopper to make ten complete revolutions. Determine the period for one revolution by dividing the measured time by ten. Record the time in the data table.

6. Repeat Step 5 two more times. Be sure to record each trial in a data table. After the third trial, calculate and record the average period of revolution.

PART 2 Designing an Experiment

7. Write your hypothesis for how a planet's period of revolution would be affected by changing its distance from the sun.

8. Design an experiment that will enable you to test your hypothesis. Write the steps you plan to follow to carry out your experiment. As you design your experiment, consider the following factors:
   • What different distances will you test?
   • What variables are involved in your experiment and how will you control them?
   • How many trials will you run for each distance?

9. Have your teacher review your step-by-step plan. After your teacher approves your plan, carry out your experiment.

Analyze and Conclude

1. **Making Models** In your experiment, what represents the planet and what represents the sun?

2. **Making Models** What force does the pull on the string represent?

3. **Interpreting Data** What happened to the period of revolution when you changed the distance in Part 2? Did your experiment prove or disprove your hypothesis?

4. **Drawing Conclusions** Which planets take less time to revolve around the sun—those closer to the sun or those farther away? Use the model to support your answer.

5. **Designing Experiments** As you were designing your experiment, which variable was the most difficult to control? How did you design your procedure to control that variable?

6. **Communicating** Write a brief summary of your experiment for a science magazine. Describe your hypothesis, procedure, and results in one or two paragraphs.

More to Explore

Develop a hypothesis for how a planet's mass might affect its period of revolution. Then, using a stopper with a different mass, modify the activity to test your hypothesis. Before you swing your stopper, have your teacher check your knots.

Comets, Asteroids, and Meteors

Reading Preview

Key Concepts
- What are the characteristics of comets?
- Where are most asteroids found?
- What are meteoroids and how do they form?

Key Terms
- comet • coma • nucleus
- Kuiper belt • Oort cloud
- asteroid • asteroid belt
- meteoroid • meteor
- meteorite

Target Reading Skill
Comparing and Contrasting
As you read, compare and contrast comets, asteroids, and meteoroids by completing a table like the one below.

Comets, Asteroids, and Meteoroids

Feature	Comets	Asteroids
Origin	Kuiper belt and Oort cloud	
Size		
Composition		

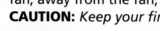

Discover Activity

Which Way Do Comet Tails Point?

1. Form a small ball out of modeling clay to represent a comet.
2. ✂ Using a pencil point, push three 10-cm lengths of string into the ball. The strings represent the comet's tail. Stick the ball onto the pencil point, as shown.
3. 🖐 Hold the ball about 1 m in front of a fan. The air from the fan represents the solar wind. Move the ball toward the fan, away from the fan, and from side to side.
   CAUTION: *Keep your fingers away from the fan blades.*

Think It Over
Inferring How does moving the ball affect the direction in which the strings point? What determines which way the tail of a comet points?

Imagine watching a cosmic collision! That's exactly what happened in July 1994. The year before, Eugene and Carolyn Shoemaker and David Levy discovered a comet that had previously broken into pieces near Jupiter. When their orbit passed near Jupiter again, the fragments crashed into Jupiter. On Earth, many people were fascinated to view images of the huge explosions—some were as large as Earth!

As this example shows, the sun, planets, and moons aren't the only objects in the solar system. There are also many smaller objects moving through the solar system. These objects are classified as comets, asteroids, or meteoroids.

FIGURE 24
Structure of a Comet
The main parts of a comet are the nucleus, the coma, and the tail. The nucleus is deep within the coma. Most comets have two tails—a bluish gas tail and a white dust tail.

Gas tail

Nucleus

Coma

Dust tail

Comets

One of the most glorious things you can see in the night sky is a comet. But what exactly is a comet? You can think of a **comet** as a "dirty snowball" about the size of a mountain. **Comets are loose collections of ice, dust, and small rocky particles whose orbits are usually very long, narrow ellipses.**

A Comet's Head When a comet gets close enough to the sun, the energy in the sunlight turns the ice into gas, releasing gas and dust. Clouds of gas and dust form a fuzzy outer layer called a **coma.** Figure 24 shows the coma and the **nucleus,** the solid inner core of a comet. The brightest part of a comet, the comet's head, is made up of the nucleus and coma.

A Comet's Tail As a comet approaches the sun and heats up, some of its gas and dust stream outward, forming a tail. The name *comet* means "long-haired star" in Greek. Most comets have two tails—a gas tail and a dust tail. Both tails usually point away from the sun, as shown in Figure 25.

A comet's tail can be more than 100 million kilometers long and stretch across most of the sky. The material is stretched out very thinly, however, so there is little mass in a comet's tail.

Origin of Comets Most comets are found in one of two distant regions of the solar system: the Kuiper belt and the Oort cloud. The **Kuiper belt** is a doughnut-shaped region that extends from beyond Neptune's orbit to about 100 times Earth's distance from the sun. The **Oort cloud** is a spherical region of comets that surrounds the solar system out to more than 1,000 times the distance between Pluto and the sun.

 **Reading Checkpoint** **What is the Oort cloud?**

Go Online
SciLINKS NSTA

For: Links on comets, asteroids, and meteors
Visit: www.SciLinks.org
Web Code: scn-0635

FIGURE 25
Comet Orbits
Most comets revolve around the sun in very long, narrow orbits. Gas and dust tails form as the comet approaches the sun. **Observing** *What shape is a comet's orbit?*

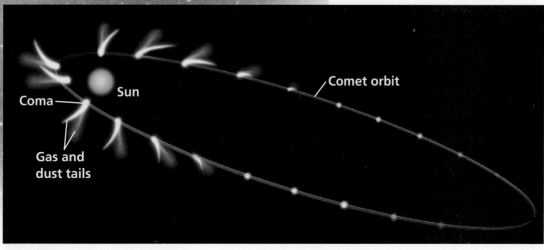

Comet orbit
Coma
Sun
Gas and dust tails

Asteroids

Between 1801 and 1807, astronomers discovered four small objects between the orbits of Mars and Jupiter. They named the objects Ceres, Pallas, Juno, and Vesta. Over the next 80 years, astronomers found 300 more. These rocky objects, called **asteroids,** are too small and too numerous to be considered full-fledged planets. **Most asteroids revolve around the sun between the orbits of Mars and Jupiter.** This region of the solar system, shown in Figure 26, is called the **asteroid belt.**

Astronomers have discovered more than 100,000 asteroids, and they are constantly finding more. Most asteroids are small—less than a kilometer in diameter. Only Ceres, Pallas, Vesta, and Hygiea are more than 300 kilometers across. The largest asteroid, Ceres, was recently classified as a dwarf planet. At one time, scientists thought that asteroids were the remains of a shattered planet. However, the combined mass of all the asteroids is too small to support this idea. Scientists now hypothesize that the asteroids are leftover pieces of the early solar system that never came together to form a planet.

Some asteroids have very elliptical orbits that bring them closer to the sun than Earth's orbit. Someday, one of these asteroids could hit Earth. One or more large asteroids did hit Earth about 65 million years ago, filling the atmosphere with dust and smoke and blocking out sunlight around the world. Scientists hypothesize that many species of organisms, including the dinosaurs, became extinct as a result.

 **Reading Checkpoint** Name the four largest asteroids.

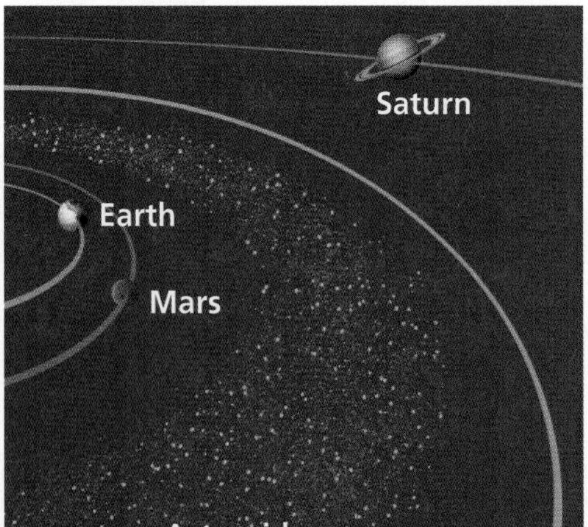

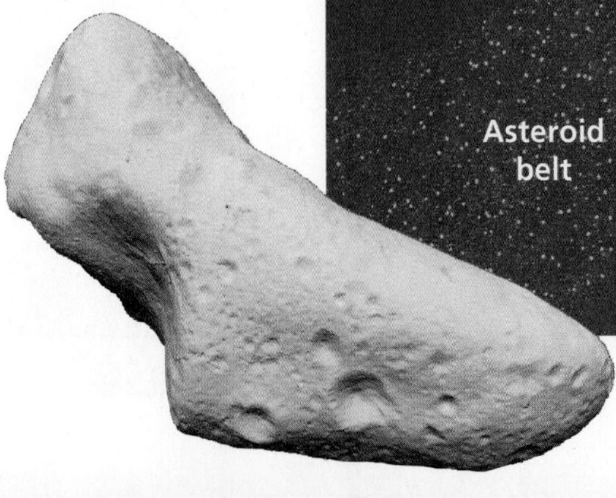

FIGURE 26
Asteroids
The asteroid belt (right) lies between Mars and Jupiter. Asteroids come in many sizes and shapes. The photo below shows the oddly shaped asteroid Eros.

Saturn

Earth

Mars

Asteroid belt

Jupiter

Meteors

It's a perfect night for stargazing—dark and clear. Suddenly, a streak of light flashes across the sky. For an hour or so, you see a streak at least once a minute. You are watching a meteor shower. Meteor showers happen regularly, several times a year.

Even when there is no meteor shower, you often can see meteors if you are far from city lights and the sky is not cloudy. On average, a meteor streaks overhead every 10 minutes.

A **meteoroid** is a chunk of rock or dust in space. **Meteoroids come from comets or asteroids.** Some meteoroids form when asteroids collide in space. Others form when a comet breaks up and creates a cloud of dust that continues to move through the solar system. When Earth passes through one of these dust clouds, bits of dust enter Earth's atmosphere.

When a meteoroid enters Earth's atmosphere, friction with the air creates heat and produces a streak of light in the sky—a **meteor.** If the meteoroid is large enough, it may not burn up completely. Meteoroids that pass through the atmosphere and hit Earth's surface are called **meteorites.** The craters on the moon were formed by meteoroids.

FIGURE 27
Meteors
Meteoroids make streaks of light called meteors, like the one above, as they burn up in the atmosphere.

 **Reading Checkpoint** What is a meteorite?

Section 5 Assessment

Target Reading Skill Comparing and Contrasting Use the information in your table about comets, asteroids, and meteoroids to help you answer the questions below.

Reviewing Key Concepts

1. **a. Defining** What is a comet?
   b. Listing What are the different parts of a comet?
   c. Relating Cause and Effect How does a comet's appearance change as it approaches the sun? Why do these changes occur?
2. **a. Describing** What is an asteroid?
   b. Explaining Where are most asteroids found?
   c. Summarizing How did the asteroids form?
3. **a. Describing** What is a meteoroid?
   b. Explaining What are the main sources of meteoroids?
   c. Comparing and Contrasting What are the differences between meteoroids, meteors, and meteorites?

Lab zone **At-Home Activity**

Observing Meteors Meteor showers occur regularly on specific dates. (The Perseid meteor shower, for example, occurs around August 12 each year.) Look in the newspaper, on the Internet, or in an almanac for information about the next meteor shower. With adult family members, go outside on that night and look for meteors. Explain to your family what causes the display.

Is There Life Beyond Earth?

Reading Preview

Key Concepts
- What conditions do living things need to exist on Earth?
- Why do scientists think Mars and Europa are good places to look for signs of life?

Key Term
- extraterrestrial life

Target Reading Skill

Asking Questions Before you read, preview the red headings. In a graphic organizer like the one below, ask a question for each heading. As you read, write the answers to your questions.

Is There Life Beyond Earth?

Question	Answer
What are the "Goldilocks" conditions?	The "Goldilocks" conditions are . . .

Discover **Activity**

Is Yeast Alive or Not?

1. Open a package of yeast and pour it into a bowl.
2. Look at the yeast carefully. Make a list of your observations.
3. Fill the bowl about halfway with warm water (about 20°C). Add a spoonful of sugar. Stir the mixture with the spoon. Wait 5 minutes.
4. Now look at the yeast again and make a list of your observations.

Think It Over
Forming Operational Definitions Which of your observations suggest that yeast is not alive? Which observations suggest that yeast is alive? How can you tell if something is alive?

Most of Antarctica is covered with snow and ice. You would not expect to see rocks lying on top of the whiteness. But surprisingly, people have found rocks lying on Antarctica's ice. When scientists examined the rocks, they found that many were meteorites. A few of these meteorites came from Mars. Astronomers think that meteoroids hitting the surface of Mars blasted chunks of rock into space. Some of these rocks eventually entered Earth's atmosphere and landed on its surface.

In 1996, a team of scientists announced that a meteorite from Mars found in Antarctica has tiny shapes that look like fossils—the remains of ancient life preserved in rock—though much smaller. Most scientists doubt that the shapes really are fossils. But if they are, it would be a sign that microscopic life-forms similar to bacteria once existed on Mars. Life other than that on Earth would be called **extraterrestrial life.**

FIGURE 28
Meteorites in Antarctica
Dr. Ursula Marvin (lying down) studies meteorites like this one in Antarctica.

Life on Earth

Sometimes it can be hard to tell whether something is alive or not. But all living things on Earth have several characteristics in common. Living things are made up of one or more cells. Living things take in energy and use it to grow and develop. They reproduce, producing new living things of the same type. Living things also give off waste.

The "Goldilocks" Conditions No one knows whether life exists anywhere other than Earth. Scientists often talk about the conditions needed by "life as we know it." **Earth has liquid water and a suitable temperature range and atmosphere for living things to survive.** Scientists sometimes call these favorable conditions the "Goldilocks" conditions. That is, the temperature is not too hot and not too cold. It is just right. If Earth were much hotter, water would always be a gas—water vapor. If Earth were much colder, water would always be solid ice.

Are these the conditions necessary for life? Or are they just the conditions that Earth's living things happen to need? Scientists have only one example to study: life on Earth. Unless scientists find evidence of life somewhere else, there is no way to answer these questions for certain.

Extreme Conditions Recently, scientists have discovered living things in places where it was once believed that life could not exist. Giant tubeworms have been found under the extremely high pressures at the bottom of the ocean. Single-celled organisms have been found in the near-boiling temperatures of hot springs. Tiny life-forms have been discovered deep inside solid rock. Scientists have even found animals that do not require the energy of sunlight, but instead get their energy from chemicals.

These astounding discoveries show that the range of conditions in which life can exist is much greater than scientists once thought. Could there be life-forms in the solar system that do not need the "Goldilocks" conditions?

 **Reading Checkpoint** What are some characteristics of all living things?

FIGURE 29
Hot Spring
Bacteria that thrive in near-boiling water help to produce the striking colors of Grand Prismatic Spring in Wyoming. **Inferring** *How does studying unusual organisms on Earth help scientists predict what extraterrestrial life might be like?*

Lab zone Skills **Activity**

Communicating You are writing a letter to a friend who lives on another planet. Your friend has never been to Earth and has no idea what the planet is like. Explain in your letter why the conditions on Earth make it an ideal place for living things.

Life Elsewhere in the Solar System?

Recall that Mars is the planet most similar to Earth. That makes Mars the most obvious place to look for living things.

Life on Mars? Spacecraft have found regions on the surface of Mars that look like streambeds with crisscrossing paths of water. Shapes like those shown in Figure 30 were almost certainly formed by flowing water. **Since life as we know it requires water, scientists hypothesize that Mars may have once had the conditions needed for life to exist.**

In 1976 twin *Viking* spacecraft reached Mars. Each of the *Viking* landers carried a small laboratory meant to search for life forms. These laboratories tested Mars's air and soil for signs of life. None of these tests showed evidence of life.

More recently, the *Spirit* and *Opportunity* rovers found rocks and other surface features on Mars that were certainly formed by liquid water. However, the rovers were not equipped to search for past or present life.

Interest in life on Mars was increased by a report in 1996 about a meteorite from Mars that may contain fossils. The scientists' report started a huge debate. What were the tube-shaped things in the meteorite? Some scientists have suggested that the tiny shapes found in the meteorite are too small to be the remains of life forms. The shapes may have come from natural processes on Mars.

The most effective way to answer these questions is to send more probes to Mars. Future Mars missions should be able to bring samples of rocks and soil back to Earth for detailed analysis. Scientists may not yet have evidence of life on Mars, but hope is growing that we can soon learn the truth.

Reading Checkpoint What did the *Spirit* and *Opportunity* rovers discover on Mars?

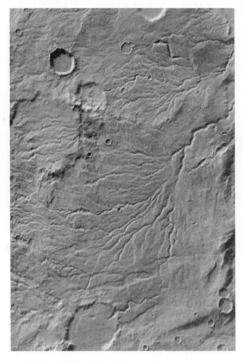

FIGURE 30
Liquid Water on Mars
The river-like patterns on the surface of Mars indicate that liquid water once flowed there.
Applying Concepts *Why does this evidence make it more likely that there may once have been life on Mars?*

FIGURE 31
Martian Fossils?
This false-color electron microscope image shows tiny fossil-like shapes found in a meteorite from Mars. These structures are less than one-hundredth the width of a human hair.

Life on Europa? Many scientists think that Europa, one of Jupiter's moons, may have the conditions necessary for life to develop. Europa has a smooth, icy crust with giant cracks. Close-up views from the *Galileo* space probe show that Europa's ice has broken up and re-formed, resulting in large twisted blocks of ice. Similar patterns occur in the ice crust over Earth's Arctic Ocean. Scientists hypothesize that there is a liquid ocean under Europa's ice. The water in the ocean could be kept liquid by heat coming from inside Europa. **If there is liquid water on Europa, there might also be life.**

How could scientists study conditions under Europa's ice sheet? Perhaps a future space probe might be able to use radar to "see" through Europa's icy crust. After that, robotic probes could be sent to drill through the ice to search for life in the water below.

FIGURE 32
Exploring Europa
Scientists have discussed sending a robotic probe to search for life in the ocean below Europa's icy crust.

Section 6 Assessment

Target Reading Skills Asking Questions Use the answers to the questions you wrote about the section headings to help answer the questions.

Reviewing Key Concepts

1. **a. Relating Cause and Effect** What conditions does life on Earth need to survive?
   b. Summarizing Why is Earth said to have the "Goldilocks" conditions?
   c. Applying Concepts Do you think there could be life as we know it on Neptune? Explain. (*Hint:* Review Section 4.)
2. **a. Explaining** Why do astronomers think there could be life on Europa?
   b. Identifying Scientists think that in the past Mars may have had the conditions needed for life to exist. What are these conditions? Do they still exist?

   c. Making Generalizations What characteristic do Mars and Europa share with Earth that makes them candidates to support extraterrestrial life?

Lab zone At-Home **Activity**

Making a Message Imagine that scientists have found intelligent extraterrestrial life. With family members, make up a message to send to the extraterrestrials. Remember that they will not understand English, so you should use only symbols and drawings in your message.

Study Guide

The **BIG Idea**   **Structure of the Solar System** The solar system includes the sun, the planets and their moons, and smaller objects such as comets, asteroids, and meteoroids.

① Observing the Solar System

Key Concepts

- In a geocentric system, Earth is perceived to be at the center of the revolving planets and stars. In a heliocentric system, Earth and the other planets revolve around the sun.
- Galileo's discoveries supported the heliocentric model. Kepler found that the orbit of each planet is an ellipse.
- The solar system consists of the sun, the planets and their moons, and a series of smaller objects that revolve around the sun.

Key Terms
• geocentric • heliocentric • ellipse

② The Sun

Key Concepts

- The sun's interior consists of the core, radiation zone, and convection zone. The sun's atmosphere consists of the photosphere, chromosphere, and corona.
- Features on or just above the sun's surface include sunspots, prominences, and solar flares.

Key Terms
• core • nuclear fusion • radiation zone
• convection zone • photosphere
• chromosphere • corona • solar wind
• sunspot • prominence • solar flare

③ The Inner Planets

Key Concepts

- The four inner planets are small and dense and have rocky surfaces.
- Earth is unique in our solar system in having liquid water at its surface.
- Mercury is the smallest terrestrial planet. Venus's internal structure is similar to Earth's.
- Scientists think that a large amount of liquid water flowed on Mars's surface in the distant past.

Key Terms
• terrestrial planets • greenhouse effect

④ The Outer Planets

Key Concepts

- Jupiter, Saturn, Uranus, and Neptune are much larger and more massive than Earth.
- Jupiter is the largest and most massive planet in the solar system.
- Saturn has the most spectacular rings of any planet.
- Uranus's axis of rotation is tilted at an angle of about 90 degrees from the vertical.
- Neptune is a cold, blue planet. Its atmosphere contains visible clouds.
- Pluto has a solid surface and is much smaller and denser than the outer planets.

Key Terms
• gas giant • ring

⑤ Comets, Asteroids, and Meteors

Key Concepts

- Comets are loose collections of ice, dust, and small rocky particles whose orbits are usually very long, narrow ellipses.
- Most asteroids revolve around the sun between the orbits of Mars and Jupiter.
- Meteoroids come from comets or asteroids.

Key Terms
• comet • coma • nucleus • Kuiper belt
• Oort cloud • asteroid • asteroid belt
• meteoroid • meteor • meteorite

⑥ Is There Life Beyond Earth?

Key Concepts

- Earth has liquid water and a suitable temperature range and atmosphere for life.
- Scientists hypothesize that Mars may have once had the conditions for life to exist.
- If there is liquid water on Europa, there might also be life.

Key Term   • extraterrestrial life

Review and Assessment

Organizing Information

Comparing and Contrasting Fill in the graphic organizer to compare and contrast the geocentric system and the heliocentric system. (For more on Comparing and Contrasting, see the Skills Handbook.)

Feature	Geocentric System	Heliocentric System
Object at center	Earth	a. _____?_____
Objects that move around center	Planets and sun	b. _____?_____
Proposed by	c. _____?_____	Copernicus
Supporters	Ptolemy	d. _____?_____

Reviewing Key Terms

Choose the letter of the best answer.

1. Copernicus thought that the solar system was
   a. an ellipse.
   b. a constellation.
   c. geocentric.
   d. heliocentric.

2. The part of the sun where nuclear fusion occurs is the
   a. photosphere.
   b. core.
   c. chromosphere.
   d. corona.

3. Pluto is a(n)
   a. inner planet.
   b. terrestrial planet.
   c. dwarf planet.
   d. gas giant.

4. The region between Mars and Jupiter where many rocky objects are found is the
   a. asteroid belt.
   b. Oort cloud.
   c. convection zone.
   d. Kuiper belt.

5. A meteoroid that reaches Earth's surface is called a(n)
   a. comet.
   b. meteorite.
   c. meteor.
   d. asteroid.

If the statement is true, write *true*. If it is false, change the underlined word or words to make the statement true.

6. The shape of the orbit of each planet is a(n) <u>ellipse</u>.

7. <u>Prominences</u> are regions of cooler gases on the sun.

8. The trapping of heat by a planet's atmosphere is called <u>nuclear fusion</u>.

9. All the <u>terrestrial planets</u> are surrounded by rings.

10. The solid inner core of a comet is its <u>coma</u>.

Writing in Science

News Report Imagine you are on a mission to explore the solar system. Write a brief news report telling the story of your trip from Earth to another terrestrial planet and to a gas giant. Include a description of each planet.

Discovery CHANNEL SCHOOL™

The Solar System

Video Preview
Video Field Trip
▶ Video Assessment

Review and Assessment

Checking Concepts

11. Describe the contributions Tycho Brahe and Johannes Kepler made to modern astronomy.

12. What is the solar wind?

13. Why does Mercury have very little atmosphere?

14. Why can astronomers see the surface of Mars clearly but not the surface of Venus?

15. What evidence do astronomers have that water once flowed on Mars?

Math Practice

16. Circumference Mars has a radius of 3,397 km at its equator. Find its circumference.

17. Circumference Jupiter has a circumference of about 449,000 km at its equator. Calculate its radius.

Thinking Critically

18. Applying Concepts Explain why Venus is hotter than it would be if it had no atmosphere.

19. Predicting Do you think astronomers have found all of the moons of the outer planets? Explain.

20. Comparing and Contrasting Compare and contrast comets, asteroids, and meteoroids.

21. Classifying Look at the diagram below. Do you think it represents the structure of a terrestrial planet or a gas giant? Explain.

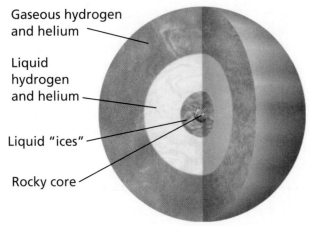

Gaseous hydrogen and helium

Liquid hydrogen and helium

Liquid "ices"

Rocky core

22. Making Generalizations Why would the discovery of liquid water on another planet be important?

Applying Skills

Use the diagram of an imaginary, newly discovered planetary system around Star X to answer Questions 23–25.

The periods of revolution of planets A, B, and C are 75 Earth days, 200 Earth days, and 300 Earth days.

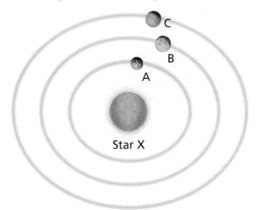

Star X

23. Interpreting Data Which planet in this new planetary system revolves around Star X in the shortest amount of time?

24. Making Models In 150 days, how far will each planet have revolved around Star X? Copy the diagram and sketch the positions of the three planets to find out. How far will each planet have revolved around Star X in 400 days? Sketch their positions.

25. Drawing Conclusions Can Planet C ever be closer to Planet A than to Planet B? Study your drawings to figure this out.

Lab zone Chapter **Project**

Performance Assessment Present your scale models of the solar system. Display your data tables showing how you did the calculations and how you checked them for accuracy.

Standardized Test Prep

Choose the letter of the best answer.

1. What characteristic do all of the inner planets share?

   A They are larger and more massive than the sun.

   B They have thick atmospheres of hydrogen and helium.

   C They have rocky surfaces.

   D They each have many moons.

2. Mercury has a daytime temperature of about 430° C and a nighttime temperature below −170° C. What is the best explanation?

   F Mercury has a greenhouse effect.

   G Global warming is occurring on Mercury.

   H Mercury is the closest planet to the sun.

   J Mercury has no real atmosphere.

The table below shows data for five planets in our solar system. Use the table and your knowledge of science to answer Questions 3–5.

Planet	Period of Rotation (Earth days)	Period of Revolution (Earth years)	Average Distance From the Sun (million km)
Mars	1.03	1.9	228
Jupiter	0.41	12	779
Saturn	0.45	29	1,434
Uranus	0.72	84	2,873
Neptune	0.67	164	4,495

3. Which of these planets' orbits is farthest from Earth's orbit?

   A Mars   **B** Jupiter

   C Uranus   **D** Neptune

4. Which planet has a "day" that is most similar in length to a day on Earth?

   F Mars   **G** Jupiter

   H Uranus   **J** Neptune

5. Light takes about 8 minutes and 20 seconds to travel from the sun to Earth, 150 million kilometers away. About how long does it take light to travel from the sun to Jupiter?

   A 10 minutes   **B** 25 minutes

   C 43 minutes   **D** 112 minutes

Constructed Response

6. Describe three major differences between the terrestrial planets and the gas giants.

Chapter 4

Stars, Galaxies, and the Universe

The BIG Idea
Structure of the Universe

Q How do astronomers learn about the structure of the universe?

The dark Horsehead Nebula is visible ▶ against red-glowing hydrogen gas.

Discovery CHANNEL SCHOOL™

Stars, Galaxies, and
the Universe
▶ Video Preview
Video Field Trip
Video Assessment

Lab zone™ Chapter **Project**

Star Stories

Many years ago, people created
stories to explain the patterns of stars
they saw in the sky. In your project,
you'll learn how the names of these
constellations reflect the cultures
of the people who named
them.

Your Goal To complete the
project you will

● learn the star patterns of
at least three constellations

● research the myths that gave
one constellation its name

● create your own star myth

Plan It! Begin by making a list of
constellations that you have heard
about. Then use the star charts in
the appendix to locate constellations in the night sky. Make a sketch
of the constellations that you locate.
Choose one constellation, and research the myths that
gave it its name. Draw a new picture for the star pattern in your constellation, and choose a name for it.
Finally, write a story about your constellation. At the
end of the chapter, you will present your constellation
and a story that explains its name.

Telescopes

Reading Preview

Key Concepts
- What are the regions of the electromagnetic spectrum?
- What are telescopes and how do they work?
- Where are most large telescopes located?

Key Terms
- telescope
- electromagnetic radiation
- visible light
- wavelength
- spectrum
- optical telescope
- refracting telescope
- convex lens
- reflecting telescope
- radio telescope
- observatory

Target Reading Skill

Building Vocabulary Carefully read the definition of each key term. Also read the neighboring sentences. Then write a definition of each key term in your own words.

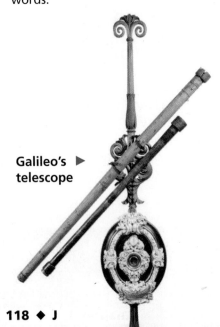

◄ Galileo's telescope

Lab zone | Discover **Activity**

How Does Distance Affect an Image?

1. Hold a plastic hand lens about 7 cm away from your eye and about 5 cm away from a printed letter on a page. Move the lens slowly back and forth until the letter is in clear focus.

2. Keep the letter about 5 cm from the lens as you move your eye back to about 20 cm from the lens. Then, keeping the distance between your eye and the lens constant, slowly move the object away from the lens.

Think It Over

Observing What did the letter look like through the lens in Step 1 compared with how it looked without the lens? How did the image change in Step 2?

Ancient peoples often gazed up in wonder at the many points of light in the night sky. But they could see few details with their eyes alone. It was not until the invention of the telescope in 1608 that people could observe objects in the sky more closely. Recall that a **telescope** is a device that makes distant objects appear to be closer. The telescope revolutionized astronomy. Scientists now had a tool that allowed them to see many objects in space for the first time.

Although Galileo was not the first to use a telescope, he soon made it famous as he turned his homemade instrument to the sky. With his telescope, Galileo saw things that no one had even dreamed of. He was the first to see sunspots, Saturn's rings, and the four large moons of Jupiter. Galileo could see fine details, such as mountains on the moon, which cannot be seen clearly by the unaided eye.

Since Galileo's time, astronomers have built ever larger and more powerful telescopes. These telescopes have opened up a whole universe of wonders that would have amazed even Galileo.

Electromagnetic Radiation

To understand how telescopes work, it's useful to understand the nature of electromagnetic radiation. Light is a form of **electromagnetic radiation** (ih lek troh mag NET ik), or energy that can travel through space in the form of waves. You can see stars when the light that they produce reaches your eyes.

Forms of Radiation Scientists call the light you can see **visible light.** Visible light is just one of many types of electromagnetic radiation. Many objects give off radiation that you can't see. For example, in addition to their reddish light, the glowing coils of an electric heater give off infrared radiation, which you feel as heat. Radio transmitters produce radio waves that carry signals to radios and televisions. Objects in space give off all types of electromagnetic radiation.

The Electromagnetic Spectrum As shown in Figure 1, the distance between the crest of one wave and the crest of the next wave is called **wavelength.** Visible light has very short wavelengths, less than one millionth of a meter. Some electromagnetic waves have even shorter wavelengths. Other waves have much longer wavelengths, even several meters long.

If you shine white light through a prism, the light spreads out to make a range of different colors with different wavelengths, called a **spectrum.** The spectrum of visible light is made of the colors red, orange, yellow, green, blue, and violet. **The electromagnetic spectrum includes the entire range of radio waves, infrared radiation, visible light, ultraviolet radiation, X-rays, and gamma rays.**

Reading Checkpoint What are two kinds of electromagnetic waves that you might experience every day?

Go Online
SciLinks NSTA

For: Links on telescopes
Visit: www.SciLinks.org
Web Code: scn-0641

FIGURE 1
The Electromagnetic Spectrum
The electromagnetic spectrum ranges from long-wavelength radio waves through short-wavelength gamma rays.
Interpreting Diagrams *Are infrared waves longer or shorter than ultraviolet waves?*

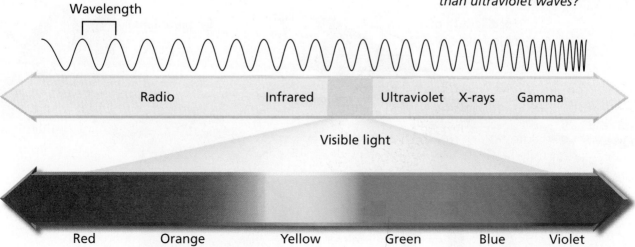

Wavelength

Radio   Infrared   Ultraviolet X-rays Gamma

Visible light

Red   Orange   Yellow   Green   Blue   Violet

Types of Telescopes

On a clear night, your eyes can see at most a few thousand stars. But with a telescope, you can see many millions. Why? The light from stars spreads out as it moves through space, and your eyes are too small to gather much light.

Telescopes are instruments that collect and focus light and other forms of electromagnetic radiation. Telescopes make distant objects appear larger and brighter. A telescope that uses lenses or mirrors to collect and focus visible light is called an **optical telescope.** The two major types of optical telescope are refracting telescopes and reflecting telescopes.

Modern astronomy is based on the detection of many forms of electromagnetic radiation besides visible light. Non-optical telescopes collect and focus different types of electromagnetic radiation, just as optical telescopes collect visible light.

Refracting Telescopes A **refracting telescope** uses convex lenses to gather and focus light. A **convex lens** is a piece of transparent glass, curved so that the middle is thicker than the edges.

Figure 2 shows a simple refracting telescope. This telescope has two convex lenses, one at each end of a long tube. Light enters the telescope through the large objective lens at the top. The objective lens focuses the light at a certain distance from the lens. This distance is the focal length of the lens. The larger the objective lens, the more light the telescope can collect. This makes it easier for astronomers to see faint objects.

The smaller lens at the lower end of a refracting telescope is the eyepiece lens. The eyepiece lens magnifies the image produced by the objective lens.

FIGURE 2
Refracting and Reflecting Telescopes
A refracting telescope uses convex lenses to focus light. A reflecting telescope has a curved mirror in place of an objective lens.

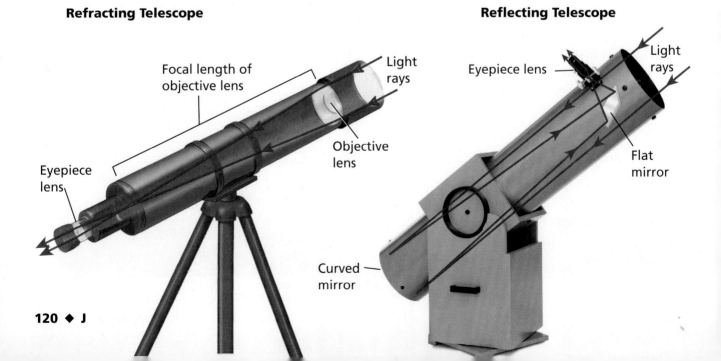

Refracting Telescope

Focal length of objective lens

Light rays

Objective lens

Eyepiece lens

Reflecting Telescope

Eyepiece lens

Light rays

Flat mirror

Curved mirror

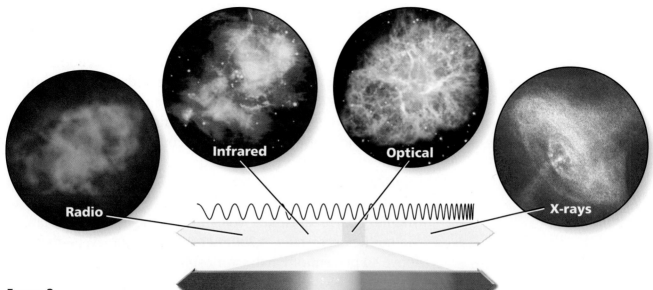

FIGURE 3
Four Views of the Crab Nebula
Different types of telescopes collect electromagnetic radiation at different wavelengths. Astronomers are able to learn a great deal about the Crab Nebula by examining these different images. The images are shown at different scales.

Reflecting Telescopes In 1668, Isaac Newton built the first reflecting telescope. A **reflecting telescope** uses a curved mirror to collect and focus light. Like the objective lens in a refracting telescope, the curved mirror in a reflecting telescope focuses a large amount of light onto a small area. The larger the mirror, the more light the telescope can collect. The largest optical telescopes today are all reflecting telescopes.

Radio Telescopes Devices used to detect radio waves from objects in space are called **radio telescopes.** Most radio telescopes have curved, reflecting surfaces—up to 305 meters in diameter. These surfaces focus radio waves the way the mirror in a reflecting telescope focuses light waves. The surfaces concentrate the faint radio waves from space onto small antennas like those on radios. As with optical telescopes, the larger a radio telescope is, the more radio waves it can collect.

Other Telescopes Some telescopes detect infrared radiation, which has longer wavelengths than visible light but shorter wavelengths than radio waves. There are also telescopes that detect the shortest wavelengths—ultraviolet radiation, X-rays, and gamma rays.

 **Reading Checkpoint** Who built the first reflecting telescope?

Lab zone Try This Activity

Locating Radio Waves
You can use an umbrella to focus radio waves.

1. Line the inside of an open umbrella with aluminum foil.
2. Turn on a small radio and tune it to a station.
3. Move the radio up and down along the umbrella handle. Find the position where the station is clearest. Radio waves reflecting off the foil focus at this point. Tape the radio to the handle.
4. Hold the umbrella at different angles. At which angle is the station the clearest?

Inferring In which direction do you think the radio station's transmitter is located? Explain.

Observatories

In general, an **observatory** is a building that contains one or more telescopes. However, some observatories are located in space. **Many large observatories are located on mountaintops or in space.** Why? Earth's atmosphere makes objects in space look blurry. The sky on some mountaintops is clearer than at sea level and is not brightened much by city lights. Unlike optical telescopes, radio telescopes do not need to be located on mountaintops.

One of the best observatory sites on Earth is on the top of Mauna Kea, a dormant volcano on the island of Hawaii. Mauna Kea is so tall—4,200 meters above sea level—that it is above 40 percent of Earth's atmosphere.

• Tech & Design in History •

Development of Modern Telescopes
During the last century, astronomers have built larger telescopes, which can collect more visible light and other types of radiation. Today's astronomers use tools that could not have been imagined 100 years ago.

1897 Yerkes Telescope
The 1-meter-diameter telescope at Yerkes Observatory in Wisconsin is the largest refracting telescope ever built. Because its main lens is so large, the Yerkes telescope can collect more light than any other refracting telescope.

1931 Beginning of Radio Astronomy
Karl Jansky, an American engineer, was trying to find the source of static that was interfering with radio communications. Using a large antenna, he discovered that the static was radio waves given off by objects in space. Jansky's accidental discovery led to the beginning of radio astronomy.

1963 Arecibo Radio Telescope
This radio telescope in Puerto Rico was built in a natural bowl in the ground. It is 305 meters in diameter, the largest radio telescope in existence.

| 1900 | | 1940 | 1960 |

Advanced Telescopes Today, many large optical telescopes are equipped with systems that significantly improve the quality of their images. Optical telescopes on Earth equipped with such systems are able to produce images of small regions of the sky that rival those of optical telescopes based in space.

Some new telescopes are equipped with computer systems that correct images for problems such as telescope movement and changes in air temperature or mirror shape. Other advanced telescopes use lasers to monitor conditions in the atmosphere. The shape of the telescope's mirror is automatically adjusted thousands of times each second in response to changes in the atmosphere.

1980 Very Large Array
The Very Large Array is a set of 27 radio telescopes in New Mexico. The telescopes can be moved close together or far apart. The telescopes are linked, so they can be used as if they were one giant radio telescope 25 kilometers in diameter.

1990 Hubble Space Telescope
The Hubble Space Telescope views objects in space from high above the atmosphere. As a result, it can produce extremely sharp images.

2003 Spitzer Space Telescope
The Spitzer Space Telescope is a powerful 0.85-meter diameter telescope that surveys the sky in the infrared range of the spectrum.

1980   **2000**   **2020**

Telescopes in Space X-rays, gamma rays, and most ultraviolet radiation are blocked by Earth's atmosphere. To detect these wavelengths, astronomers have placed telescopes in space. Some space telescopes are designed to detect visible light or infrared radiation, since Earth's atmosphere interferes with the transmission of these forms of radiation.

The Hubble Space Telescope is a reflecting telescope with a mirror 2.4 meters in diameter. Because the Hubble telescope orbits Earth above the atmosphere, it can produce very detailed images in visible light. It also collects ultraviolet and infrared radiation. The spectacular Hubble telescope images have changed how astronomers view the universe.

The hottest objects in space give off X-rays. The Chandra X-ray Observatory produces images in the X-ray portion of the spectrum. Chandra's X-ray images are much more detailed than those of earlier X-ray telescopes.

The most recent addition to NASA's lineup of telescopes in space is the Spitzer Space Telescope. Launched in 2003, the Spitzer telescope produces images in the infrared portion of the spectrum.

 **Reading Checkpoint** What is an observatory?

FIGURE 4
Repairing Hubble
Astronauts have repaired and upgraded the Hubble Space Telescope on several occasions.

Section 1 Assessment

Target Reading Skill Building Vocabulary
Use your definitions to help answer the questions below.

Reviewing Key Concepts

1. a. Sequencing List the main types of electromagnetic waves, from longest wavelength to shortest.
  b. Applying Concepts Why are images from the Hubble Space Telescope clearer than images from telescopes on Earth?
2. a. Identifying What are the two major types of optical telescope?
  b. Explaining How does a refracting telescope work?
  c. Comparing and Contrasting Use Figure 2 to explain the major differences between reflecting and refracting telescopes.

3. a. Summarizing How does the atmosphere affect electromagnetic radiation?
  b. Explaining Why are many large optical telescopes located on mountaintops?
  c. Applying Concepts Would it make sense to place an X-ray or gamma ray telescope on a mountaintop? Explain why or why not.

Writing in Science

Writing Instructions Write a short explanation of how to build a reflecting telescope for a booklet to be included in a model telescope kit. Be sure to describe the shape and position of each of the lenses or mirrors. You may include drawings.

Design and Build a Telescope

Foam holder

Eyepiece

Paper towel tubes

Objective lens (tape to the end of tube)

Problem
Can you design and build a telescope?

Skills Focus
evaluating the design, redesigning

Materials
- 2 paper towel tubes of slightly different diameters
- several plastic objective lenses
- several plastic eyepiece lenses
- meter stick
- foam holder for eyepiece
- transparent tape

Procedure
1. Fit one of the paper towel tubes inside the other. Make sure you can move the tubes but that they will not slide on their own.

2. Place the large objective lens flat against the end of the outer tube. Tape the lens in place.

3. Insert the small eyepiece lens into the opening in the foam holder.

4. Place the foam eyepiece lens holder into the inner tube at the end of the telescope opposite to the objective lens.

5. Tape a meter stick to the wall. Look through the eyepiece at the meter stick from 5 m away. Slide the tubes in and out to focus your telescope so that you can clearly read the numbers on the meter stick. Draw your telescope. On the drawing, mark the tube position that allows you to read the numbers most clearly.

6. Use your telescope to look at other objects at different distances, both in your classroom and through the window. For each object you view, draw your telescope, marking the tube position at which you see the object most clearly. **CAUTION:** *Do not look at the sun. You will damage your eyes.*

7. Design and build a better telescope. Your new telescope should make objects appear larger than your first model from the same observing distance. It should have markings on the inner tube to enable you to pre-focus the telescope for a given observing distance.

8. Draw a design for your new telescope. List the materials you'll need. Obtain your teacher's approval. Then build your new model.

Analyze and Conclude
1. **Inferring** Why do you need two tubes?

2. **Observing** If you focus on a nearby object and then focus on something farther away, do you have to move the tubes together or apart?

3. **Evaluating the Design** How could you improve on the design of your new telescope? What effects would different lenses or tubes have on its performance?

4. **Redesigning** Describe the most important factors in redesigning your telescope.

Communicate
Write a product brochure for your new telescope. Be sure to describe in detail why your new telescope is better than the first telescope.

Characteristics of Stars

Reading Preview

Key Concepts
- How are stars classified?
- How do astronomers measure distances to the stars?
- What is an H-R diagram and how do astronomers use it?

Key Terms
- constellation
- spectrograph
- apparent brightness
- absolute brightness
- light-year
- parallax
- Hertzsprung-Russell diagram
- main sequence

Target Reading Skill
Using Prior Knowledge Before you read, write what you know about the characteristics of stars in a graphic organizer like the one below. As you read, write what you learn.

What You Know
1. Stars are bright and hot.
2.

What You Learned
1.
2.

Lab zone

Discover **Activity**

How Does Your Thumb Move?

1. Stand facing a wall, at least an arm's length away. Stretch your arm out with your thumb up and your fingers curled.

2. Close your right eye and look at your thumb with your left eye. Line your thumb up with something on the wall.

3. Now close your left eye and open your right eye. How does your thumb appear to move along the wall?

4. Bring your thumb closer to your eye, about half the distance as before. Repeat Steps 2 and 3.

Think It Over
Observing How does your thumb appear to move in Step 4 compared to Step 3? How are these observations related to how far away your thumb is at each step? How could you use this method to estimate distances?

When ancient observers around the world looked up at the night sky, they imagined that groups of stars formed pictures of people or animals. Today, we call these imaginary patterns of stars **constellations.**

Different cultures gave different names to the constellations. For example, a large constellation in the winter sky is named Orion, the Hunter, after a Greek myth. In this constellation, Orion is seen with a sword in his belt and an upraised arm. The ancient Sumerians thought that the stars in Orion formed the outline of a sheep. In ancient China, this group of stars was called "three," probably because of the three bright stars in Orion's belt.

Astronomers use the patterns of the constellations to locate objects in the night sky. But although the stars in a constellation look as if they are close to one another, they generally are not. They just happen to lie in the same part of the sky as seen from Earth.

Illustration of Orion ▼

Classifying Stars

Like the sun, all stars are huge spheres of glowing gas. They are made up mostly of hydrogen, and they produce energy through the process of nuclear fusion. This energy makes stars shine brightly. Astronomers classify stars according to their physical characteristics. **Characteristics used to classify stars include color, temperature, size, composition, and brightness.**

Color and Temperature If you look at the night sky, you can see slight differences in the colors of the stars. For example, Betelgeuse (BAY tul jooz), the bright star in Orion's shoulder, looks reddish. Rigel, the star in Orion's heel, is blue-white.

Like hot objects on Earth, a star's color reveals its surface temperature. If you watch a toaster heat up, you can see the wires glow red-hot. The wires inside a light bulb are even hotter and glow white. Similarly, the coolest stars—with a surface temperature of about 3,200 degrees Celsius—appear reddish in the sky. With a surface temperature of about 5,500 degrees Celsius, the sun appears yellow. The hottest stars in the sky, with surface temperatures of over 20,000 degrees Celsius, appear bluish.

Size When you look at stars in the sky, they all appear to be points of light of the same size. Many stars are actually about the size of the sun, which is a medium-sized star. However, some stars are much larger than the sun. Very large stars are called giant stars or supergiant stars. If the supergiant star Betelgeuse were located where our sun is, it would be large enough to fill the solar system as far out as Jupiter.

Most stars are much smaller than the sun. White dwarf stars are about the size of Earth. Neutron stars are even smaller, only about 20 kilometers in diameter.

Go Online
PHSchool.com

For: More on types of stars
Visit: PHSchool.com
Web Code: cfd-5042

FIGURE 5
Star Size
Stars vary greatly in size. Giant stars are typically 10 to 100 times larger than the sun and more than 1,000 times the size of a white dwarf. **Calculating** *Betelgeuse has a diameter of 420 million kilometers. How many times larger is this than the sun, which has a diameter of 1.4 million kilometers?*

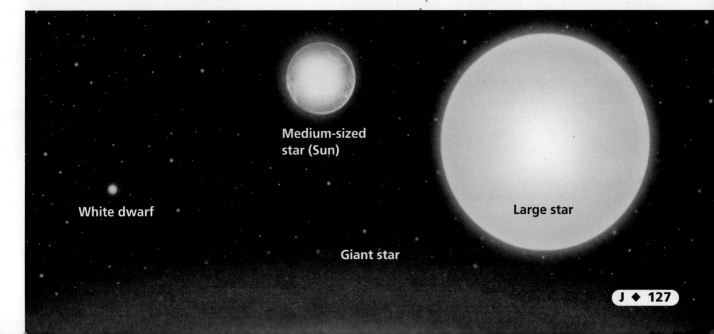

White dwarf

Medium-sized star (Sun)

Giant star

Large star

FIGURE 6

Spectrums of Four Stars
Astronomers can use line spectrums to identify the chemical elements in a star. Each element produces a characteristic pattern of spectral lines.

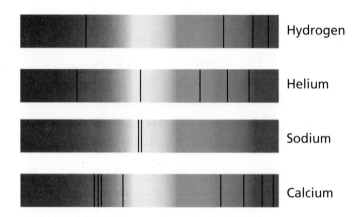

Hydrogen

Helium

Sodium

Calcium

Inferring

The lines on the spectrums below are from three different stars. Each of these star spectrums is made up of an overlap of spectrums from the individual elements shown in Figure 6. In star A, which elements have the strongest lines? Which are the strongest in star B? In star C?

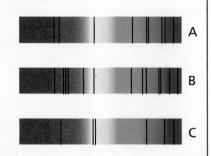

A

B

C

Chemical Composition Stars vary in their chemical composition. The chemical composition of most stars is about 73 percent hydrogen, 25 percent helium, and 2 percent other elements by mass. This is similar to the composition of the sun.

Astronomers use spectrographs to determine the elements found in stars. A **spectrograph** (SPEK truh graf) is a device that breaks light into colors and produces an image of the resulting spectrum. Most large telescopes have spectrographs.

The gases in a star's atmosphere absorb some wavelengths of light produced within the star. When the star's light is seen through a spectrograph, each absorbed wavelength is shown as a dark line on a spectrum. Each chemical element absorbs light at particular wavelengths. Just as each person has a unique set of fingerprints, each element has a unique set of lines for a given temperature. Figure 6 shows the spectral lines of four elements. By comparing a star's spectrum with the spectrums of known elements, astronomers can infer how much of each element is found in the star.

 **Reading Checkpoint** What is a spectrograph?

Brightness of Stars

Stars also differ in brightness, the amount of light they give off. **The brightness of a star depends upon both its size and temperature.** Recall that the photosphere is the layer of a star that gives off light. Betelgeuse is fairly cool, so a square meter of its photosphere doesn't give off much light. But Betelgeuse is very large, so it shines brightly.

Rigel, on the other hand, is very hot, so each square meter of Rigel's photosphere gives off a lot of light. Even though it is smaller than Betelgeuse, Rigel shines more brightly.

How bright a star looks from Earth depends on both its distance from Earth and how bright the star truly is. Because of these two factors, the brightness of a star can be described in two ways: apparent brightness and absolute brightness.

Apparent Brightness A star's **apparent brightness** is its brightness as seen from Earth. Astronomers can measure apparent brightness fairly easily using electronic devices. However, astronomers can't tell how much light a star gives off just from the star's apparent brightness. Just as a flashlight looks brighter the closer it is to you, a star looks brighter the closer it is to Earth. For example, the sun looks very bright. This does not mean that the sun gives off more light than all other stars. The sun looks so bright simply because it is so close. In reality, the sun is a star of only average brightness.

Absolute Brightness A star's **absolute brightness** is the brightness the star would have if it were at a standard distance from Earth. Finding a star's absolute brightness is more complex than finding its apparent brightness. An astronomer must first find out both the star's apparent brightness and its distance from Earth. The astronomer can then calculate the star's absolute brightness.

Astronomers have found that the absolute brightness of stars can vary tremendously. The brightest stars are more than a billion times brighter than the dimmest stars!

Reading Checkpoint **What is a star's absolute brightness?**

Lab zone Try This Activity

Star Bright

You can compare absolute and apparent brightness.

1. Dim the lights. Put two equally bright flashlights next to each other on a table. Turn them on.
2. Look at the flashlights from the other side of the room. Think of the flashlights as two stars. Then compare them in terms of absolute and apparent brightness.
3. Move one of the flashlights closer to you and repeat Step 2.
4. Replace one of the flashlights with a brighter one. Repeat Steps 1 and 2 with the unequally bright flashlights.

Making Models How could you place the flashlights in Step 4 so that they have the same apparent brightness? Try it.

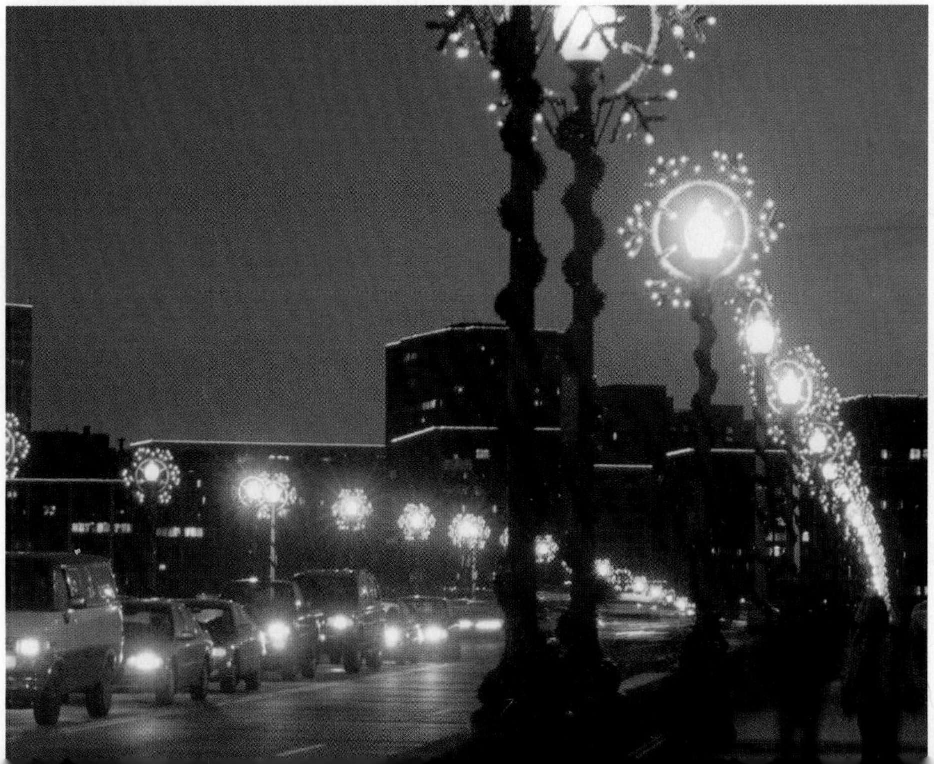

FIGURE 7
Absolute Brightness
The streetlights in this photo all give off about the same amount of light, and so have about the same absolute brightness.
Applying Concepts *Why do the closer streetlights appear brighter than the more distant lights?*

Measuring Distances to Stars

Imagine that you could travel to the stars at the speed of light. To travel from Earth to the sun would take about 8 minutes, not very much time for such a long trip. The next nearest star, Proxima Centauri, is much farther away. A trip to Proxima Centauri at the speed of light would take 4.2 years!

The Light-Year Distances on Earth's surface are often measured in kilometers. However, distances to the stars are so large that kilometers are not very practical units. **Astronomers use a unit called the light-year to measure distances between the stars.** In space, light travels at a speed of about 300,000 kilometers per second. A **light-year** is the distance that light travels in one year, about 9.5 million million kilometers.

Note that the light-year is a unit of distance, not time. To help you understand this, consider an everyday example. If you bicycle at 10 kilometers per hour, it would take you 1 hour to go to a mall 10 kilometers away. You could say that the mall is "1 bicycle-hour" away.

Parallax Standing on Earth looking up at the sky, it may seem as if there is no way to tell how far away the stars are. However, astronomers have found ways to measure those distances. **Astronomers often use parallax to measure distances to nearby stars.**

Parallax is the apparent change in position of an object when you look at it from different places. For example, imagine that you and a friend have gone to a movie. A woman with a large hat sits down in front of you, as shown in Figure 8. Because you and your friend are sitting in different places, the woman's hat blocks different parts of the screen. If you are sitting on her left, the woman's hat appears to be in front of the large dinosaur. But to your friend on the right, she appears to be in front of the bird.

Have the woman and her hat moved? No. But because you changed your position, she appears to have moved. This apparent movement when you look from two different directions is parallax.

FIGURE 8
Parallax at the Movies
You and your friend are sitting behind a woman with a large hat. **Applying Concepts** *Why is your view of the screen different from your friend's view?*

Your view

Your friend's view

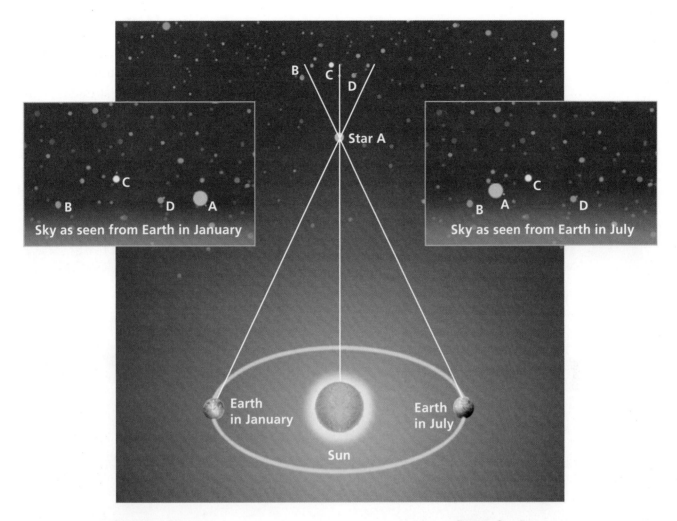

Sky as seen from Earth in January

Sky as seen from Earth in July

Star A

Earth in January

Earth in July

Sun

Parallax in Astronomy Astronomers are able to measure the parallax of nearby stars to determine their distances. As shown in Figure 9, astronomers look at a nearby star when Earth is on one side of the sun. Then they look at the same star again six months later, when Earth is on the opposite side of the sun. Astronomers measure how much the nearby star appears to move against a background of stars that are much farther away. They can then use this measurement to calculate the distance to the nearby star. The less the nearby star appears to move, the farther away it is.

Astronomers can use parallax to measure distances up to a few hundred light-years from Earth. The parallax of any star that is farther away is too small to measure accurately.

 **Reading Checkpoint** How is parallax useful in astronomy?

FIGURE 9
Parallax of Stars
The apparent movement of a star when seen from a different position is called parallax. Astronomers use parallax to calculate the distance to nearby stars. Note that the diagram is not to scale.
Interpreting Diagrams *Why do nearby stars appear to change position between January and July?*

The Hertzsprung-Russell Diagram

About 100 years ago, two scientists working independently made the same discovery. Both Ejnar Hertzsprung (EYE nahr HURT sprung) in Denmark and Henry Norris Russell in the United States made graphs to find out if the temperature and the absolute brightness of stars are related. They plotted the surface temperatures of stars on the *x*-axis and their absolute brightness on the *y*-axis. The points formed a pattern. The graph they made is still used by astronomers today. It is called the **Hertzsprung-Russell diagram,** or H-R diagram.

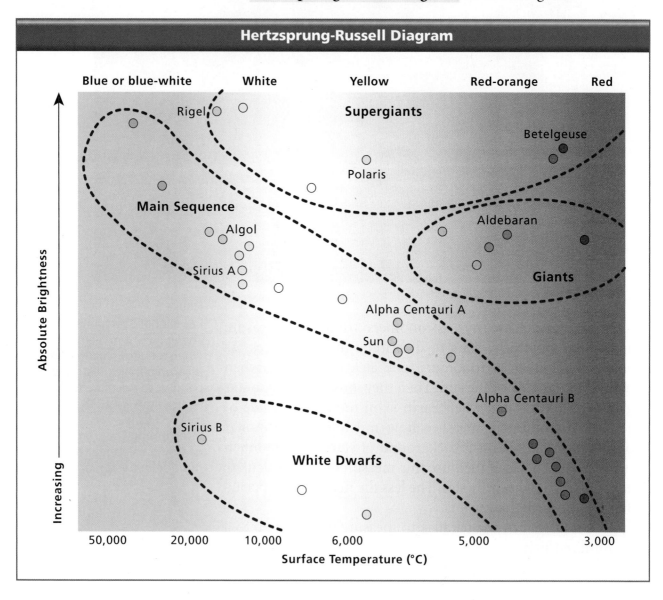

FIGURE 10

The Hertzsprung-Russell diagram shows the relationship between the surface temperature and absolute brightness of stars.
Interpreting Diagrams *Which star has a hotter surface: Rigel or Aldebaran?*

Astronomers use H-R diagrams to classify stars and to understand how stars change over time. As you can see in Figure 10, most of the stars in the H-R diagram form a diagonal area called the **main sequence.** More than 90 percent of all stars, including the sun, are main-sequence stars. Within the main sequence, surface temperature increases as absolute brightness increases. Thus, hot bluish stars are located at the left of an H-R diagram and cooler reddish stars are located at the right of the diagram.

The brightest stars are located near the top of an H-R diagram, while the dimmest stars are located at the bottom. Giant and supergiant stars are very bright. They can be found near the top center and right of the diagram. White dwarfs are hot, but not very bright, so they appear at the bottom left or bottom center of the diagram.

 **Reading Checkpoint** What is the main sequence?

FIGURE 11
Orion
Orion includes the red supergiant Betelgeuse, the blue supergiant Rigel, and many other main-sequence and giant stars.

Section 2 Assessment

Target Reading Skill Using Prior Knowledge Review your graphic organizer and revise it based on what you just learned in the section.

Reviewing Key Concepts

1. a. Listing Name three characteristics used to classify stars.
  b. Comparing and Contrasting What is the difference between apparent brightness and absolute brightness?
  c. Applying Concepts Stars A and B have about the same apparent brightness, but Star A is about twice as far from Earth as Star B. Which star has the greater absolute brightness? Explain your answer.

2. a. Measuring What is a light-year?
  b. Defining What is parallax?
  c. Predicting Vega is 25.3 light-years from Earth and Arcturus is 36.7 light-years away. Which star would have a greater parallax? Explain.

3. a. Summarizing What two characteristics of stars are shown in an H-R diagram?
  b. Identifying Identify two ways in which astronomers can use an H-R diagram.
  c. Classifying The star Procyon B has a surface temperature of 6,600°C and an absolute brightness that is much less than the sun's. What type of star is Procyon B? (*Hint:* Refer to the H-R diagram.)

Lab zone At-Home **Activity**

Observing Orion With adult family members, go outside on a clear, dark night. Determine which way is south. Using the star charts in the appendix, look for the constellation Orion, which is visible in the evening during winter and spring. Find the stars Betelgeuse and Rigel in Orion and explain to your family why they are different colors.

Skills Lab

How Far Is That Star?

Problem

How can parallax be used to determine distances?

Skills Focus

inferring, calculating, predicting

Materials

- masking tape • paper clips • pen
- black and red pencils • metric ruler • paper
- meter stick • calculator
- lamp without a shade, with 100-watt light bulb
- copier paper box (without the lid)
- flat rectangular table, about 1 m wide

Procedure

PART 1 Telescope Model

1. Place the lamp on a table in the middle of the classroom.

2. Carefully use the tip of the pen to make a small hole in the middle of one end of the box. The box represents a telescope.

3. At the front of the classroom, place the box on a flat table so the hole points toward the lamp. Line the left side of the box up with the left edge of the table.

4. Put a small piece of tape on the table below the hole. Use the pen to make a mark on the tape directly below the hole. The mark represents the position of the telescope when Earth is on one side of its orbit.

PART 2 Star 1

5. Label a sheet of paper Star 1 and place it inside the box as shown in the drawing. Hold the paper in place with two paper clips. The paper represents the film in a telescope.

6. Darken the room. Turn on the light to represent the star.

7. With the red pencil, mark the paper where you see a dot of light. Label this dot A. Dot A represents the image of the star on the film.

8. Move the box so the right edge of the box lines up with the right edge of the table. Repeat Step 4. The mark on the tape represents the position of the telescope six months later, when Earth is on the other side of its orbit.

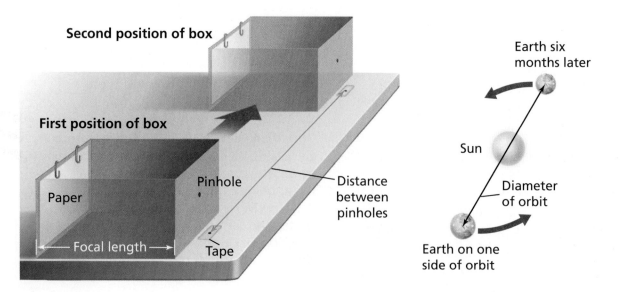

Second position of box

First position of box

Paper

Pinhole

Distance between pinholes

Focal length

Tape

Earth six months later

Sun

Diameter of orbit

Earth on one side of orbit

Data Table						
Star	Parallax Shift (mm)	Focal Length (mm)	Diameter of Orbit (mm)	Calculated Distance to Star (mm)	Calculated Distance to Star (m)	Actual Distance to Star (m)

9. Repeat Step 7, using a black pencil to mark the second dot B. Dot B represents the image of the star as seen 6 months later from the other side of Earth's orbit.

10. Remove the paper. Before you continue, copy the data table into your notebook.

11. Measure and record the distance in millimeters between dots A and B. This distance represents the parallax shift for Star 1.

12. Measure and record the distance from the hole in the box to the lamp. This distance represents the actual distance to the star.

13. Measure and record the distance from the hole (lens) to the back of the box in millimeters. This distance represents the focal length of your telescope.

14. Measure and record the distance in millimeters between the marks on the two pieces of masking tape. This distance represents the diameter of Earth's orbit.

PART 3 Stars 2 and 3

15. Move the lamp away from the table—about half the distance to the back of the room. The bulb now represents Star 2. Predict what you think will happen to the light images on your paper.

16. Repeat Steps 6–12 with a new sheet of paper to find the parallax shift for Star 2.

17. Move the lamp to the back of the classroom. The bulb now represents Star 3. Repeat Steps 6–12 with a new sheet of paper to find the parallax shift for Star 3.

Analyze and Conclude

1. **Inferring** What caused the apparent change in position of the dots of light for each star? Explain.

2. **Calculating** Use the following formula to calculate the distance from the telescope to Star 1.

$$\text{Distance} = \frac{\text{Diameter} \times \text{Focal length}}{\text{Parallax shift}}$$

3. **Calculating** Divide your result from Question 2 by 1,000 to get the distance to the light bulb in meters.

4. **Calculating** Repeat Questions 2 and 3 for Stars 2 and 3.

5. **Predicting** Was your prediction in Step 15 correct? Why or why not?

6. **Interpreting Data** How did your calculation for Star 3 compare with the actual distance? What could you do to improve your results?

7. **Communicating** Write a paragraph that explains how parallax shift varies with distance. Relate each star's parallax shift to its distance from Earth.

Design an Experiment

What would happen if you kept moving the lamp away from the box? Is there a distance at which you can no longer find the distance to the star? Design an experiment to find out.

Reading Preview

Key Concepts
- How does a star form?
- What determines how long a star will exist?
- What happens to a star when it runs out of fuel?

Key Terms
- nebula • protostar
- white dwarf • supernova
- neutron star • pulsar
- black hole

Target Reading Skill

Sequencing As you read, make a flowchart like the one below that shows the stages in the life of a star like the sun. Write each step of the process in a separate box in the flowchart in the order that it occurs.

Life Cycle of a Sun-like Star

| Protostar forms from a nebula. |

↓

| A star is born as fusion begins. |

↓

Lab zone | Discover **Activity**

What Determines How Long Stars Live?

1. This graph shows how the mass of a star is related to its lifetime—how long the star lives before it runs out of fuel.

2. How long does a star with 0.75 times the mass of the sun live? How long does a star with 3 times the mass of the sun live?

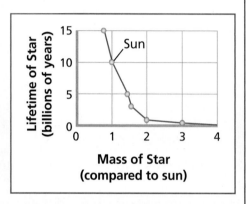

Think It Over
Drawing Conclusions Describe the general relationship between a star's mass and its lifetime.

Imagine that you want to study how people age. You wish you could watch a few people for 50 years, but your project is due next week! You have to study a lot of people for a short time, and classify the people into different age groups. You may come up with groups like *babies, young adults,* and *elderly people.* You don't have time to see a single person go through all these stages, but you know the stages exist.

Astronomers have a similar problem in trying to understand how stars age. They can't watch a single star for billions of years. Instead, they study many stars and other objects in space. Over time, astronomers have figured out that these objects represent different stages in the lives of stars.

◀ **Three generations**

The Lives of Stars

Stars do not last forever. Each star is born, goes through its life cycle, and eventually dies. (Of course, stars are not really alive. The words *born, live,* and *die* are just helpful comparisons.)

A Star Is Born All stars begin their lives as parts of nebulas. A **nebula** is a large cloud of gas and dust spread out in an immense volume. A star, on the other hand, is made up of a large amount of gas in a relatively small volume.

In the densest part of a nebula, gravity pulls gas and dust together. A contracting cloud of gas and dust with enough mass to form a star is called a **protostar.** *Proto* means "earliest" in Greek, so a protostar is the earliest stage of a star's life.

A star is born when the contracting gas and dust from a nebula become so dense and hot that nuclear fusion starts. Recall that nuclear fusion is the process by which atoms combine to form heavier atoms. In the sun, for example, hydrogen atoms combine to form helium. During nuclear fusion, enormous amounts of energy are released. Nuclear fusion has not yet begun in a protostar.

Lifetimes of Stars How long a star lives depends on its mass. You might think that stars with more mass would last longer than stars with less mass. But the reverse is true. You can think of stars as being like cars. A small car has a small gas tank, but it also has a small engine that burns gas slowly. A large car has a larger gas tank, but it also has a larger engine that burns gas rapidly. So the small car can travel farther on a tank of gas than the larger car. Small-mass stars use up their fuel more slowly than large-mass stars, so they have much longer lives.

Generally, stars that have less mass than the sun use their fuel slowly, and can live for up to 200 billion years. Medium-mass stars like the sun live for about 10 billion years. Astronomers think the sun is about 4.6 billion years old, so it is almost halfway through its lifetime.

Stars that have more mass than the sun have shorter lifetimes. A star that is 15 times as massive as the sun may live only about ten million years. That may seem like a long time, but it is only one tenth of one percent of the lifetime of the sun.

 **Reading Checkpoint** How long will a star that is the mass of the sun live?

FIGURE 12
Young Stars
New stars are forming in the nebula on top. The bottom photo shows a protostar in the Orion Nebula. **Applying Concepts** *How do some of the gas and dust in a nebula become a protostar?*

DISCOVERY
CHANNEL
SCHOOL

Stars, Galaxies, and the Universe

Video Preview
▶ Video Field Trip
Video Assessment

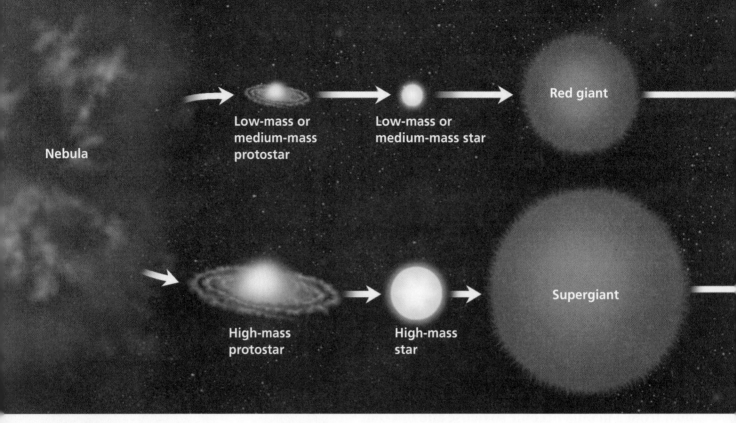

Low-mass or
medium-mass
protostar

Low-mass or
medium-mass star

Red giant

Nebula

High-mass
protostar

High-mass
star

Supergiant

FIGURE 13

FIGURE 13
The Lives of Stars

A star's life history depends on its mass. A low-mass main-sequence star uses up its fuel slowly and eventually becomes a white dwarf. A high-mass star uses up its fuel quickly. After its supergiant stage, it will explode as a supernova, producing a neutron star or a black hole.

Interpreting Diagrams *What type of star produces a planetary nebula?*

Skills Activity

Predicting

Find Algol, Sirius B, and Polaris in Figure 10, the H-R diagram. What type of star is each of these now? Predict what the next stage in each star's life will be.

Deaths of Stars

When a star begins to run out of fuel, its core shrinks and its outer portion expands. Depending on its mass, the star becomes either a red giant or a supergiant. All main-sequence stars eventually become red giants or supergiants. As shown in Figure 13, red giants and supergiants evolve in very different ways. **After a star runs out of fuel, it becomes a white dwarf, a neutron star, or a black hole.**

White Dwarfs Low-mass stars and medium-mass stars like the sun take billions of years to use up their nuclear fuel. As they start to run out of fuel, their outer layers expand, and they become red giants. Eventually, the outer parts grow larger still and drift out into space, forming a glowing cloud of gas called a planetary nebula. The blue-white core of the star that is left behind cools and becomes a **white dwarf.**

White dwarfs are only about the size of Earth, but they have about as much mass as the sun. Since a white dwarf has the same mass as the sun but only one millionth the volume, it is one million times as dense as the sun. A spoonful of material from a white dwarf has as much mass as a large truck. White dwarfs have no fuel, but they glow faintly from leftover energy. After billions of years, a white dwarf eventually stops glowing. Then it is called a black dwarf.

Reading Checkpoint What is a white dwarf?

Planetary nebula

White dwarf

Black dwarf

Neutron star

Supernova

Black hole

Supernovas The life cycle of a high-mass star is quite different from the life cycle of a low-mass or medium-mass star. High-mass stars quickly evolve into brilliant supergiants. When a supergiant runs out of fuel, it can explode suddenly. Within hours, the star blazes millions of times brighter. The explosion is called a **supernova.** After a supernova, some of the material from the star expands into space. This material may become part of a nebula. This nebula can then contract to form a new, partly recycled star. Astronomers think the sun began as a nebula that contained material from a supernova.

Neutron Stars After a supergiant explodes, some of the material from the star is left behind. This material may form a neutron star. **Neutron stars** are the remains of high-mass stars. They are even smaller and denser than white dwarfs. A neutron star may contain as much as three times the mass of the sun but be only about 25 kilometers in diameter, the size of a city.

In 1967, Jocelyn Bell, a British astronomy student, detected an object in space that appeared to give off regular pulses of radio waves. Some astronomers hypothesized that the pulses might be a signal from an extraterrestrial civilization. At first, astronomers even named the source LGM, for the "Little Green Men" in early science-fiction stories. Soon, however, astronomers concluded that the source of the radio waves was really a rapidly spinning neutron star. Spinning neutron stars are called **pulsars,** short for pulsating radio sources. Some pulsars spin hundreds of times per second!

Go **O**nline
active art

For: The Lives of Stars activity
Visit: PHSchool.com
Web Code: cfp-5043

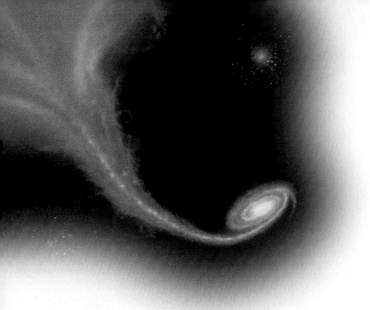

Black Holes The most massive stars—those having more than 40 times the mass of the sun—may become black holes when they die. A **black hole** is an object with gravity so strong that nothing, not even light, can escape. After a very massive star dies in a supernova explosion, more than five times the mass of the sun may be left. The gravity of this mass is so strong that the gas is pulled inward, packing the gas into a smaller and smaller space. The gas becomes so densely packed that its intense gravity will not allow even light to escape. The remains of the star have become a black hole.

No light, radio waves, or any other form of radiation can ever get out of a black hole, so it is not possible to detect a black hole directly. But astronomers can detect black holes indirectly. For example, gas near a black hole is pulled so strongly that it revolves faster and faster around the black hole. Friction heats the gas up. Astronomers can detect X-rays coming from the hot gas and infer that a black hole is present. Similarly, if another star is near a black hole, astronomers can calculate the mass of the black hole from the effect of its gravity on the star. Scientists have detected dozens of star-size black holes with the Chandra X-ray Observatory. They have also detected huge black holes that are millions or billions of times the sun's mass.

FIGURE 14
Black Holes
The remains of the most massive stars collapse into black holes. This artist's impression shows a black hole pulling matter from a companion star. The material glows as it is pulled into the black hole. **Applying Concepts** *If it is impossible to detect a black hole directly, how do astronomers find them?*

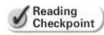 **Reading Checkpoint** What is a black hole?

Section 3 Assessment

Target Reading Skill Sequencing Refer to your flowchart as you answer the questions.

Reviewing Key Concepts

1. a. **Defining** What is a nebula?
   b. **Explaining** How does a star form from a nebula?
   c. **Comparing and Contrasting** How is a protostar different from a star?

2. a. **Identifying** What factor determines how long a star lives?
   b. **Applying Concepts** A star is twice as massive as the sun. Will its lifespan be longer, shorter, or the same as that of the sun?

3. a. **Comparing and Contrasting** What is a white dwarf? How is it different from a neutron star?

   b. **Relating Cause and Effect** Why do some stars become white dwarfs and others become neutron stars or black holes?
   c. **Predicting** What will happen to the sun when it runs out of fuel? Explain.

Writing in Science

Descriptive Paragraph Write a description of one of the stages in the life of a star, such as a nebula, red giant, supernova, or white dwarf. Include information on how it formed and what will happen next in the star's evolution.

Star Systems and Galaxies

Reading Preview

Key Concepts
- What is a star system?
- What are the major types of galaxies?
- How do astronomers describe the scale of the universe?

Key Terms
- binary star
- eclipsing binary • open cluster
- globular cluster • galaxy
- spiral galaxy • elliptical galaxy
- irregular galaxy • quasar
- universe • scientific notation

Target Reading Skill
Building Vocabulary Carefully read the definition of each key term. Also read the neighboring sentences. Then write a definition of each key term in your own words.

Discover **Activity**

Why Does the Milky Way Look Hazy?

1. Using a pencil, carefully poke at least 20 holes close together in a sheet of white paper.
2. Tape the paper to a chalkboard or dark-colored wall.
3. Go to the other side of the room and look at the paper. From the far side of the room, what do the dots look like? Can you see individual dots?

Think It Over
Making Models How is looking at the paper from the far side of the room like trying to see many very distant stars that are close together? How does your model compare to the photograph of the Milky Way below?

On a clear, dark night in the country, you can see a hazy band of light stretched across the sky. This band of stars is called the Milky Way. It looks as if the Milky Way is very far away. Actually, though, Earth is inside the Milky Way! The Milky Way looks milky or hazy from Earth because the stars are too close together for your eyes to see them individually. The dark blotches in the Milky Way are clouds of dust that block light from stars behind them.

The Milky Way

Star Systems and Clusters

Our solar system has only one star, the sun. But this is not the most common situation for stars. **Most stars are members of groups of two or more stars, called star systems.** If you were on a planet in one of these star systems, at times you might see two or more suns in the sky! At other times, one or more of these suns would be below the horizon.

Multiple Star Systems Star systems that have two stars are called double stars or **binary stars.** (The prefix *bi* means "two.") Those with three stars are called triple stars. The nearby star Proxima Centauri may be part of a triple star system. The other two stars in the system, Alpha Centauri A and Alpha Centauri B, form a double star. Scientists are not sure whether Proxima Centauri is really part of the system or is just passing close to the other two stars temporarily.

Often one star in a binary star is much brighter and more massive than the other. Astronomers can sometimes detect a binary star even if only one of the stars can be seen from Earth. Astronomers can often tell that there is a dim star in a binary system by observing the effects of its gravity. As the dim companion star revolves around a bright star, the dim star's gravity causes the bright star to wobble back and forth. Imagine watching a pair of dancers who are twirling each other around. Even if one dancer were invisible, you could tell that the invisible dancer was there from watching the motion of the visible dancer.

Eclipsing Binaries A wobble is not the only clue that a star has a dim companion. A dim star in a binary star may pass in front of a brighter star and eclipse it. From Earth, the binary star would suddenly look much dimmer. A system in which one star periodically blocks the light from another is called an **eclipsing binary.** As Figure 16 shows, the star Algol is actually an eclipsing binary star system.

FIGURE 15
Invisible Partners
If you saw someone dancing but couldn't see a partner, you could infer that the partner was there by watching the dancer you could see. Astronomers use a similar method to detect faint stars in star systems.

FIGURE 16
Eclipsing Binary
Algol is an eclipsing binary star system consisting of a bright star and a dim companion. Each time the dimmer star passes in front of the brighter one, Algol appears less bright.
Interpreting Diagrams *When does Algol appear brighter?*

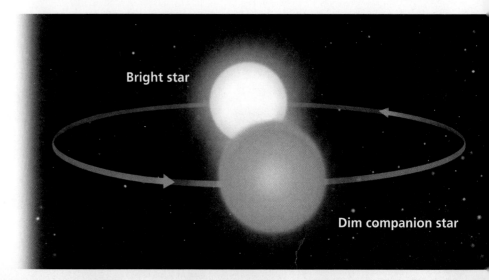

Bright star

Dim companion star

Planets Around Other Stars In 1995, astronomers first discovered a planet revolving around another ordinary star. They used a method similar to the one used in studying binary stars. The astronomers observed that a star was moving slightly toward and away from us. They knew that the invisible object causing the movement didn't have enough mass to be a star. They inferred that it must be a planet.

Since then, astronomers have discovered more than 100 planets around other stars, and new ones are being discovered all of the time. Most of these new planets are very large, with at least half of the mass of Jupiter. A small planet would be hard to detect because it would have little gravitational effect on the star it orbited.

Could there be life on planets in other solar systems? Some scientists think it is possible. A few astronomers are using radio telescopes to search for signals that could not have come from natural sources. Such a signal might be evidence that an extraterrestrial civilization was sending out radio waves.

Star Clusters Many stars belong to larger groupings called star clusters. All of the stars in a particular cluster formed from the same nebula at about the same time and are about the same distance from Earth.

There are two major types of star clusters: open clusters and globular clusters. **Open clusters** have a loose, disorganized appearance and contain no more than a few thousand stars. They often contain many bright supergiants and much gas and dust. In contrast, **globular clusters** are large groupings of older stars. Globular clusters are round and densely packed with stars—some may contain more than a million stars.

 **What is a globular cluster?**

FIGURE 17
Star Clusters
The stars in a globular cluster (above) are all about the same age and the same distance from Earth. The Pleiades (left), also called the *Seven Sisters*, is an open cluster.

Spiral Galaxy

Elliptical Galaxy

Irregular Galaxy

FIGURE 18
Types of Galaxies
There are three major types of galaxies: spiral, elliptical, and irregular.

Galaxies

A **galaxy** is a huge group of single stars, star systems, star clusters, dust, and gas bound together by gravity. There are billions of galaxies in the universe. The largest galaxies have more than a trillion stars. **Astronomers classify most galaxies into the following types: spiral, elliptical, and irregular.** Figure 18 shows examples of these three.

Spiral Galaxies Some galaxies appear to have a bulge in the middle and arms that spiral outward, like pinwheels. Such galaxies are called **spiral galaxies.** The spiral arms contain many bright, young stars as well as gas and dust. Most new stars in spiral galaxies form in these spiral arms. Relatively few new stars are forming in the central bulge. Some spiral galaxies, called barred-spiral galaxies, have a huge bar-shaped region of stars and gas that passes through their center.

Elliptical Galaxies Not all galaxies have spiral arms. **Elliptical galaxies** look like round or flattened balls. These galaxies contain billions of stars but have little gas and dust between the stars. Because there is little gas or dust, stars are no longer forming. Most elliptical galaxies contain only old stars.

Irregular Galaxies Some galaxies do not have regular shapes. These are known as **irregular galaxies.** Irregular galaxies are typically smaller than other types of galaxies. They generally have many bright, young stars and lots of gas and dust to form new stars.

Quasars In the 1960s, astronomers discovered objects that are very bright, but also very far away. Many of these objects are 10 billion light-years or more away, making them among the most distant objects in the universe. These distant, enormously bright objects looked almost like stars. Since *quasi* means "something like" in Latin, these objects were given the name quasi-stellar objects, or **quasars.**

What could be so bright at such a great distance from Earth? Astronomers have concluded that quasars are active young galaxies with giant black holes at their centers. Each of these black holes has a mass a billion times or more as great as that of the sun. As enormous amounts of gas revolve around the black hole, the gas heats up and shines brightly.

 **Reading Checkpoint** What is a quasar?

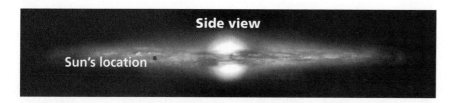

Side view

Sun's location

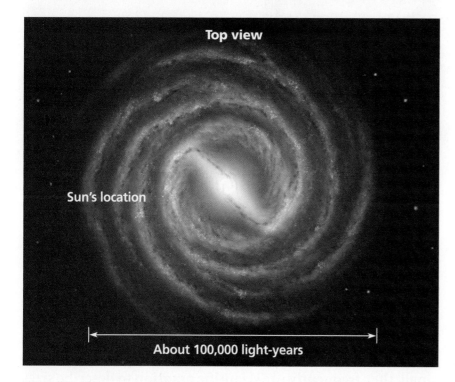

Top view

Sun's location

About 100,000 light-years

FIGURE 19

Structure of the Milky Way
From the side, the Milky Way appears to be a narrow disk with a bulge in the middle. The galaxy's spiral structure is visible only from above or below the galaxy.
Interpreting Diagrams *Where in the galaxy is the sun located?*

The Milky Way

Our solar system is located in a spiral galaxy called the Milky Way. As Figure 19 shows, the shape of the Milky Way varies depending on your vantage point. From the side, the Milky Way would look like a narrow disk with a large bulge in the middle. But from the top or bottom, the Milky Way would have a spiral, pinwheel shape. You can't see the spiral shape of the Milky Way from Earth because our solar system is inside the galaxy in one of the spiral arms.

The Milky Way is usually thought of as a standard spiral galaxy. However, recent evidence suggests that the Milky Way is a barred-spiral galaxy instead.

When you see the Milky Way at night during the summer, you are looking toward the center of our galaxy. The center of the galaxy is about 25,000 light-years away, but it is hidden from view by large clouds of dust and gas. However, astronomers can study the center using X-rays, infrared radiation, and radio waves.

Reading Checkpoint How far away is the center of the galaxy?

Lab zone Try This **Activity**

A Spiral Galaxy

You can make a model of our galaxy.

1. Using pipe cleaners, make a pinwheel with two spirals.

2. View the spirals along the surface of the table. Sketch what you see.

3. Next, view the spirals from above the table and sketch them.

Observing The sun is inside a flat spiral galaxy. From Earth's position on the flat surface, is it possible to get a good view of stars in the spiral arms? Why or why not?

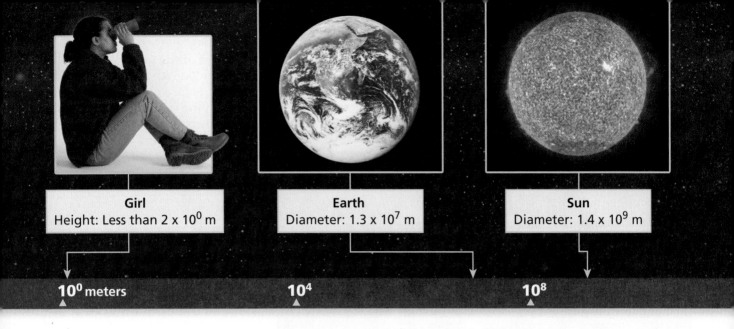

Girl
Height: Less than 2×10^0 m

Earth
Diameter: 1.3×10^7 m

Sun
Diameter: 1.4×10^9 m

10^0 meters

10^4

10^8

The Scale of the Universe

Astronomers define the **universe** as all of space and everything in it. The universe is enormous, almost beyond imagination. Astronomers study objects as close as the moon and as far away as quasars. They study incredibly large objects, such as galaxies that are millions of light-years across. They also study the behavior of tiny particles, such as the atoms within stars. **Since the numbers astronomers use are often very large or very small, they frequently use scientific notation to describe sizes and distances in the universe.**

Scientific Notation **Scientific notation** uses powers of ten to write very large or very small numbers in shorter form. Each number is written as the product of a number between 1 and 10 and a power of 10. For example: 1,200 is written as 1.2×10^3. One light-year is about 9,500,000,000,000,000 meters. Since there are 15 digits after the first digit, in scientific notation this number is written as 9.5×10^{15} meters.

The Immensity of Space The structures in the universe vary greatly in scale. To understand the scale of these structures, imagine that you are going on a journey through the universe. Refer to Figure 20 as you take your imaginary trip. Start at the left with something familiar—a girl looking through binoculars. She is about 1.5 meters tall. Now shift to the right and change the scale by 10,000,000 or 10^7. You're now close to the diameter of Earth, 1.28×10^7 meters. As you move from left to right across Figure 20, the scale increases. The diameter of the sun is about 100 times that of Earth.

Cat's Eye Nebula
Diameter: 3×10^{16} m

Andromeda Galaxy
Diameter: 2×10^{21} m

Virgo Supercluster
Diameter: 9×10^{23} m

10^{16} 10^{20} 10^{24}

Beyond the solar system, the sizes of observable objects become much larger. For example, within our galaxy, the beautiful Cat's Eye Nebula is about 3×10^{16} meters across.

Beyond our galaxy are billions of other galaxies, many of which contain billions of stars. For example, the nearby spiral galaxy Andromeda is about 2×10^{21} meters across. The Milky Way is part of a cluster of 50 or so galaxies called the Local Group. The Local Group is part of the Virgo Supercluster, which contains hundreds of galaxies. The size of the observable universe is about 10^{10} light years, or 10^{26} meters.

FIGURE 20
Scientific Notation
Scientists often use scientific notation to help describe the vast sizes and distances in space.
Calculating *About how many times larger is the Cat's Eye Nebula than Earth?*

Section 4 Assessment

Target Reading Skill **Building Vocabulary** Use your definitions to help answer the questions.

Reviewing Key Concepts

1. a. Defining What is a binary star?
  b. Classifying Are all binary stars part of star systems? Explain.
  c. Applying Concepts Some binary stars are called eclipsing binaries. Explain why this term is appropriate. (*Hint:* Think about Algol as you write your answer.)
2. a. Listing Name the main types of galaxies.
  b. Classifying What type of galaxy is the Milky Way?
  c. Classifying Suppose astronomers discover a galaxy that contains only old stars. What type of galaxy is it likely to be?

3. a. Reviewing What is scientific notation?
  b. Explaining How is scientific notation useful to astronomers?
  c. Calculating How large is the Cat's Eye Nebula in light-years? (*Hint:* Refer to Figure 20.)

Math Practice

4. Scientific Notation The star Betelgeuse has a diameter of 940,000,000 km. Betelgeuse is 427 light-years from Earth. Write each of these figures in scientific notation.

The Expanding Universe

Reading Preview

Key Concepts
- What is the big bang theory?
- How did the solar system form?
- What do astronomers predict about the future of the universe?

Key Terms
- big bang • Hubble's law
- cosmic background radiation
- solar nebula • planetesimal
- dark matter • dark energy

Target Reading Skill

Identifying Supporting Evidence As you read, identify the evidence that supports the big bang theory. Write the evidence in a graphic organizer like the one below.

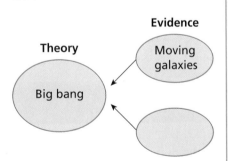

Theory

Big bang

Evidence

Moving galaxies

Discover Activity

How Does the Universe Expand?

1. Use a marker to put 10 dots on an empty balloon. The dots represent galaxies.
2. Blow up the balloon. What happens to the distances between galaxies that are close together? Galaxies that are far apart?

Think It Over

Inferring If the universe is expanding, do galaxies that are close together move apart faster or slower than galaxies that are far apart? Explain.

The Andromeda Galaxy is the most distant object that the human eye can see. Light from this galaxy has traveled for about 3 million years before reaching Earth. When that light finally reaches your eye, you are seeing how the galaxy looked 3 million years ago. It is as though you are looking back in time.

Astronomers have photographed galaxies that are billions of light-years away. Light from these galaxies traveled for billions of years before it reached Earth. From these observations, astronomers are able to infer the age of the universe.

How the Universe Formed

Astronomers theorize that the universe began billions of years ago. At that time, the part of the universe we can now see was no larger than the period at the end of this sentence. This tiny universe was incredibly hot and dense. The universe then exploded in what astronomers call the **big bang.**

◀ Nearly every visible object in this image is a distant galaxy.

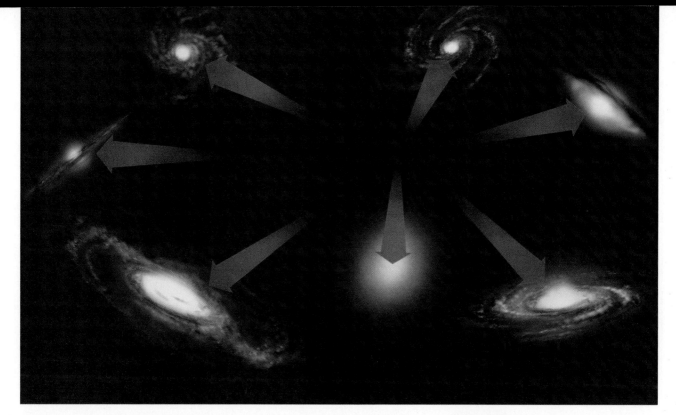

FIGURE 21
Retreating Galaxies
All of the distant galaxies
astronomers have observed are
moving rapidly away from our
galaxy and from each other.

According to the big bang theory, the universe formed in an instant, billions of years ago, in an enormous explosion. Since the big bang, the size of the universe has been increasing rapidly. The universe is billions of times larger now than it was early in its history.

As the universe expanded, it gradually cooled. After a few hundred thousand years, atoms formed. About 200 million years after the big bang, the first stars and galaxies formed.

If the big bang theory is accurate, what evidence might you expect to find in today's universe? You might expect that the matter that had been hurled apart by the big bang would still be moving apart. You might also expect to find evidence of energy left over from the explosion.

Moving Galaxies An American astronomer, Edwin Hubble, discovered important evidence that later helped astronomers to develop the big bang theory. In the 1920s, Hubble studied the spectrums of many galaxies at various distances from Earth. By examining a galaxy's spectrum, Hubble could tell how fast the galaxy is moving and whether it is moving toward our galaxy or away from it.

Hubble discovered that, with the exception of a few nearby galaxies, all galaxies are moving away from us and from each other. Hubble found that there is a relationship between the distance to a galaxy and its speed. **Hubble's law** states that the farther away a galaxy is, the faster it is moving away from us. Hubble's law strongly supports the big bang theory.

Speeding Galaxies

Use the graph to answer the questions below about moving clusters of galaxies.

1. **Reading Graphs** How far away is the Bootes cluster? How fast is it moving?

2. **Reading Graphs** Which galaxy is moving away the fastest? Which galaxy is closest to Earth?

3. **Drawing Conclusions** How are the distance and speed of a galaxy related?

4. **Predicting** Predict the speed of a galaxy that is 5 billion light-years from Earth.

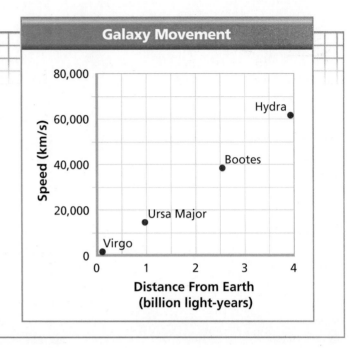

Galaxy Movement

Graph: Speed (km/s) vs. Distance From Earth (billion light-years)

Virgo, Ursa Major, Bootes, Hydra

To understand how the galaxies are moving, think of raisin bread dough that is rising. If you could shrink yourself to sit on a raisin, you would see all the other raisins moving away from you. The farther a raisin was from you, the faster it would move away, because there would be more bread dough to expand between you and the raisin. No matter which raisin you sat on, all the other raisins would seem to be moving away from you. You could tell that the bread dough was expanding by watching the other raisins.

The universe is like the bread dough. Like the raisins in the dough, the galaxies in the universe are moving away from each other. In the universe, it is space that is expanding, like the dough between the raisins.

Cosmic Background Radiation In 1965, two American physicists, Arno Penzias and Robert Wilson, accidentally detected faint radiation on their radio telescope. This mysterious glow was coming from all directions in space. Scientists later concluded that this glow, now called **cosmic background radiation,** is the leftover thermal energy from the big bang. This energy was distributed in every direction as the universe expanded.

Age of the Universe Since astronomers can measure approximately how fast the universe is expanding now, they can infer how long it has been expanding. Based on careful measurements of how fast distant galaxies are moving away from us and the cosmic background radiation, astronomers estimate that the universe is about 13.7 billion years old.

FIGURE 22
Rising Dough
The galaxies in the universe are like the raisins in rising bread dough. **Making Models** *How does rising raisin bread dough resemble the expanding universe?*

Formation of the Solar System

After the big bang, matter in the universe separated into galaxies. Gas and dust spread throughout space. Where the solar system is now, there was only cold, dark gas and dust. How did the solar system form? The leading hypothesis is explained below.

The Solar Nebula **About five billion years ago, a giant cloud of gas and dust collapsed to form our solar system.** A large cloud of gas and dust such as the one that formed our solar system is called a **solar nebula.** Slowly, gravity began to pull the solar nebula together. As the solar nebula shrank, it spun faster and faster. The solar nebula flattened, forming a rotating disk. Gravity pulled most of the gas into the center of the disk, where the gas eventually became hot and dense enough for nuclear fusion to begin. The sun was born.

Planetesimals In the outer parts of the disk, gas and dust formed small asteroid-like and comet-like bodies called **planetesimals.** These formed the building blocks of the planets. Planetesimals collided and grew larger by sticking together, eventually combining to form the planets.

The Inner Planets When the solar system formed, temperatures were very high. It was so hot close to the sun that most water and other ice-forming materials simply vaporized. Most gases escaped the gravity of the planets that were forming in this region. As a result, the inner planets, Mercury, Venus, Earth, and Mars, are relatively small and rocky.

The Outer Planets In contrast, farther from the sun it was much cooler. As the planets in this region grew, their gravity increased and they were able to capture much of the hydrogen and helium gas in the surrounding space. As a result, the planets Jupiter, Saturn, Uranus, and Neptune became very large. Most comets formed near Jupiter and Saturn. They were later flung out to the outer solar system. Beyond the gas giants, a huge disk of ice and other substances formed. Pluto also formed in this region.

A cloud of gas and dust formed a spinning disk.

Gas in the center of the disk collapsed to form the sun.

The remaining gas and dust formed the planets.

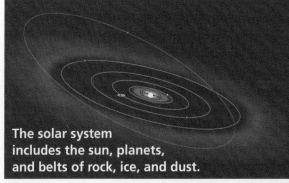
The solar system includes the sun, planets, and belts of rock, ice, and dust.

Figure 23
How the Solar System Formed
The solar system formed from a collapsing cloud of gas and dust.

 **Reading Checkpoint** What is a solar nebula?

FIGURE 24
Vera Rubin
Astronomer Vera Rubin's observations proved the existence of dark matter.

The Future of the Universe

What will happen to the universe in the future? One possibility is that the universe will continue to expand, as it is doing now. All of the stars will eventually run out of fuel and burn out, and the universe will be cold and dark. Another possibility is that the force of gravity will begin to pull the galaxies back together. The result would be a reverse big bang, or "big crunch." All of the matter in the universe would be crushed into an enormous black hole.

Which of these possibilities is more likely? Recent discoveries have produced a surprising new view of the universe that is still not well understood. **New observations lead many astronomers to conclude that the universe will likely expand forever.**

Dark Matter Until fairly recently, astronomers assumed that the universe consisted solely of the matter they could observe directly. But this idea was disproved by the American astronomer Vera Rubin. Rubin made detailed observations of the rotation of spiral galaxies. She discovered that the matter that astronomers can see, such as stars and nebulas, makes up as little as ten percent of the mass in galaxies. The remaining mass exists in the form of dark matter.

Dark matter is matter that does not give off electromagnetic radiation. Dark matter cannot be seen directly. However, its presence can be inferred by observing the effect of its gravity on visible objects, such as stars, or on light.

Astronomers still don't know much about dark matter—what it is made of or all of the places where it is found. But astronomers estimate that about 23 percent of the universe's mass is made of dark matter.

An Accelerating Expansion In the late 1990s, astronomers observed that the expansion of the universe appears to be accelerating. That is, galaxies seem to be moving apart at a faster rate now than in the past. This observation was puzzling, as no known force could account for it. Astronomers infer that a mysterious new force, which they call **dark energy,** is causing the expansion of the universe to accelerate. Current estimates indicate that most of the universe is made of dark energy and dark matter.

Astronomy is one of the oldest sciences, but there are still many discoveries to be made and puzzles to be solved about this universe of ours!

 **Reading Checkpoint** What is the effect of dark energy?

FIGURE 25
Dark Matter
Astronomers measured the effect of gravity on light to produce this computer image of how dark matter (in blue) is distributed across a cluster of galaxies.

Section 5 Assessment

 **Target Reading Skill** Identifying Supporting Evidence Refer to your graphic organizer about the big bang theory as you answer Question 1 below.

Reviewing Key Concepts

1. a. **Defining** What was the big bang?
   b. **Summarizing** When did the big bang occur?
   c. **Describing** Describe two pieces of evidence that support the big bang theory.
2. a. **Summarizing** How old is the solar system?
   b. **Relating Cause and Effect** What force caused the solar system to form?
   c. **Sequencing** Place the following events in the proper order: planets form; planetesimals form; solar nebula shrinks; nuclear fusion begins in the sun.

3. a. **Defining** What is dark matter?
   b. **Explaining** How do scientists know that dark matter exists?
   c. **Predicting** What evidence has led scientists to predict that the universe will continue to expand forever?

Lab zone At-Home **Activity**

Stargazing Plan an evening of stargazing with adult family members. Choose a dark, clear night. Use binoculars if available and the star charts in the appendix to locate the Milky Way and some interesting stars that you have learned about. Explain to your family what you know about the Milky Way and each constellation that you observe.

Study Guide

Chapter 4

The BIG Idea **Structure of the Universe** Astronomers learn about the structure of the universe and how it has changed over time by studying stars, galaxies, and other objects in space.

1 Telescopes

Key Concepts

- The electromagnetic spectrum includes radio waves, infrared radiation, visible light, ultraviolet radiation, X-rays, and gamma rays.
- Telescopes are instruments that collect and focus light and other forms of electromagnetic radiation.
- Many large observatories are located on mountaintops or in space.

Key Terms

- telescope
- visible light
- wavelength
- spectrum
- optical telescope
- electromagnetic radiation
- refracting telescope
- convex lens
- reflecting telescope
- radio telescope
- observatory

2 Characteristics of Stars

Key Concepts

- Characteristics used to classify stars include color, temperature, size, composition, and brightness.
- The brightness of a star depends upon both its size and temperature.
- Astronomers use a unit called the light-year to measure distances between the stars.
- Astronomers often use parallax to measure distances to nearby stars.
- Astronomers use H-R diagrams to classify stars and to understand how stars change over time.

Key Terms

- constellation
- spectrograph
- apparent brightness
- absolute brightness
- light-year
- parallax
- Hertzsprung-Russell diagram
- main sequence

3 Lives of Stars

Key Concepts

- A star is born when nuclear fusion starts.
- How long a star lives depends on its mass.
- After a star runs out of fuel, it becomes a white dwarf, a neutron star, or a black hole.

Key Terms

- nebula
- protostar
- white dwarf
- supernova
- neutron star
- pulsar
- black hole

4 Star Systems and Galaxies

Key Concepts

- Most stars are members of groups of two or more stars called star systems.
- Astronomers classify most galaxies into the following types: spiral, elliptical, and irregular.
- Our solar system is located in a spiral galaxy called the Milky Way.
- Astronomers often use scientific notation to describe sizes and distances in the universe.

Key Terms

- binary star
- eclipsing binary
- open cluster
- globular cluster
- galaxy
- spiral galaxy
- elliptical galaxy
- irregular galaxy
- quasar
- universe
- scientific notation

5 The Expanding Universe

Key Concepts

- According to the big bang theory, the universe formed in an instant, billions of years ago, in an enormous explosion.
- About five billion years ago, a giant cloud of gas and dust collapsed to form our solar system.
- New observations lead astronomers to conclude that the universe will likely expand forever.

Key Terms

- big bang
- Hubble's law
- cosmic background radiation
- solar nebula
- planetesimal
- dark matter
- dark energy

Review and Assessment

Go Online
PHSchool.com

For: Self-Assessment
Visit: PHSchool.com
Web Code: cfa-5040

Organizing Information

Concept Mapping Copy the concept map about telescopes onto a separate sheet of paper. Then complete it and add a title. (For more on Concept Mapping, see the Skills Handbook.)

Telescopes

can be

On Earth — collect types of radiation

In space only — collect types of radiation

a. ___?___   b. ___?___   Visible light   c. ___?___   d. ___?___   Gamma rays

Reviewing Key Terms

Choose the letter of the best answer.

1. Visible light is a form of
   a. spectrum.
   b. electromagnetic radiation.
   c. wavelength.
   d. cosmic background radiation.

2. An H-R diagram is a graph of stars' temperature and
   a. apparent brightness.
   b. main sequence.
   c. absolute brightness.
   d. parallax.

3. A low-mass main sequence star will eventually evolve into a
   a. white dwarf.   b. protostar.
   c. black hole.   d. nebula.

4. A star system in which one star blocks the light from another is called a(n)
   a. open cluster.
   b. quasar.
   c. binary star.
   d. eclipsing binary.

5. Astronomers theorize that the universe began in an enormous explosion called the
   a. solar nebula.
   b. supernova.
   c. big bang.
   d. big crunch.

If the statement is true, write *true*. If it is false, change the underlined word or words to make the statement true.

6. A <u>reflecting telescope</u> uses convex lenses to gather and focus light.

7. Astronomers use <u>spectrographs</u> to determine the chemical composition of stars.

8. Pulsars are a kind of <u>neutron star</u>.

9. A galaxy shaped like a ball and containing only older stars is most likely a <u>spiral galaxy</u>.

10. <u>Globular clusters</u> are small asteroid-like bodies that formed the building blocks of the planets.

Writing in Science

News Article Imagine that you are a journalist covering current research in astronomy, including stars and black holes. Write an article explaining what black holes are, how they form, and how they can be detected.

Discovery CHANNEL **SCHOOL**

Stars, Galaxies, and the Universe
Video Preview
Video Field Trip
▶ Video Assessment

Review and Assessment

Checking Concepts

11. Is a light-year a unit of distance or a unit of time? Explain.

12. Why can't astronomers measure the parallax of a star that is a million light-years away?

13. At what point in the evolution of a star is the star actually born?

14. Where in our galaxy does most star formation take place?

15. What is Hubble's law?

16. How can astronomers detect dark matter if they cannot observe it directly?

Math Practice

17. **Calculating** The bright star Spica is 262 light-years from our solar system. How many kilometers is this?

18. **Scientific Notation** The star Antares is approximately 604 light-years from Earth. Write this distance in scientific notation.

Thinking Critically

19. **Inferring** What advantage might there be to locating a telescope, such as the one shown below, on the moon?

20. **Applying Concepts** Describe a real-world situation involving absolute and apparent brightness. (*Hint:* Think about riding in a car at night.)

21. **Relating Cause and Effect** How does a star's mass affect its lifetime?

22. **Comparing and Contrasting** Compare the conditions that led to the formation of the terrestrial planets with those that led to the formation of the gas giants.

Applying Skills

Use the data in the H-R diagram below to answer Questions 23–26.

Hertzsprung-Russell Diagram

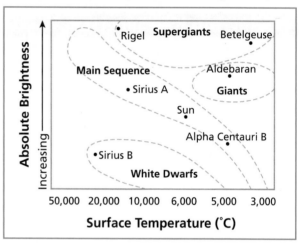

23. **Interpreting Diagrams** Which star has a greater absolute brightness, Aldebaran or Sirius B?

24. **Interpreting Diagrams** Which stars have higher surface temperatures than Sirius A?

25. **Applying Concepts** Which star is most likely to be red: Rigel, Sirius B, or Betelgeuse?

26. **Comparing and Contrasting** Compare Aldebaran and the sun in terms of size, temperature, and absolute brightness.

Lab zone Chapter Project

Performance Assessment Check the final draft of your constellation story for correct spelling, grammar, punctuation, and usage. Then decide how you will present your story. For example, you could make a poster, read your story aloud, or perform it as a skit or a play.

Standardized Test Prep

Choose the letter of the best answer.

1. The most common chemical element in most stars is
   A oxygen.
   B hydrogen.
   C helium.
   D nitrogen.

2. The main factor that affects the evolution of a star is its
   F color.
   G apparent brightness.
   H mass.
   J parallax.

3. The color of a star is related to its temperature. Which of the following color sequences correctly identifies the temperatures of stars in order from hottest to coldest?
   A red, red-orange, yellow, white, blue
   B yellow, white, blue, red, red-orange
   C blue, yellow, red-orange, red, white
   D blue, white, yellow, red-orange, red

The table below gives an estimate of the distribution of stars in the Milky Way galaxy. Use the table and your knowledge of science to answer Questions 4 and 5.

Type of Star	Percentage of Total
Main sequence	90.75%
Red Giant	0.50%
Supergiant	< 0.0001%
White Dwarf	8.75%

4. According to the table, the most common type of stars in the Milky Way is
   F main-sequence stars.
   G red giants.
   H supergiants.
   J white dwarfs.

5. If there are a total of 400 billion stars in the Milky Way, about how many white dwarfs are there in the galaxy?
   A 8.75 billion
   B 35 billion
   C 87.5 billion
   D 3,500 billion

Constructed Response

6. Describe the appearance of the Milky Way as you would see it both from Earth and from a point directly above or below the galaxy. Why does the galaxy look different from different vantage points?

Journey to Mars

The six-wheeled rover inched onto
the surface of Mars.
Scientists on Earth held their breaths.
Then, *Spirit* hummed into action.

Spirit was the first star of the 2004 Mars mission. Engineers at the Jet Propulsion Laboratory in Pasadena, California, guided the rover from Earth by remote control. *Spirit* carried a high-tech microscope, cameras, and geologic instruments. Within hours of landing in Gusev Crater, *Spirit* was beaming images of the rocks and red soil back to Earth. Engineers on Earth "drove" *Spirit* to its first target, a large rock that they named "Adirondack."

A major goal of the Mars Exploration Mission was to look for evidence of past liquid water on Mars. Earlier photos of the red planet lead scientists to believe that Gusev Crater was once a dried-up lake bed. The presence of water increases the likelihood that life may have once existed on Mars.

Just three weeks later, another rover called *Opportunity* landed on the opposite side of Mars in a strange, flat landscape. It sent back images of a shallow red crater with bedrock in the distance.

***Spirit* Rover**
The artwork below shows *Spirit* exploring Mars. The image of the Martian landscape at right was taken by *Spirit*.

When People Go to Mars

In 1983, Sally Ride became the first American woman in space as a crew member on the space shuttle *Challenger*. Since retiring from NASA in 1987, she has encouraged young people to explore their interests in science, math, and technology. Sally continues to dream of future achievements in space. The following passage is from *The Mystery of Mars*, a book Sally Ride co-wrote with Tam O'Shaughnessy.

Dr. Sally Ride at NASA

When the first astronauts visit Mars, what will they find? Though an astronaut could not survive without a spacesuit, she would feel more at home on Mars than anywhere else in the solar system. She could stand on a rocky surface, scoop up a gloveful of dirt, and explore extinct volcanoes and ancient canyons.

She would need the spacesuit to protect her from the thin Martian air and the extreme cold. The spacesuit would be bulky, but not heavy. Because Mars is smaller than Earth, the pull of gravity on its surface is lower. She and her spacesuit would weigh about one-third what they weighed on Earth.

As the astronaut hiked across the rugged, rocky terrain, her boots would leave deep footprints in the dusty red soil. Fine red dust would cling to her spacesuit. Even on days when the wind was calm, she would look up at a pink sky loaded with red dust. As she headed back to the warmth of her spacecraft at the end of the day, she would look past the silhouettes of crater rims at a dimmer setting sun.

The planet she was exploring would seem strangely familiar. But it would be missing the air and water that make Earth habitable, and the plants and animals that share her home world.

Language Arts Activity

Suppose you are a member of the team that has sent Sally Ride's imaginary astronaut to Mars. What is your job? Did you design the spacesuit or outfit the spacecraft? Were you a scientist or an engineer or a different team member? Write a description of your job. Include as many details as you can.

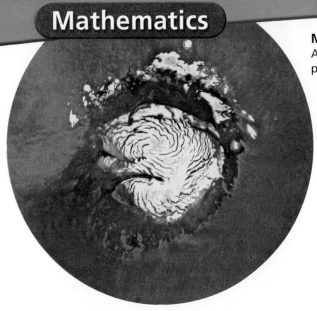

Mathematics

Mars Polar Cap
An ice cap covers the northern polar region of Mars.

Math Activity

There are 669 sols (Martian days) in a Martian year. Knowing the number of sols in a season, you can figure the percent of the year that is winter. For example, winter in the northern hemisphere is 156 sols ÷ 669 sols ≈ 0.233 ≈ 23%.

Martian Seasons in Sols (Martian Days)		
	Northern Hemisphere	Southern Hemisphere
Winter	156	177
Spring	194	142
Summer	177	156
Fall	142	194

Northern Hemisphere **Southern Hemisphere**

Northern: 23%, ?, ?, 27%
Southern: 27%, ?, 23%, ?

Winter ◼ Spring ◼ Summer ◼ Fall

- Use the table and circle graphs above to figure out what percent of the Martian year in each hemisphere is spring and fall. Round to the nearest hundredth.

- Make two circle graphs like those shown here. Label, color, and write the percent for each season in the northern and southern hemispheres.

- Choose a different color for each.

If you had a choice, which hemisphere would you choose to live in?

Sols of Mars

Mars is the planet most like Earth. But its smaller size, greater distance from the sun, and different orbit cause some immense differences. A Martian day, called a sol, is only about 40 minutes longer than an Earth day. The Martian year, however, is much longer—669 sols.

Mars, like Earth, tilts on its axis, so it has seasons. Each Martian season lasts longer than an Earth season because the Martian year is longer. The shape of Mars's orbit makes the seasons unequal in length (see the table at right).

The climate in the southern hemisphere is more extreme than in the northern hemisphere. Winters in the south are longer and colder, while summers are shorter and warmer. Winter in the south, for instance, lasts 177 sols. In the northern hemisphere, winter lasts only 156 sols.

Seasonal changes affect Mars's north and south poles, which are covered with polar ice caps made of water and carbon dioxide. During winter in the southern hemisphere, the polar cap covers almost half the hemisphere. Here the ice cap is mainly frozen carbon dioxide—like dry ice. In spring, the ice cap partially melts, releasing carbon dioxide into the air. In a similar way, when spring comes in the northern hemisphere, the north polar cap melts. But in the north, the frozen core is made mainly of water ice.

Partners in Space

Many engineers and scientists are sure that humans will travel to Mars sometime in the next 20 years. Meanwhile, people have gotten a preview of a space voyage from astronauts and cosmonauts traveling on space shuttles, on *Mir* (Russia's space station), and most recently, aboard the International Space Station.

For years, the United States and the Soviet Union competed in the race to send missions into space. Now the race has become a cooperative effort. On *Mir*, astronauts worked with cosmonauts to solve problems, make repairs, take space walks, and run the ship's computers. Since 2000, cosmonauts and astronauts have lived and worked together on the International Space Station, which is in orbit about 354 kilometers above the surface of Earth.

What's it like for crew members from different backgrounds to live and work together in a cramped spacecraft? Besides having cultural and language differences, Russian and American crews have different training and different equipment. Still, it seems they have learned how to get along. They even celebrated the first-ever space wedding together in August of 2003!

This experience of living and working together and solving problems will be invaluable should we ever send a manned expedition to Mars.

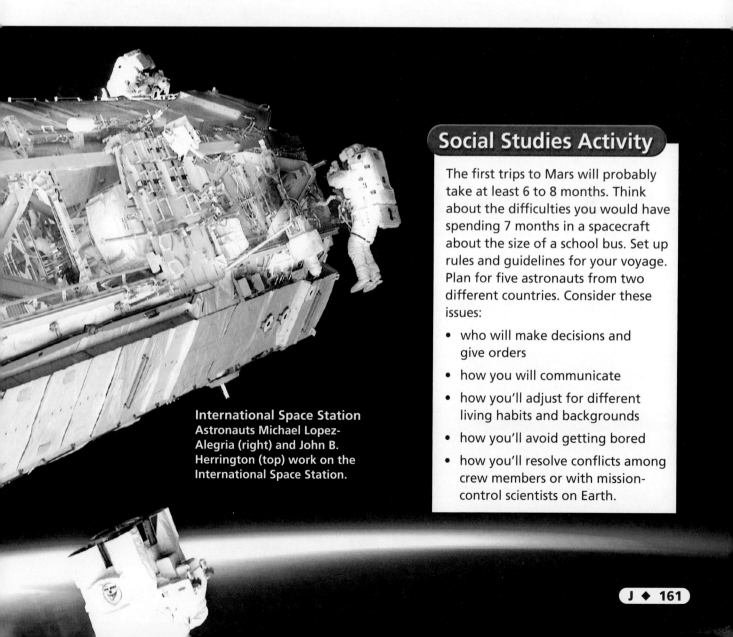

International Space Station
Astronauts Michael Lopez-Alegria (right) and John B. Herrington (top) work on the International Space Station.

Social Studies Activity

The first trips to Mars will probably take at least 6 to 8 months. Think about the difficulties you would have spending 7 months in a spacecraft about the size of a school bus. Set up rules and guidelines for your voyage. Plan for five astronauts from two different countries. Consider these issues:

- who will make decisions and give orders
- how you will communicate
- how you'll adjust for different living habits and backgrounds
- how you'll avoid getting bored
- how you'll resolve conflicts among crew members or with mission-control scientists on Earth.

Future Space Colony
In this painting, an artist imagines a human colony on another planet.

Essentials for Survival

You step out of your spacecraft onto a dusty red landscape under a pinkish-red sky. Now you know why Mars is called the "red planet." Water vapor in the air forms thin clouds, even fog. Because the air is so thin, the sun glares down. It's windy, too. Thick clouds of reddish dust, rich in iron, blow around you.

Without a pressurized spacesuit, you would not survive for long in the thin Martian air. Unlike the thick layers of atmosphere around Earth, this atmosphere gives almost no protection against harmful ultraviolet radiation. You also must carry oxygen. Martian air is about 95 percent carbon dioxide, which humans can't breathe.

Your spacesuit must keep you warm. Even at the Martian equator, daytime temperatures are generally below freezing. At night they plunge as low as −140°C. Walk carefully, too, because Martian gravity is weak. You'll feel only 38 percent of your Earth weight!

Mars Landscape
This is the first 360-degree image taken on Mars by *Spirit* in 2004.

Science Activity

Any human settlement on Mars would have to grow some of its own food. Experiment with a method called hydroponics—growing plants mainly in water, without soil. Set up two plant containers to grow tomatoes or peppers.

- Decide what variables to control.

- In one container, use just water and plant food, with a wire mesh support.

- In the other, add sand or gravel to root plants; add water and plant food.

- Record the rate of growth and strength of each plant over a two-to three-week period.

Which technique worked best? How do you think hydroponics would work on Mars?

Plant Grown in Water

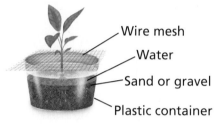

Wire mesh

Water

Plastic container

Plant Grown in Gravel

Wire mesh

Water

Sand or gravel

Plastic container

Tie It Together

Plan a Martian Station

At last, you will be going to Mars to set up the first human research station. For an expedition this long, good planning is essential. Review the major problems that Mars presents to humans, such as a thin atmosphere, a lack of oxygen, and extreme temperatures.

Remember that it's too expensive to send most supplies to Mars. Work in groups to make a plan for setting up Earth's research station. Include maps and drawings. As you make your plan, consider questions such as these:

- How will you supply oxygen? Water? Fuel?

- What site will you choose for your settlement? Consider the landscape and climate on Mars.

- What supplies will you bring with you?

- What will you use for building materials?

- What kinds of food will you get? How will you get food?

Rocky Plains of Mars
This painting shows a future scene in which humans walk on Mars.

Think Like a Scientist

Scientists have a particular way of looking at the world, or scientific habits of mind. Whenever you ask a question and explore possible answers, you use many of the same skills that scientists do. Some of these skills are described on this page.

Observing

When you use one or more of your five senses to gather information about the world, you are **observing.** Hearing a dog bark, counting twelve green seeds, and smelling smoke are all observations. To increase the power of their senses, scientists sometimes use microscopes, telescopes, or other instruments that help them make more detailed observations.

An observation must be an accurate report of what your senses detect. It is important to keep careful records of your observations in science class by writing or drawing in a notebook. The information collected through observations is called evidence, or data.

Inferring

When you interpret an observation, you are **inferring,** or making an inference. For example, if you hear your dog barking, you may infer that someone is at your front door. To make this inference, you combine the evidence— the barking dog—and your experience or knowledge—you know that your dog barks when strangers approach—to reach a logical conclusion.

Notice that an inference is not a fact; it is only one of many possible interpretations for an observation. For example, your dog may be barking because it wants to go for a walk. An inference may turn out to be incorrect even if it is based on accurate observations and logical reasoning. The only way to find out if an inference is correct is to investigate further.

Predicting

When you listen to the weather forecast, you hear many predictions about the next day's weather—what the temperature will be, whether it will rain, and how windy it will be. Weather forecasters use observations and knowledge of weather patterns to predict the weather. The skill of **predicting** involves making an inference about a future event based on current evidence or past experience.

Because a prediction is an inference, it may prove to be false. In science class, you can test some of your predictions by doing experiments. For example, suppose you predict that larger paper airplanes can fly farther than smaller airplanes. How could you test your prediction?

Activity

Use the photograph to answer the questions below.

Observing Look closely at the photograph. List at least three observations.

Inferring Use your observations to make an inference about what has happened. What experience or knowledge did you use to make the inference?

Predicting Predict what will happen next. On what evidence or experience do you base your prediction?

Classifying

Could you imagine searching for a book in the library if the books were shelved in no particular order? Your trip to the library would be an all-day event! Luckily, librarians group together books on similar topics or by the same author. Grouping together items that are alike in some way is called **classifying.** You can classify items in many ways: by size, by shape, by use, and by other important characteristics.

Like librarians, scientists use the skill of classifying to organize information and objects. When things are sorted into groups, the relationships among them become easier to understand.

> **Activity**
>
> Classify the objects in the photograph into two groups based on any characteristic you choose. Then use another characteristic to classify the objects into three groups.

Making Models

Have you ever drawn a picture to help someone understand what you were saying? Such a drawing is one type of model. A model is a picture, diagram, computer image, or other representation of a complex object or process. **Making models** helps people understand things that they cannot observe directly.

Scientists often use models to represent things that are either very large or very small, such as the planets in the solar system, or the parts of a cell. Such models are physical models—drawings or three-dimensional structures that look like the real thing. Other models are mental models—mathematical equations or words that describe how something works.

> **Activity**
>
> This student is using a model to demonstrate what causes day and night on Earth. What do the flashlight and the tennis ball in the model represent?

Communicating

Whenever you talk on the phone, write a report, or listen to your teacher at school, you are communicating. **Communicating** is the process of sharing ideas and information with other people. Communicating effectively requires many skills, including writing, reading, speaking, listening, and making models.

Scientists communicate to share results, information, and opinions. Scientists often communicate about their work in journals, over the telephone, in letters, and on the Internet.

They also attend scientific meetings where they share their ideas with one another in person.

> **Activity**
>
> On a sheet of paper, write out clear, detailed directions for tying your shoe. Then exchange directions with a partner. Follow your partner's directions exactly. How successful were you at tying your shoe? How could your partner have communicated more clearly?

Making Measurements

By measuring, scientists can express their observations more precisely and communicate more information about what they observe.

Measuring in SI

The standard system of measurement used by scientists around the world is known as the International System of Units, which is abbreviated as SI (**Système International d'Unités,** in French). SI units are easy to use because they are based on powers of 10. Each unit is ten times larger than the next smallest unit and one tenth the size of the next largest unit. The table lists the prefixes used to name the most common SI units.

Length To measure length, or the distance between two points, the unit of measure is the **meter (m).** The distance from the floor to a doorknob is approximately one meter. Long distances, such as the distance between two cities, are measured in kilometers (km). Small lengths are measured in centimeters (cm) or millimeters (mm). Scientists use metric rulers and meter sticks to measure length.

Common Conversions

1 km	=	1,000 m
1 m	=	100 cm
1 m	=	1,000 mm
1 cm	=	10 mm

Common SI Prefixes

Prefix	Symbol	Meaning
kilo-	k	1,000
hecto-	h	100
deka-	da	10
deci-	d	0.1 (one tenth)
centi-	c	0.01 (one hundredth)
milli-	m	0.001 (one thousandth)

Liquid Volume To measure the volume of a liquid, or the amount of space it takes up, you will use a unit of measure known as the **liter (L).** One liter is the approximate volume of a medium-size carton of milk. Smaller volumes are measured in milliliters (mL). Scientists use graduated cylinders to measure liquid volume.

Activity

The larger lines on the metric ruler in the picture show centimeter divisions, while the smaller, unnumbered lines show millimeter divisions. How many centimeters long is the shell? How many millimeters long is it?

Activity

The graduated cylinder in the picture is marked in milliliter divisions. Notice that the water in the cylinder has a curved surface. This curved surface is called the *meniscus.* To measure the volume, you must read the level at the lowest point of the meniscus. What is the volume of water in this graduated cylinder?

Common Conversion

1 L = 1,000 mL

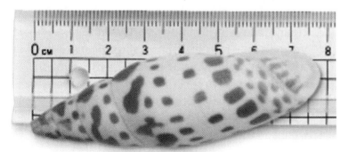

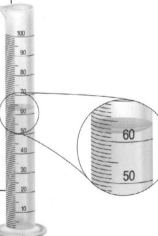

Mass To measure mass, or the amount of matter in an object, you will use a unit of measure known as the **gram (g).** One gram is approximately the mass of a paper clip. Larger masses are measured in kilograms (kg). Scientists use a balance to find the mass of an object.

Common Conversion
1 kg = 1,000 g

Activity

The mass of the potato in the picture is measured in kilograms. What is the mass of the potato? Suppose a recipe for potato salad called for one kilogram of potatoes. About how many potatoes would you need?

`0.25 KG`

Temperature To measure the temperature of a substance, you will use the **Celsius scale.** Temperature is measured in degrees Celsius (°C) using a Celsius thermometer. Water freezes at 0°C and boils at 100°C.

Time The unit scientists use to measure time is the **second (s).**

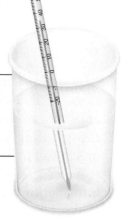

Activity

What is the temperature of the liquid in degrees Celsius?

Converting SI Units

To use the SI system, you must know how to convert between units. Converting from one unit to another involves the skill of **calculating,** or using mathematical operations. Converting between SI units is similar to converting between dollars and dimes because both systems are based on powers of ten.

Suppose you want to convert a length of 80 centimeters to meters. Follow these steps to convert between units.

1. Begin by writing down the measurement you want to convert—in this example, 80 centimeters.

2. Write a conversion factor that represents the relationship between the two units you are converting. In this example, the relationship is 1 meter = 100 centimeters. Write this conversion factor as a fraction, making sure to place the units you are converting from (centimeters, in this example) in the denominator.

3. Multiply the measurement you want to convert by the fraction. When you do this, the units in the first measurement will cancel out with the units in the denominator. Your answer will be in the units you are converting to (meters, in this example).

Example

80 centimeters = ▨ meters

$$80 \text{ centimeters} \times \frac{1 \text{ meter}}{100 \text{ centimeters}} = \frac{80 \text{ meters}}{100}$$

$$= 0.8 \text{ meters}$$

Activity

Convert between the following units.
1. 600 millimeters = ▨ meters
2. 0.35 liters = ▨ milliliters
3. 1,050 grams = ▨ kilograms

Conducting a Scientific Investigation

In some ways, scientists are like detectives, piecing together clues to learn about a process or event. One way that scientists gather clues is by carrying out experiments. An experiment tests an idea in a careful, orderly manner. Although experiments do not all follow the same steps in the same order, many follow a pattern similar to the one described here.

Posing Questions

Experiments begin by asking a scientific question. A scientific question is one that can be answered by gathering evidence. For example, the question "Which freezes faster—fresh water or salt water?" is a scientific question because you can carry out an investigation and gather information to answer the question.

Developing a Hypothesis

The next step is to form a hypothesis. A **hypothesis** is a possible explanation for a set of observations or answer to a scientific question. In science, a hypothesis must be something that can be tested. A hypothesis can be worded as an *If . . . then . . .* statement. For example, a hypothesis might be *"If I add table salt to fresh water, then the water will freeze at a lower temperature."* A hypothesis worded this way serves as a rough outline of the experiment you should perform.

Designing an Experiment

Next you need to plan a way to test your hypothesis. Your plan should be written out as a step-by-step procedure and should describe the observations or measurements you will make.

Two important steps involved in designing an experiment are controlling variables and forming operational definitions.

Controlling Variables In a well-designed experiment, you need to keep all variables the same except for one. A **variable** is any factor that can change in an experiment. The factor that you change is called the **manipulated variable**. In this experiment, the manipulated variable is the amount of table salt added to the water. Other factors, such as the amount of water or the starting temperature, are kept constant.

The factor that changes as a result of the manipulated variable is called the **responding variable.** The responding variable is what you measure or observe to obtain your results. In this experiment, the responding variable is the temperature at which the water freezes.

An experiment in which all factors except one are kept constant is called a **controlled experiment.** Most controlled experiments include a test called the control. In this experiment, Container 3 is the control. Because no salt is added to Container 3, you can compare the results from the other containers to it. Any difference in results must be due to the addition of salt alone.

Forming Operational Definitions Another important aspect of a well-designed experiment is having clear operational definitions. An **operational definition** is a statement that describes how a particular variable is to be measured or how a term is to be defined. For example, in this experiment, how will you determine if the water has frozen? You might decide to insert a stick in each container at the start of the experiment. Your operational definition of "frozen" would be the time at which the stick can no longer move.

Experimental Procedure
1. Fill 3 containers with 300 milliliters of cold tap water.
2. Add 10 grams of salt to Container 1; stir. Add 20 grams of salt to Container 2; stir. Add no salt to Container 3.
3. Place the 3 containers in a freezer.
4. Check the containers every 15 minutes. Record your observations.

Interpreting Data

The observations and measurements you make in an experiment are called **data.** At the end of an experiment, you need to analyze the data to look for any patterns or trends. Patterns often become clear if you organize your data in a data table or graph. Then think through what the data reveal. Do they support your hypothesis? Do they point out a flaw in your experiment? Do you need to collect more data?

Drawing Conclusions

A **conclusion** is a statement that sums up what you have learned from an experiment. When you draw a conclusion, you need to decide whether the data you collected support your hypothesis or not. You may need to repeat an experiment several times before you can draw any conclusions from it. Conclusions often lead you to pose new questions and plan new experiments to answer them.

Activity

Is a ball's bounce affected by the height from which it is dropped? Using the steps just described, plan a controlled experiment to investigate this problem.

Technology Design Skills

Engineers are people who use scientific and technological knowledge to solve practical problems. To design new products, engineers usually follow the process described here, even though they may not follow these steps in the exact order. As you read the steps, think about how you might apply them in technology labs.

Identify a Need

Before engineers begin designing a new product, they must first identify the need they are trying to meet. For example, suppose you are a member of a design team in a company that makes toys. Your team has identified a need: a toy boat that is inexpensive and easy to assemble.

Research the Problem

Engineers often begin by gathering information that will help them with their new design. This research may include finding articles in books, magazines, or on the Internet. It may also include talking to other engineers who have solved similar problems. Engineers often perform experiments related to the product they want to design.

For your toy boat, you could look at toys that are similar to the one you want to design. You might do research on the Internet. You could also test some materials to see whether they will work well in a toy boat.

Drawing for a boat design ▼

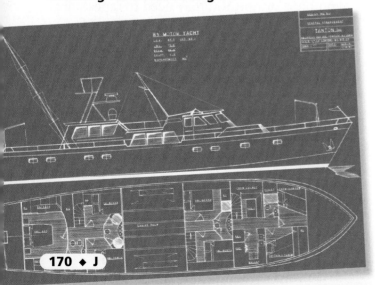

Design a Solution

Research gives engineers information that helps them design a product. When engineers design new products, they usually work in teams.

Generating Ideas Often design teams hold brainstorming meetings in which any team member can contribute ideas. **Brainstorming** is a creative process in which one team member's suggestions often spark ideas in other group members. Brainstorming can lead to new approaches to solving a design problem.

Evaluating Constraints During brainstorming, a design team will often come up with several possible designs. The team must then evaluate each one.

As part of their evaluation, engineers consider constraints. **Constraints** are factors that limit or restrict a product design. Physical characteristics, such as the properties of materials used to make your toy boat, are constraints. Money and time are also constraints. If the materials in a product cost a lot, or if the product takes a long time to make, the design may be impractical.

Making Trade-offs Design teams usually need to make trade-offs. In a **trade-off,** engineers give up one benefit of a proposed design in order to obtain another. In designing your toy boat, you will have to make trade-offs. For example, suppose one material is sturdy but not fully waterproof. Another material is more waterproof, but breakable. You may decide to give up the benefit of sturdiness in order to obtain the benefit of waterproofing.

Build and Evaluate a Prototype

Once the team has chosen a design plan, the engineers build a prototype of the product. A **prototype** is a working model used to test a design. Engineers evaluate the prototype to see whether it works well, is easy to operate, is safe to use, and holds up to repeated use.

Think of your toy boat. What would the prototype be like? Of what materials would it be made? How would you test it?

Troubleshoot and Redesign

Few prototypes work perfectly, which is why they need to be tested. Once a design team has tested a prototype, the members analyze the results and identify any problems. The team then tries to **troubleshoot,** or fix the design problems. For example, if your toy boat leaks or wobbles, the boat should be redesigned to eliminate those problems.

Communicate the Solution

A team needs to communicate the final design to the people who will manufacture and use the product. To do this, teams may use sketches, detailed drawings, computer simulations, and word descriptions.

Activity

You can use the technology design process to design and build a toy boat.

Research and Investigate

1. Visit the library or go online to research toy boats.
2. Investigate how a toy boat can be powered, including wind, rubber bands, or baking soda and vinegar.
3. Brainstorm materials, shapes, and steering for your boat.

Design and Build

4. Based on your research, design a toy boat that
   • is made of readily available materials
   • is no larger than 15 cm long and 10 cm wide
   • includes a power system, a rudder, and an area for cargo
   • travels 2 meters in a straight line carrying a load of 20 pennies
5. Sketch your design and write a step-by-step plan for building your boat. After your teacher approves your plan, build your boat.

Evaluate and Redesign

6. Test your boat, evaluate the results, and troubleshoot any problems.
7. Based on your evaluation, redesign your toy boat so it performs better.

Creating Data Tables and Graphs

How can you make sense of the data in a science experiment?
The first step is to organize the data to help you understand them.
Data tables and graphs are helpful tools for organizing data.

Data Tables

You have gathered your materials and set up your experiment. But before you start, you need to plan a way to record what happens during the experiment. By creating a data table, you can record your observations and measurements in an orderly way.

Suppose, for example, that a scientist conducted an experiment to find out how many Calories people of different body masses burn while doing various activities. The data table shows the results.

Notice in this data table that the manipulated variable (body mass) is the heading of one column. The responding variable (for

Calories Burned in 30 Minutes			
Body Mass	Experiment 1: Bicycling	Experiment 2: Playing Basketball	Experiment 3: Watching Television
30 kg	60 Calories	120 Calories	21 Calories
40 kg	77 Calories	164 Calories	27 Calories
50 kg	95 Calories	206 Calories	33 Calories
60 kg	114 Calories	248 Calories	38 Calories

Experiment 1, the number of Calories burned while bicycling) is the heading of the next column. Additional columns were added for related experiments.

Bar Graphs

To compare how many Calories a person burns doing various activities, you could create a bar graph. A bar graph is used to display data in a number of separate, or distinct, categories. In this example, bicycling, playing basketball, and watching television are the three categories.

To create a bar graph, follow these steps.

1. On graph paper, draw a horizontal, or *x*-, axis and a vertical, or *y*-, axis.

2. Write the names of the categories to be graphed along the horizontal axis. Include an overall label for the axis as well.

3. Label the vertical axis with the name of the responding variable. Include units of measurement. Then create a scale along the axis by marking off equally spaced numbers that cover the range of the data collected.

4. For each category, draw a solid bar using the scale on the vertical axis to determine the height. Make all the bars the same width.

5. Add a title that describes the graph.

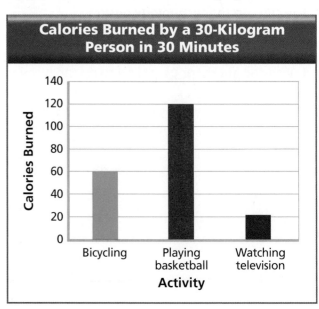

Calories Burned by a 30-Kilogram Person in 30 Minutes

Line Graphs

To see whether a relationship exists between body mass and the number of Calories burned while bicycling, you could create a line graph. A line graph is used to display data that show how one variable (the responding variable) changes in response to another variable (the manipulated variable). You can use a line graph when your manipulated variable is **continuous,** that is, when there are other points between the ones that you tested. In this example, body mass is a continuous variable because there are other body masses between 30 and 40 kilograms (for example, 31 kilograms). Time is another example of a continuous variable.

Line graphs are powerful tools because they allow you to estimate values for conditions that you did not test in the experiment. For example, you can use the line graph to estimate that a 35-kilogram person would burn 68 Calories while bicycling.

To create a line graph, follow these steps.

1. On graph paper, draw a horizontal, or *x*-, axis and a vertical, or *y*-, axis.

2. Label the horizontal axis with the name of the manipulated variable. Label the vertical axis with the name of the responding variable. Include units of measurement.

3. Create a scale on each axis by marking off equally spaced numbers that cover the range of the data collected.

4. Plot a point on the graph for each piece of data. In the line graph above, the dotted lines show how to plot the first data point (30 kilograms and 60 Calories). Follow an imaginary vertical line extending up from the horizontal axis at the 30-kilogram mark. Then follow an imaginary horizontal line extending across from the vertical axis at the 60-Calorie mark. Plot the point where the two lines intersect.

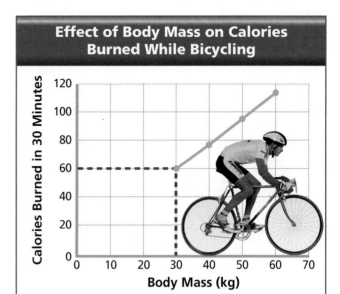

Effect of Body Mass on Calories Burned While Bicycling

5. Connect the plotted points with a solid line. (In some cases, it may be more appropriate to draw a line that shows the general trend of the plotted points. In those cases, some of the points may fall above or below the line. Also, not all graphs are linear. It may be more appropriate to draw a curve to connect the points.)

6. Add a title that identifies the variables or relationship in the graph.

Activity

Create line graphs to display the data from Experiment 2 and Experiment 3 in the data table.

Activity

You read in the newspaper that a total of 4 centimeters of rain fell in your area in June, 2.5 centimeters fell in July, and 1.5 centimeters fell in August. What type of graph would you use to display these data? Use graph paper to create the graph.

Circle Graphs

Like bar graphs, circle graphs can be used to display data in a number of separate categories. Unlike bar graphs, however, circle graphs can only be used when you have data for *all* the categories that make up a given topic. A circle graph is sometimes called a pie chart. The pie represents the entire topic, while the slices represent the individual categories. The size of a slice indicates what percentage of the whole a particular category makes up.

The data table below shows the results of a survey in which 24 teenagers were asked to identify their favorite sport. The data were then used to create the circle graph at the right.

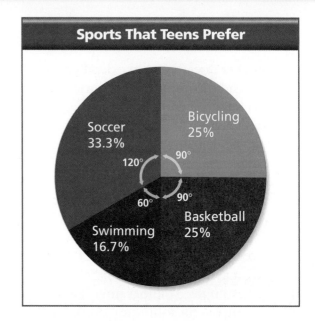

Favorite Sports

Sport	Students
Soccer	8
Basketball	6
Bicycling	6
Swimming	4

To create a circle graph, follow these steps.

1. Use a compass to draw a circle. Mark the center with a point. Then draw a line from the center point to the top of the circle.

2. Determine the size of each "slice" by setting up a proportion where x equals the number of degrees in a slice. (*Note:* A circle contains 360 degrees.) For example, to find the number of degrees in the "soccer" slice, set up the following proportion:

$$\frac{\text{Students who prefer soccer}}{\text{Total number of students}} = \frac{x}{\text{Total number of degrees in a circle}}$$

$$\frac{8}{24} = \frac{x}{360}$$

Cross-multiply and solve for x.

$$24x = 8 \times 360$$
$$x = 120$$

The "soccer" slice should contain 120 degrees.

3. Use a protractor to measure the angle of the first slice, using the line you drew to the top of the circle as the 0° line. Draw a line from the center of the circle to the edge for the angle you measured.

4. Continue around the circle by measuring the size of each slice with the protractor. Start measuring from the edge of the previous slice so the wedges do not overlap. When you are done, the entire circle should be filled in.

5. Determine the percentage of the whole circle that each slice represents. To do this, divide the number of degrees in a slice by the total number of degrees in a circle (360), and multiply by 100%. For the "soccer" slice, you can find the percentage as follows:

$$\frac{120}{360} \times 100\% = 33.3\%$$

6. Use a different color for each slice. Label each slice with the category and with the percentage of the whole it represents.

7. Add a title to the circle graph.

Activity

In a class of 28 students, 12 students take the bus to school, 10 students walk, and 6 students ride their bicycles. Create a circle graph to display these data.

Math Review

Scientists use math to organize, analyze, and present data. This appendix will help you review some basic math skills.

Mean, Median, and Mode

The **mean** is the average, or the sum of the data divided by the number of data items. The middle number in a set of ordered data is called the **median**. The **mode** is the number that appears most often in a set of data.

Example

A scientist counted the number of distinct songs sung by seven different male birds and collected the data shown below.

Male Bird Songs							
Bird	A	B	C	D	E	F	G
Number of Songs	36	29	40	35	28	36	27

To determine the mean number of songs, add the total number of songs and divide by the number of data items—in this case, the number of male birds.

$$\text{Mean} = \frac{231}{7} = 33 \text{ songs}$$

To find the median number of songs, arrange the data in numerical order and find the number in the middle of the series.

27 28 29 35 36 36 40

The number in the middle is 35, so the median number of songs is 35.

The mode is the value that appears most frequently. In the data, 36 appears twice, while each other item appears only once. Therefore, 36 songs is the mode.

Practice

Find out how many minutes it takes each student in your class to get to school. Then find the mean, median, and mode for the data.

Probability

Probability is the chance that an event will occur. Probability can be expressed as a ratio, a fraction, or a percentage. For example, when you flip a coin, the probability that the coin will land heads up is 1 in 2, or $\frac{1}{2}$, or 50 percent.

The probability that an event will happen can be expressed in the following formula.

$$P(\text{event}) = \frac{\text{Number of times the event can occur}}{\text{Total number of possible events}}$$

Example

A paper bag contains 25 blue marbles, 5 green marbles, 5 orange marbles, and 15 yellow marbles. If you close your eyes and pick a marble from the bag, what is the probability that it will be yellow?

$$P(\text{yellow marbles}) = \frac{15 \text{ yellow marbles}}{50 \text{ marbles total}}$$

$$P = \frac{15}{50}, \text{ or } \frac{3}{10}, \text{ or } 30\%$$

Practice

Each side of a cube has a letter on it. Two sides have *A*, three sides have *B*, and one side has *C*. If you roll the cube, what is the probability that *A* will land on top?

Area

The **area** of a surface is the number of square units that cover it. The front cover of your textbook has an area of about 600 cm^2.

Area of a Rectangle and a Square To find the area of a rectangle, multiply its length times its width. The formula for the area of a rectangle is

$$A = \ell \times w, \text{ or } A = \ell w$$

Since all four sides of a square have the same length, the area of a square is the length of one side multiplied by itself, or squared.

$$A = s \times s, \text{ or } A = s^2$$

Example

A scientist is studying the plants in a field that measures 75 m $\times$ 45 m. What is the area of the field?

$$A = \ell \times w$$

$$A = 75 \text{ m} \times 45 \text{ m}$$

$$A = 3,375 \text{ m}^2$$

Area of a Circle The formula for the area of a circle is

$$A = \pi \times r \times r, \text{ or } A = \pi r^2$$

The length of the radius is represented by r, and the value of π is approximately $\frac{22}{7}$.

Example

Find the area of a circle with a radius of 14 cm.

$$A = \pi r^2$$

$$A = 14 \times 14 \times \frac{22}{7}$$

$$A = 616 \text{ cm}^2$$

Practice

Find the area of a circle that has a radius of 21 m.

Circumference

The distance around a circle is called the circumference. The formula for finding the circumference of a circle is

$$C = 2 \times \pi \times r, \text{ or } C = 2\pi r$$

Example

The radius of a circle is 35 cm. What is its circumference?

$$C = 2\pi r$$

$$C = 2 \times 35 \times \frac{22}{7}$$

$$C = 220 \text{ cm}$$

Practice

What is the circumference of a circle with a radius of 28 m?

Volume

The volume of an object is the number of cubic units it contains. The volume of a wastebasket, for example, might be about 26,000 cm^3.

Volume of a Rectangular Object To find the volume of a rectangular object, multiply the object's length times its width times its height.

$$V = \ell \times w \times h, \text{ or } V = \ell w h$$

Example

Find the volume of a box with length 24 cm, width 12 cm, and height 9 cm.

$$V = \ell w h$$

$$V = 24 \text{ cm} \times 12 \text{ cm} \times 9 \text{ cm}$$

$$V = 2,592 \text{ cm}^3$$

Practice

What is the volume of a rectangular object with length 17 cm, width 11 cm, and height 6 cm?

Fractions

A **fraction** is a way to express a part of a whole. In the fraction $\frac{4}{7}$, 4 is the numerator and 7 is the denominator.

Adding and Subtracting Fractions To add or subtract two or more fractions that have a common denominator, first add or subtract the numerators. Then write the sum or difference over the common denominator.

To find the sum or difference of fractions with different denominators, first find the least common multiple of the denominators. This is known as the least common denominator. Then convert each fraction to equivalent fractions with the least common denominator. Add or subtract the numerators. Then write the sum or difference over the common denominator.

Example

$$\frac{5}{6} - \frac{3}{4} = \frac{10}{12} - \frac{9}{12} = \frac{10 - 9}{12} = \frac{1}{12}$$

Multiplying Fractions To multiply two fractions, first multiply the two numerators, then multiply the two denominators.

Example

$$\frac{5}{6} \times \frac{2}{3} = \frac{5 \times 2}{6 \times 3} = \frac{10}{18} = \frac{5}{9}$$

Dividing Fractions Dividing by a fraction is the same as multiplying by its reciprocal. Reciprocals are numbers whose numerators and denominators have been switched. To divide one fraction by another, first invert the fraction you are dividing by—in other words, turn it upside down. Then multiply the two fractions.

Example

$$\frac{2}{5} \div \frac{7}{8} = \frac{2}{5} \times \frac{8}{7} = \frac{2 \times 8}{5 \times 7} = \frac{16}{35}$$

Practice

Solve the following: $\frac{3}{7} \div \frac{4}{5}$.

Decimals

Fractions whose denominators are 10, 100, or some other power of 10 are often expressed as decimals. For example, the fraction $\frac{9}{10}$ can be expressed as the decimal 0.9, and the fraction $\frac{7}{100}$ can be written as 0.07.

Adding and Subtracting With Decimals To add or subtract decimals, line up the decimal points before you carry out the operation.

Example

$$\begin{array}{r} 27.4 \\ +\ 6.19 \\ \hline 33.59 \end{array} \qquad \begin{array}{r} 278.635 \\ -\ 191.4 \\ \hline 87.235 \end{array}$$

Multiplying With Decimals When you multiply two numbers with decimals, the number of decimal places in the product is equal to the total number of decimal places in each number being multiplied.

Example

$$\begin{array}{r} 46.2 \text{ (one decimal place)} \\ \times\ 2.37 \text{ (two decimal places)} \\ \hline 109.494 \text{ (three decimal places)} \end{array}$$

Dividing With Decimals To divide a decimal by a whole number, put the decimal point in the quotient above the decimal point in the dividend.

Example

$$15.5 \div 5$$
$$\begin{array}{r} 3.1 \\ 5 \overline{)15.5} \end{array}$$

To divide a decimal by a decimal, you need to rewrite the divisor as a whole number. Do this by multiplying both the divisor and dividend by the same multiple of 10.

Example

$$1.68 \div 4.2 = 16.8 \div 42$$
$$\begin{array}{r} 0.4 \\ 42 \overline{)16.8} \end{array}$$

Practice

Multiply 6.21 by 8.5.

Ratio and Proportion

A **ratio** compares two numbers by division. For example, suppose a scientist counts 800 wolves and 1,200 moose on an island. The ratio of wolves to moose can be written as a fraction, $\frac{800}{1,200}$, which can be reduced to $\frac{2}{3}$. The same ratio can also be expressed as 2 to 3 or 2 : 3.

A **proportion** is a mathematical sentence saying that two ratios are equivalent. For example, a proportion could state that $\frac{800 \text{ wolves}}{1,200 \text{ moose}} = \frac{2 \text{ wolves}}{3 \text{ moose}}$. You can sometimes set up a proportion to determine or estimate an unknown quantity. For example, suppose a scientist counts 25 beetles in an area of 10 square meters. The scientist wants to estimate the number of beetles in 100 square meters.

Example

1. Express the relationship between beetles and area as a ratio: $\frac{25}{10}$, simplified to $\frac{5}{2}$.

2. Set up a proportion, with x representing the number of beetles. The proportion can be stated as $\frac{5}{2} = \frac{x}{100}$.

3. Begin by cross-multiplying. In other words, multiply each fraction's numerator by the other fraction's denominator.

$$5 \times 100 = 2 \times x, \text{ or } 500 = 2x$$

4. To find the value of x, divide both sides by 2. The result is 250, or 250 beetles in 100 square meters.

Practice

Find the value of x in the following proportion: $\frac{6}{7} = \frac{x}{49}$.

Percentage

A **percentage** is a ratio that compares a number to 100. For example, there are 37 granite rocks in a collection that consists of 100 rocks. The ratio $\frac{37}{100}$ can be written as 37%. Granite rocks make up 37% of the rock collection.

You can calculate percentages of numbers other than 100 by setting up a proportion.

Example

Rain falls on 9 days out of 30 in June. What percentage of the days in June were rainy?

$$\frac{9 \text{ days}}{30 \text{ days}} = \frac{d\%}{100\%}$$

To find the value of d, begin by cross-multiplying, as for any proportion:

$$9 \times 100 = 30 \times d \qquad d = \frac{900}{30} \qquad d = 30$$

Practice

There are 300 marbles in a jar, and 42 of those marbles are blue. What percentage of the marbles are blue?

Significant Figures

The **precision** of a measurement depends on the instrument you use to take the measurement. For example, if the smallest unit on the ruler is millimeters, then the most precise measurement you can make will be in millimeters.

The sum or difference of measurements can only be as precise as the least precise measurement being added or subtracted. Round your answer so that it has the same number of digits after the decimal as the least precise measurement. Round up if the last digit is 5 or more, and round down if the last digit is 4 or less.

Example

Subtract a temperature of 5.2°C from the temperature 75.46°C.

75.46 − 5.2 = 70.26

5.2 has the fewest digits after the decimal, so it is the least precise measurement. Since the last digit of the answer is 6, round up to 3. The most precise difference between the measurements is 70.3°C.

Practice

Add 26.4 m to 8.37 m. Round your answer according to the precision of the measurements.

Significant figures are the number of nonzero digits in a measurement. Zeroes between nonzero digits are also significant. For example, the measurements 12,500 L, 0.125 cm, and 2.05 kg all have three significant figures. When you multiply and divide measurements, the one with the fewest significant figures determines the number of significant figures in your answer.

Example

Multiply 110 g by 5.75 g.

110 × 5.75 = 632.5

Because 110 has only two significant figures, round the answer to 630 g.

Scientific Notation

A **factor** is a number that divides into another number with no remainder. In the example, the number 3 is used as a factor four times.

An **exponent** tells how many times a number is used as a factor. For example, $3 \times 3 \times 3 \times 3$ can be written as 3^4. The exponent 4 indicates that the number 3 is used as a factor four times. Another way of expressing this is to say that 81 is equal to 3 to the fourth power.

Example

$$3^4 = 3 \times 3 \times 3 \times 3 = 81$$

Scientific notation uses exponents and powers of ten to write very large or very small numbers in shorter form. When you write a number in scientific notation, you write the number as two factors. The first factor is any number between 1 and 10. The second factor is a power of 10, such as 10^3 or 10^6.

Example

The average distance between the planet Mercury and the sun is 58,000,000 km. To write the first factor in scientific notation, insert a decimal point in the original number so that you have a number between 1 and 10. In the case of 58,000,000, the number is 5.8.

To determine the power of 10, count the number of places that the decimal point moved. In this case, it moved 7 places.

58,000,000 km = 5.8×10^7 km

Practice

Express 6,590,000 in scientific notation.

Reading Comprehension Skills

Each section in your textbook introduces a Target Reading Skill. You will improve your reading comprehension by using the Target Reading Skills described below.

Using Prior Knowledge

Your prior knowledge is what you already know before you begin to read about a topic. Building on what you already know gives you a head start on learning new information. Before you begin a new assignment, think about what you know. You might look at the headings and the visuals to spark your memory. You can list what you know. Then, as you read, consider questions like these.

• How does what you learn relate to what you know?

• How did something you already know help you learn something new?

• Did your original ideas agree with what you have just learned?

Asking Questions

Asking yourself questions is an excellent way to focus on and remember new information in your textbook. For example, you can turn the text headings into questions. Then your questions can guide you to identify the important information as you read. Look at these examples:

Heading: Using Seismographic Data

Question: How are seismographic data used?

Heading: Kinds of Faults

Question: What are the kinds of faults?

You do not have to limit your questions to text headings. Ask questions about anything that you need to clarify or that will help you understand the content. *What* and *how* are probably the most common question words, but you may also ask *why, who, when,* or *where* questions.

Previewing Visuals

Visuals are photographs, graphs, tables, diagrams, and illustrations. Visuals contain important information. Before you read, look at visuals and their labels and captions. This preview will help you prepare for what you will be reading.

Often you will be asked what you want to learn about a visual. For example, after you look at the normal fault diagram below, you might ask: What is the movement along a normal fault? Questions about visuals give you a purpose for reading—to answer your questions.

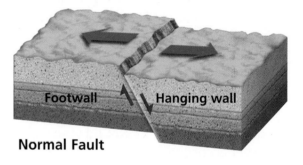

Footwall   Hanging wall

Normal Fault

Outlining

An outline shows the relationship between main ideas and supporting ideas. An outline has a formal structure. You write the main ideas, called topics, next to Roman numerals. The supporting ideas, called subtopics, are written under the main ideas and labeled A, B, C, and so on. An outline looks like this:

Technology and Society
I. Technology through history
II. The impact of technology on society
A.
B.

Identifying Main Ideas

When you are reading science material, it is important to try to understand the ideas and concepts that are in a passage. Each paragraph has a lot of information and detail. Good readers try to identify the most important—or biggest—idea in every paragraph or section. That's the main idea. The other information in the paragraph supports or further explains the main idea.

Sometimes main ideas are stated directly. In this book, some main ideas are identified for you as key concepts. These are printed in bold-face type. However, you must identify other main ideas yourself. In order to do this, you must identify all the ideas within a paragraph or section. Then ask yourself which idea is big enough to include all the other ideas.

Comparing and Contrasting

When you compare and contrast, you examine the similarities and differences between things. You can compare and contrast in a Venn diagram or in a table.

Venn Diagram A Venn diagram consists of two overlapping circles. In the space where the circles overlap, you write the characteristics that the two items have in common. In one of the circles outside the area of overlap, you write the differing features or characteristics of one of the items. In the other circle outside the area of overlap, you write the differing characteristics of the other item.

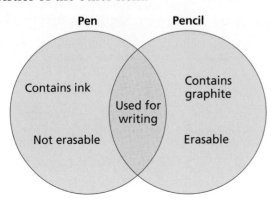

Table In a compare/contrast table, you list the characteristics or features to be compared across the top of the table. Then list the items to be compared in the left column. Complete the table by filling in information about each characteristic or feature.

Blood Vessel	Function	Structure of Wall
Artery	Carries blood away from heart	
Capillary		
Vein		

Identifying Supporting Evidence

A hypothesis is a possible explanation for observations made by scientists or an answer to a scientific question. Scientists must carry out investigations and gather evidence that either supports or disproves the hypothesis.

Identifying the supporting evidence for a hypothesis or theory can help you understand the hypothesis or theory. Evidence consists of facts—information whose accuracy can be confirmed by testing or observation.

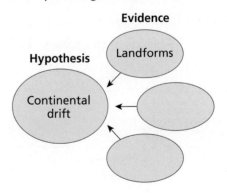

Sequencing

A sequence is the order in which a series of events occurs. A flowchart or a cycle diagram can help you visualize a sequence.

Flowchart To make a flowchart, write a brief description of each step or event in a box. Place the boxes in order, with the first event at the top of the chart. Then draw an arrow to connect each step or event to the next.

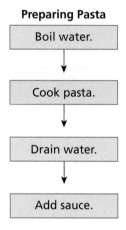

Preparing Pasta

Boil water. → Cook pasta. → Drain water. → Add sauce.

Cycle Diagram A cycle diagram shows a sequence that is continuous, or cyclical. A continuous sequence does not have an end because when the final event is over, the first event begins again. To create a cycle diagram, write the starting event in a box placed at the top of a page in the center. Then, moving in a clockwise direction, write each event in a box in its proper sequence. Draw arrows that connect each event to the one that occurs next.

Seasons of the Year

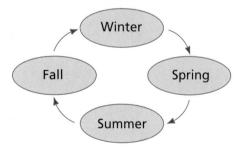

Relating Cause and Effect

Science involves many cause-and-effect relationships. A cause makes something happen. An effect is what happens. When you recognize that one event causes another, you are relating cause and effect.

Words like *cause, because, effect, affect,* and *result* often signal a cause or an effect. Sometimes an effect can have more than one cause, or a cause can produce several effects.

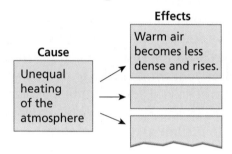

Cause Unequal heating of the atmosphere

Effects Warm air becomes less dense and rises.

Concept Mapping

Concept maps are useful tools for organizing information on any topic. A concept map begins with a main idea or core concept and shows how the idea can be subdivided into related subconcepts or smaller ideas.

You construct a concept map by placing concepts (usually nouns) in ovals and connecting them with linking words (usually verbs). The biggest concept or idea is placed in an oval at the top of the map. Related concepts are arranged in ovals below the big idea. The linking words connect the ovals.

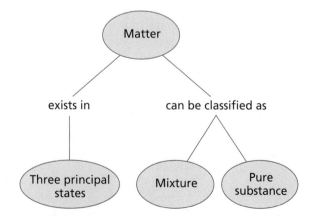

Matter
exists in — Three principal states
can be classified as — Mixture, Pure substance

Building Vocabulary

Knowing the meaning of these prefixes, suffixes, and roots will help you understand the meaning of words you do not recognize.

Word Origins Many science words come to English from other languages, such as Greek and Latin. By learning the meaning of a few common Greek and Latin roots, you can determine the meaning of unfamiliar science words.

Prefixes A prefix is a word part that is added at the beginning of a root or base word to change its meaning.

Suffixes A suffix is a word part that is added at the end of a root word to change the meaning.

Greek and Latin Roots		
Greek Roots	**Meaning**	**Example**
ast-	star	astronaut
geo-	Earth	geology
metron-	measure	kilometer
opt-	eye	optician
photo-	light	photograph
scop-	see	microscope
therm-	heat	thermostat
Latin Roots	**Meaning**	**Example**
aqua-	water	aquarium
aud-	hear	auditorium
duc-, duct-	lead	conduct
flect-	bend	reflect
fract-, frag-	break	fracture
ject-	throw	reject
luc-	light	lucid
spec-	see	inspect

Prefixes and Suffixes		
Prefix	**Meaning**	**Example**
com-, con-	with	communicate, concert
de-	from; down	decay
di-	two	divide
ex-, exo-	out	exhaust
in-, im-	in, into; not	inject, impossible
re-	again; back	reflect, recall
trans-	across	transfer
Suffix	**Meaning**	**Example**
-al	relating to	natural
-er, -or	one who	teacher, doctor
-ist	one who practices	scientist
-ity	state of	equality
-ology	study of	biology
-tion, -sion	state or quality of	reaction, tension

Safety Symbols

These symbols warn of possible dangers in the laboratory and remind you to work carefully.

 Safety Goggles Wear safety goggles to protect your eyes in any activity involving chemicals, flames or heating, or glassware.

 Lab Apron Wear a laboratory apron to protect your skin and clothing from damage.

 Breakage Handle breakable materials, such as glassware, with care. Do not touch broken glassware.

 Heat-Resistant Gloves Use an oven mitt or other hand protection when handling hot materials such as hot plates or hot glassware.

 Plastic Gloves Wear disposable plastic gloves when working with harmful chemicals and organisms. Keep your hands away from your face, and dispose of the gloves according to your teacher's instructions.

 Heating Use a clamp or tongs to pick up hot glassware. Do not touch hot objects with your bare hands.

 Flames Before you work with flames, tie back loose hair and clothing. Follow instructions from your teacher about lighting and extinguishing flames.

 No Flames When using flammable materials, make sure there are no flames, sparks, or other exposed heat sources present.

 Corrosive Chemical Avoid getting acid or other corrosive chemicals on your skin or clothing or in your eyes. Do not inhale the vapors. Wash your hands after the activity.

 Poison Do not let any poisonous chemical come into contact with your skin, and do not inhale its vapors. Wash your hands when you are finished with the activity.

 Fumes Work in a ventilated area when harmful vapors may be involved. Avoid inhaling vapors directly. Only test an odor when directed to do so by your teacher, and use a wafting motion to direct the vapor toward your nose.

 Sharp Object Scissors, scalpels, knives, needles, pins, and tacks can cut your skin. Always direct a sharp edge or point away from yourself and others.

 Animal Safety Treat live or preserved animals or animal parts with care to avoid harming the animals or yourself. Wash your hands when you are finished with the activity.

 Plant Safety Handle plants only as directed by your teacher. If you are allergic to certain plants, tell your teacher; do not do an activity involving those plants. Avoid touching harmful plants such as poison ivy. Wash your hands when you are finished with the activity.

 Electric Shock To avoid electric shock, never use electrical equipment around water, or when the equipment is wet or your hands are wet. Be sure cords are untangled and cannot trip anyone. Unplug equipment not in use.

 Physical Safety When an experiment involves physical activity, avoid injuring yourself or others. Alert your teacher if there is any reason you should not participate.

 Disposal Dispose of chemicals and other laboratory materials safely. Follow the instructions from your teacher.

 Hand Washing Wash your hands thoroughly when finished with the activity. Use soap and warm water. Rinse well.

 General Safety Awareness When this symbol appears, follow the instructions provided. When you are asked to develop your own procedure in a lab, have your teacher approve your plan before you go further.

Science Safety Rules

General Precautions

Follow all instructions. Never perform activities without the approval and supervision of your teacher. Do not engage in horseplay. Never eat or drink in the laboratory. Keep work areas clean and uncluttered.

Dress Code

Wear safety goggles whenever you work with chemicals, glassware, heat sources such as burners, or any substance that might get into your eyes. If you wear contact lenses, notify your teacher.

Wear a lab apron or coat whenever you work with corrosive chemicals or substances that can stain. Wear disposable plastic gloves when working with organisms and harmful chemicals. Tie back long hair. Remove or tie back any article of clothing or jewelry that can hang down and touch chemicals, flames, or equipment. Roll up long sleeves. Never wear open shoes or sandals.

First Aid

Report all accidents, injuries, or fires to your teacher, no matter how minor. Be aware of the location of the first-aid kit, emergency equipment such as the fire extinguisher and fire blanket, and the nearest telephone. Know whom to contact in an emergency.

Heating and Fire Safety

Keep all combustible materials away from flames. When heating a substance in a test tube, make sure that the mouth of the tube is not pointed at you or anyone else. Never heat a liquid in a closed container. Use an oven mitt to pick up a container that has been heated.

Using Chemicals Safely

Never put your face near the mouth of a container that holds chemicals. Never touch, taste, or smell a chemical unless your teacher tells you to.

Use only those chemicals needed in the activity. Keep all containers closed when chemicals are not being used. Pour all chemicals over the sink or a container, not over your work surface. Dispose of excess chemicals as instructed by your teacher.

Be extra careful when working with acids or bases. When mixing an acid and water, always pour the water into the container first and then add the acid to the water. Never pour water into an acid. Wash chemical spills and splashes immediately with plenty of water.

Using Glassware Safely

If glassware is broken or chipped, notify your teacher immediately. Never handle broken or chipped glass with your bare hands.

Never force glass tubing or thermometers into a rubber stopper or rubber tubing. Have your teacher insert the glass tubing or thermometer if required for an activity.

Using Sharp Instruments

Handle sharp instruments with extreme care. Never cut material toward you; cut away from you.

Animal and Plant Safety

Never perform experiments that cause pain, discomfort, or harm to animals. Only handle animals if absolutely necessary. If you know that you are allergic to certain plants, molds, or animals, tell your teacher before doing an activity in which these are used. Wash your hands thoroughly after any activity involving animals, animal parts, plants, plant parts, or soil.

During field work, wear long pants, long sleeves, socks, and closed shoes. Avoid poisonous plants and fungi as well as plants with thorns.

End-of-Experiment Rules

Unplug all electrical equipment. Clean up your work area. Dispose of waste materials as instructed by your teacher. Wash your hands after every experiment.

Use these star charts to locate bright stars and major constellations in the night sky at different times of year. Choose the appropriate star chart for the current season.

Autumn Sky

This chart works best at the following dates and times: September 1 at 10:00 P.M., October 1 at 8:00 P.M., or November 1 at 6:00 P.M. Look for the constellations Ursa Minor (the Little Dipper) and Cassiopeia in the northern sky, and for the star Deneb, which is nearly overhead in autumn.

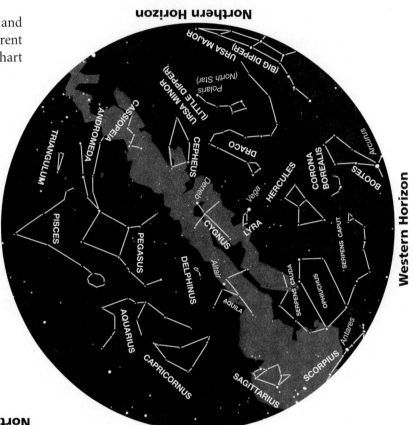

Northern Horizon

Eastern Horizon

Western Horizon

Southern Horizon

Winter Sky

This chart works best at the following dates and times: December 1 at 10:00 P.M., January 1 at 8:00 P.M., or February 1 at 6:00 P.M. Look for the constellations Orion and Gemini, the bright star Sirius, and the Pleiades, a star cluster, in the winter sky.

Northern Horizon

Eastern Horizon

Western Horizon

Southern Horizon

Using a flashlight and a compass, hold the appropriate chart and turn it so that the direction you are facing is at the bottom of the chart. These star charts work best at 34° north latitude, but can be used at other central latitudes.

Spring Sky

This chart works best at the following dates and times: March 1 at 10:00 P.M., March 15 at 9:00 P.M., or April 1 at 8:00 P.M. Look for the constellations Ursa Major (which contains the Big Dipper), Bootes, and Leo in the spring sky. The bright stars Arcturus and Spica can be seen in the east.

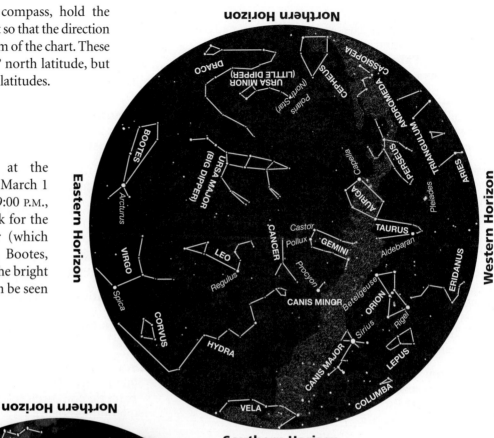

Summer Sky

This chart works best at the following dates and times: May 15 at 11:00 P.M., June 1 at 10:00 P.M., or June 15 at 9:00 P.M. Look for the bright star Arcturus in the constellation Bootes overhead in early summer. Towards the east look for the bright stars Vega, Altair, and Deneb, which form a triangle.

English and Spanish Glossary

A

absolute brightness The brightness a star would have if it were at a standard distance from Earth. (p. 129)
magnitud absoluta Brillo que tendría una estrella si estuviera a una distancia estándar de la Tierra.

apparent brightness The brightness of a star as seen from Earth. (p. 129)
magnitud aparente Brillo de una estrella visto desde la Tierra.

asteroid belt The region of the solar system between the orbits of Mars and Jupiter, where many asteroids are found. (p. 106)
cinturón de asteroides Región del sistema solar entre las órbitas de Marte y Júpiter, donde se encuentran muchos asteroides.

asteroids Rocky objects revolving around the sun that are too small and numerous to be considered planets. (p. 106)
asteroides Objetos rocosos que se mueven alrededor del Sol y que son demasiado pequeños y numerosos como para ser considerados planetas.

astronomy The study of the moon, stars, and other objects in space. (p. 6)
astronomía Estudio de la luna, las estrellas y otros objetos del espacio.

axis An imaginary line that passes through Earth's center and the North and South poles, about which Earth rotates. (p. 7)
eje Línea imaginaria que pasa a través del centro de la Tierra, por los polos Norte y Sur, sobre el cual gira la Tierra.

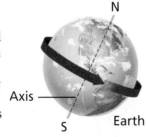

B

big bang The initial explosion that resulted in the formation and expansion of the universe. (p. 148)
big bang Explosión inicial que dio como resultado la formación y expansión del universo.

binary star A star system with two stars. (p. 142)
estrella binaria Sistema de estrellas con dos estrellas.

black hole An object whose gravity is so strong that nothing, not even light, can escape. (p. 140)
agujero negro Objeto cuya gravedad es tan fuerte que nada, ni siquiera la luz, puede escapar.

C

calendar A system of organizing time that defines the beginning, length, and divisions of a year. (p. 8)
calendario Sistema de organización del tiempo que define el principio, la duración y las divisiones de un año.

chromosphere The middle layer of the sun's atmosphere. (p. 80)
cromosfera Capa central en la atmósfera del Sol.

coma The fuzzy outer layer of a comet. (p. 105)
coma Capa exterior y difusa de un cometa.

comet A loose collection of ice, dust, and small rocky particles, typically with a long, narrow orbit. (p. 105)
cometa Conjunto no compacto de hielo, polvo y partículas rocosas pequeñas, que normalmente tiene una órbita larga y estrecha.

constellation An imaginary pattern of stars in the sky. (p. 126)
constelación Patrón imaginario de estrellas en el cielo.

convection zone The outermost layer of the sun's interior. (p. 79)
zona de convección Capa más superficial del interior del Sol.

convex lens A piece of transparent glass curved so that the middle is thicker than the edges. (p. 120)
lente convexa Trozo de cristal transparente curvado de tal manera que el centro es más grueso que los extremos.

core The central region of the sun, where nuclear fusion takes place. (p. 79)
núcleo Región central del Sol, donde ocurre la fusión nuclear.

corona The outer layer of the sun's atmosphere. (p. 80)
corona Capa externa de la atmósfera del Sol.

cosmic background radiation The electromagnetic radiation left over from the big bang. (p. 150)
radiación cósmica de fondo Radiación electromagnética que quedó del big bang.

crater A large round pit caused by the impact of a meteoroid. (p. 31)
cráter Gran cuenca redonda causada por el impacto de un meteoroide.

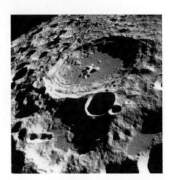

D

dark energy A mysterious force that appears to be causing the expansion of the universe to accelerate. **energía negra** Misteriosa fuerza que parece acelerar la expansión del universo. (p. 152)

dark matter Matter that does not give off electromagnetic radiation but is quite abundant in the universe. (p. 152) **materia negra** Materia que no despide radiación electromagnética, pero que es muy abundante en el universo.

E

eclipse The partial or total blocking of one object in space by another. (p. 23) **eclipse** Bloqueo parcial o total de un objeto en el espacio por otro.

eclipsing binary A binary star system in which one star periodically blocks the light from the other. (p. 142) **eclipse binario** Sistema de estrella binaria en el que una estrella bloquea periódicamente la luz de la otra.

electromagnetic radiation Energy that travels through space in the form of waves. (p. 119) **radiación electromagnética** Energía que viaja a través del espacio en forma de ondas.

ellipse An oval shape, which may be elongated or nearly circular; the shape of the planets' orbits. (p. 75) **elipse** Figura ovalada, alargada o casi circular; la forma de las órbitas de los planetas.

elliptical galaxy A galaxy shaped like a round or flattened ball, generally containing only old stars. (p. 144) **galaxia elíptica** Galaxia con forma de pelota aplastada, que generalmente está formada sólo de estrellas viejas.

equinox The two days of the year on which neither hemisphere is tilted toward or away from the sun. (p. 13) **equinoccio** Los dos días del año en los que ningún hemisferio está inclinado hacia el Sol ni más lejos de él.

escape velocity The velocity an object must reach to fly beyond a planet's or moon's gravitational pull. (p. 43) **velocidad de escape** Velocidad que debe alcanzar un objeto para salir del campo de gravedad de un planeta o luna.

extraterrestrial life Life that exists other than that on Earth. (p. 108) **vida extraterrestre** Vida que existe fuera de la Tierra.

F

force A push or a pull exerted on an object. (p. 16) **fuerza** Empuje o atracción ejercida sobre un objeto.

G

galaxy A huge group of single stars, star systems, star clusters, dust, and gas bound together by gravity. **galaxia** Enorme grupo de estrellas individuales, sistemas de estrellas, cúmulos de estrellas, polvo y gas unidos por la gravedad. (p. 144)

gas giants The name often given to the first four outer planets: Jupiter, Saturn, Uranus, and Neptune. (p. 95) **gigantes gaseosos** Nombre que normalmente se da a los cuatro primeros planetas exteriores: Júpiter, Saturno, Urano y Neptuno.

geocentric A model of the universe in which Earth is at the center of the revolving planets and stars. (p. 73) **geocéntrico** Modelo del universo en el que la Tierra es el centro de los planetas y estrellas que giran alrededor de ella.

geostationary orbit An orbit in which a satellite orbits Earth at the same rate as Earth rotates and thus stays over the same place all the time. (p. 62) **órbita geoestacionario** Órbita en la que un satélite orbita la Tierra a la misma velocidad que rota la Tierra y que, por lo tanto, permanece sobre ese lugar permanentemente.

globular cluster A large, round, densely-packed grouping of older stars. (p. 143) **cúmulo globular** Conjunto grande y redondo de estrellas viejas densamente apretadas.

gravity The attractive force between objects; its strength depends on their masses and the distance between them. (p. 16) **gravedad** Fuerza de atracción entre los objetos; su fuerza depende de sus masas y de la distancia que les separa.

greenhouse effect The trapping of heat by a planet's atmosphere. (p. 88) **efecto invernadero** Acumulación de calor en la atmósfera de un planeta.

English and Spanish Glossary

heliocentric A model of the solar system in which Earth and the other planets revolve around the sun. (p. 74)
heliocéntrico Modelo del sistema solar en el que la Tierra y otros planetas giran alrededor del Sol.

Hertzsprung-Russell diagram A graph relating the surface temperatures and absolute brightnesses of stars. (p. 132)
diagrama Hertzsprung-Russel Gráfica que muestra la relación entre las temperaturas en la superficie de las estrellas y su magnitud absoluta.

Hubble's law The observation that the farther away a galaxy is, the faster it is moving away. (p. 149)
ley de Hubble Observación que enuncia que mientras más lejos de nosotros se encuentra una galaxia, más rápido se está alejando.

inertia The tendency of an object to resist a change in motion. (p. 18)
inercia Tendencia de un objeto a resistir un cambio en su movimiento.

irregular galaxy A galaxy that does not have a regular shape. (p. 144)
galaxia irregular Galaxia que no tiene una forma regular.

Kuiper belt A doughnut-shaped region that stretches from around Pluto's orbit to about 100 times Earth's distance from the sun. (p. 105)
cinturón de Kuiper Región en forma de disco que se extiende desde la órbita de Plutón hasta alrededor de 100 veces la distancia de la Tierra al Sol.

law of universal gravitation The scientific law that states that every object in the universe attracts every other object. (p. 16)
ley de la gravitación universal Ley científica que establece que todos los objetos del universo se atraen entre ellos.

light-year The distance that light travels in one year, about 9.5 million million kilometers. (p. 130)
año luz Distancia a la que viaja la luz en un año; alrededor de 9.5 millones de millones de kilómetros.

lunar eclipse The blocking of sunlight to the moon that occurs when Earth is directly between the sun and the moon. (p. 25)
eclipse lunar Bloqueo de la luz solar sobre la Luna llena que ocurre cuando la Tierra se interpone entre el Sol y la Luna.

main sequence A diagonal area on an H-R diagram that includes more than 90 percent of all stars.
secuencia principal Área diagonal en un diagrama de H-R que incluye más del 90 por ciento de todas las estrellas. (p. 133)

maria Dark, flat areas on the moon's surface formed from huge ancient lava flows. (p. 31)
maria Áreas oscuras y llanas en la superficie de la Luna formadas por enormes flujos de lava antiguos.

mass The amount of matter in an object. (p. 17)
masa Cantidad de materia que hay en un objeto.

meteor A streak of light in the sky produced by the burning of a meteoroid in Earth's atmosphere. (p. 107)
meteoro Rayo de luz en el cielo producido por el incendio de un meteoroide en la atmósfera de la Tierra.

meteorite A meteoroid that passes through the atmosphere and hits Earth's surface. (p. 107)
meteorito Meteoroide que pasa por la atmósfera y golpea la superficie de la Tierra.

meteoroid A chunk of rock or dust in space. (pp. 31, 107)
meteoroide Pedazo de roca o polvo en el espacio.

microgravity The condition of experiencing weightlessness in orbit. (p. 59)
microgravedad Condición de experimentar falta de peso en órbita.

neap tide The tide with the least difference between consecutive low and high tides. (p. 27)
marea muerta Marea con la mínima diferencia entre marea alta y marea baja consecutivas.

nebula A large cloud of gas and dust in space, spread out in an immense volume. (p. 137)
nebulosa Gran nube de gas y polvo en el espacio, expandida en un volumen inmenso.

neutron star The small, dense remains of a high-mass star after a supernova. (p. 139)
estrella de neutrones Restos pequeños y densos de una estrella de gran masa después de una supernova.

Newton's first law of motion The scientific law that states that an object at rest will stay at rest and an object in motion will stay in motion with a constant speed and direction unless acted on by a force. (p. 18)
primera ley de Newton del movimiento Ley científica que establece que un objeto en reposo se mantendrá en reposo y un objeto en movimiento se mantendrá en movimiento con una velocidad y dirección constante a menos que se ejerza una fuerza sobre él.

nuclear fusion The process by which hydrogen atoms join together in the sun's core to form helium. (p. 79)
fusión nuclear Proceso por el cual los átomos de hidrógeno se unen en el núcleo del Sol para formar helio.

nucleus The solid inner core of a comet. (p. 105)
núcleo Centro interno sólido de un cometa.

observatory A building that contains one or more telescopes. (p. 122)
observatorio Edificio que contiene uno o más telescopios.

Oort cloud A spherical region of comets that surrounds the solar system. (p. 105)
nube de Oort Región esférica de cometas que rodea el sistema solar.

open cluster A star cluster that has a loose, disorganized appearance and contains no more than a few thousand stars. (p. 143)
cúmulo abierto Cúmulo de estrellas que tiene una apariencia no compacta y desorganizada, y que no contiene más de unos pocos miles de estrellas.

optical telescope A telescope that uses lenses or mirrors to collect and focus visible light. (p. 120)
telescopio óptico Telescopio que usa lentes o espejos para captar y enfocar la luz visible.

orbit The path of an object as it revolves around another object in space. (p. 7)
órbita Trayectoria de un objeto a medida que gira alrededor de otro en el espacio.

orbital velocity The velocity a rocket must achieve to establish an orbit around a body in space. (p. 42)
velocidad orbital Velocidad que un cohete debe alcanzar para establecer una órbita alrededor de un cuerpo en el espacio.

parallax The apparent change in position of an object when seen from different places. (p. 130)
paralaje Cambio aparente en la posición de un objeto cuando es visto desde diferentes lugares.

penumbra The part of a shadow surrounding the darkest part. (p. 24)
penumbra Parte de una sombra que rodea la parte más oscura.

phase One of the different apparent shapes of the moon as seen from Earth. (p. 21)
fase Una de las diferentes formas aparentes de la Luna según se ve desde la Tierra.

photosphere The inner layer of the sun's atmosphere that gives off its visible light (p. 80)
fotosfera Capa más interna de la atmósfera del Sol que provoca la luz que vemos; superficie del Sol.

planetesimal One of the small asteroid-like bodies that formed the building blocks of the planets. (p. 151)
planetésimo Uno de los cuerpos pequeños parecidos a asteroides que dieron origen a los planetas.

prominence A huge, reddish loop of gas that protrudes from the sun's surface, linking parts of sunspot regions. (p. 82)
protuberencia solar Enorme arco rojizo de gas que sobresale de la superficie del Sol, que une partes de las regiones de las manchas solares.

protostar A contracting cloud of gas and dust with enough mass to form a star. (p. 137)
protoestrella Nube de gas y polvo que se contrae, con suficiente masa como para formar una estrella.

pulsar A rapidly spinning neutron star that produces radio waves. (p. 139)
púlsar Estrella de neutrones que gira rápidamente y produce ondas de radio.

English and Spanish Glossary

Q

quasar An enormously bright, distant galaxy with a giant black hole at its center. (p. 144)
quásar Galaxia extraordinariamente luminosa y distante con un agujero negro gigante en el centro.

R

radiation zone A region of very tightly packed gas in the sun's interior where energy is transferred mainly in the form of light. (p. 79)
zona radiactiva Región de gases estrechamente comprimidos en el interior del Sol en donde se transfiere la energía principalmente en forma de luz.

radio telescope A device used to detect radio waves from objects in space. (p. 121)
radiotelescopio Aparato usado para detectar ondas de radio de los objetos en el espacio.

reflecting telescope A telescope that uses a curved mirror to collect and focus light. (p. 121)
telescopio reflector Telescopio que usa un espejo curvado para captar y enfocar la luz.

refracting telescope A telescope that uses convex lenses to gather and focus light. (p. 120)
telescopio refractor Telescopio que usa lentes convexas para captar y enfocar la luz.

remote sensing The collection of information about Earth and other objects in space using satellites or probes. (p. 62)
percepción remota Recolección de información sobre la Tierra y otros objetos en el espacio usando satélites o sondas.

revolution The movement of an object around another object. (p. 7)
revolución Movimiento de un objeto alrededor de otro.

ring A thin disk of small ice and rock particles surrounding a planet. (p. 95)
anillo Disco fino de pequeñas partículas de hielo y roca que rodea un planeta.

rocket A device that expels gas in one direction to move in the opposite direction. (p. 41)
cohete Aparato que expulsa gas en una dirección para moverse en la dirección opuesta.

rotation The spinning motion of a planet on its axis. (p. 7)
rotación Movimiento giratorio de un planeta sobre su eje.

rover A small robotic space probe that can move about the surface of a planet or moon. (p. 56)
róver Pequeña sonda espacial robótica que puede moverse sobre la superficie de un planeta o sobre la Luna.

S

satellite An object that revolves around another object in space. (p. 49)
satélite Objeto que gira alrededor de otro objeto en el espacio.

scientific notation A mathematical method of writing numbers using powers of ten. (p. 146)
notación científica Método matemático de escritura de números que usa la potencia de diez.

solar eclipse The blocking of sunlight to Earth that occurs when the moon is directly between the sun and Earth. (p. 24)
eclipse solar Bloqueo de la luz solar en su camino a la Tierra que ocurre cuando la Luna se interpone entre el Sol y la Tierra.

solar flare An eruption of gas from the sun's surface that occurs when the loops in sunspot regions suddenly connect. (p. 82)
fulguración solar Erupción de gas desde la superficie del Sol que ocurre cuando los arcos en las regiones de las manchas solares se unen repentinamente.

solar nebula A large cloud of gas and dust, such as the one that formed our solar system. (p. 151)
nebulosa solar Gran nube de gas y polvo como de la que formó nuestro sistema solar.

solar wind A stream of electrically charged particles that emanate from the sun's corona. (p. 80)
viento solar Flujo de partículas cargadas eléctricamente que emanan de la corona del Sol.

solstice The two days of the year on which the sun reaches its greatest distance north or south of the equator. (p. 12)
solsticio Los dos días del año en que el Sol está a mayor distancia hacia el norte o hacia el sur del ecuador.

space probe A spacecraft that has various scientific instruments that can collect data, including visual images, but has no human crew. (p. 56)
sonda espacial Nave espacial que tiene varios instrumentos científicos que pueden reunir datos, incluyendo imágenes, pero que no lleva tripulación.

space shuttle A spacecraft that can carry a crew into space, return to Earth, and then be reused for the same purpose. (p. 54)
transbordador espacial Nave espacial que puede llevar a una tripulación al espacio, volver a la Tierra, y luego volver a ser usada para el mismo propósito.

space spinoff An item that has uses on Earth but was originally developed for use in space. (p. 60)
derivación espacial Objeto que se puede usar en la Tierra, pero que originalmente se construyó para ser usado en el espacio.

space station A large artificial satellite on which people can live and work for long periods. (p. 55)
estación espacial Enorme satélite artificial en el que la gente puede vivir y trabajar durante largos períodos.

spectrograph An instrument that separates light into colors and makes an image of the resulting spectrum. (p. 128)
espectrógrafo Instrumento que separa la luz en colores y crea una imagen del espectro resultante.

spectrum The range of wavelengths of electromagnetic waves. (p. 119)
espectro Gama de longitudes de ondas electromagnéticas.

spiral galaxy A galaxy with a bulge in the middle and arms that spiral outward in a pinwheel pattern. (p. 144)
galaxia espiral Galaxia con una protuberancia en el centro y brazos que giran en espiral hacia el exterior, como un remolino.

spring tide The tide with the greatest difference between consecutive low and high tides. (p. 27)
marea viva Marea con la mayor diferencia entre mareas alta y baja consecutivas.

sunspot A dark area of gas on the sun's surface that is cooler than surrounding gases. (p. 80)
mancha solar Área oscura de gas en la superficie del Sol, que está más fría que los gases que la rodean.

supernova The brilliant explosion of a dying supergiant star. (p. 139)
supernova Explosión brillante de una estrella supergigante en extinción.

telescope A device built to observe distant objects by making them appear closer. (pp. 30, 118)
telescopio Aparato construido para observar objetos distantes que hace que aparezcan más cercanos.

terrestrial planets The name often given to the four inner planets: Mercury, Venus, Earth, and Mars. (p. 84)
planetas telúricos Nombre dado normalmente a los cuatro planetas interiores: Mercurio, Venus, Tierra y Marte.

thrust The reaction force that propels a rocket forward. (p. 42)
empuje Fuerza de reacción que propulsa un cohete hacia delante.

tide The periodic rise and fall of the level of water in the ocean. (p. 26)
marea La subida y bajada periódica del nivel de agua en el océano.

umbra The darkest part of a shadow. (p. 24)
umbra La parte más oscura de una sombra.

universe All of space and everything in it. (p. 146)
universo Todo el espacio y todo lo que hay en él.

vacuum A place that is empty of all matter. (p. 59)
vacío Lugar en donde no existe materia.

velocity Speed in a given direction. (p. 42)
velocidad Rapidez en una dirección dada.

visible light Electromagnetic radiation that can be seen with the unaided eye. (p. 119)
luz visible Radiación electromagnética que se puede ver a simple vista.

wavelength The distance between the crest of one wave and the crest of the next wave. (p. 119)
longitud de onda Distancia entre la cresta de una onda y la cresta de la siguiente onda.

weight The force of gravity on an object. (p. 17)
peso Fuerza de la gravedad que actúa sobre un objeto.

white dwarf The blue-white hot core of a star that is left behind after its outer layers have expanded and drifted out into space. (p. 138)
enana blanca Núcleo caliente azul blanquecino de una estrella, que queda después de que sus capas externas se han expandido y dispersado por el espacio.

Index

Index

Acknowledgments

Grateful acknowledgment is made to the following for copyrighted material:

Activity on page 42 is from *Exploring Planets in the Classroom* by Hawaii Space Grant Consortium. Based on a concept developed by Dale Olive.

Quote on page 53 by Janet Kavandi is from *Space Shuttle: The First 20 Years*, edited by Tony Reichhardt for Air & Space/Smithsonian Magazine. Published in the United States by DK Publishing, Inc.

Excerpt on page 159 is from *The Mystery of Mars* by Sally Ride and Tam O'Shaughnessy. Copyright © 1999 by Sally K. Ride and Tam E. O'Shaughnessy. Reprinted by permission of Crown Publishers, an imprint of Random House Children's Books, a division of Random House, Inc.

Note: Every effort has been made to locate the copyright owner of material reproduced in this component. Omissions brought to our attention will be corrected in subsequent editions.

Staff Credits

Diane Alimena, Scott Andrews, Jennifer Angel, Michele Angelucci, Laura Baselice, Carolyn Belanger, Barbara A. Bertell, Suzanne Biron, Peggy Bliss, Stephanie Bradley, James Brady, Anne M. Bray, Sarah M. Carroll, Kerry Cashman, Jonathan Cheney, Joshua D. Clapper, Lisa J. Clark, Bob Craton, Patricia Cully, Patricia M. Dambry, Kathy Dempsey, Leanne Esterly, Emily Ellen, Thomas Ferreira, Jonathan Fisher, Patricia Fromkin, Paul Gagnon, Kathy Gavilanes, Holly Gordon, Robert Graham, Ellen Granter, Diane Grossman, Barbara Hollingdale, Linda Johnson, Anne Jones, John Judge, Kevin Keane, Kelly Kelliher, Toby Klang, Sue Langan, Russ Lappa, Carolyn Lock, Rebecca Loveys, Constance J. McCarty, Carolyn B. McGuire, Ranida Touranont McKneally, Anne McLaughlin, Eve Melnechuk, Natania Mlawer, Janet Morris, Karyl Murray, Francine Neumann, Baljit Nijjar, Marie Opera, Jill Ort, Kim Ortell, Joan Paley, Dorothy Preston, Maureen Raymond, Laura Ross, Rashid Ross, Siri Schwartzman, Melissa Shustyk, Laurel Smith, Emily Soltanoff, Jennifer A. Teece, Elizabeth Torjussen, Amanda M. Watters, Merce Wilczek, Amy Winchester, Char Lyn Yeakley. **Additional Credits:** Tara Alamilla, Louise Gachet, Allen Gold, Andrea Golden, Terence Hegarty, Etta Jacobs, Meg Montgomery, Stephanie Rogers, Kim Schmidt, Adam Teller, Joan Tobin.

Illustration

All art developed and produced by **Morgan Cain & Associates**, unless otherwise noted. **Kerry Cashman**: 26, 69, 86–87, 89, 98–99, 101, 104, 117, 120, 146–147. **Richard McMahon**: 8, 122.

Photography

Photo Research John Judge

Cover Image top, © 2003 Jerry Lodriguss; **bottom**, Bill Brooks/Masterfile Corporation.

Page vi, SOHO/ESA and NASA; **vii,** Richard Haynes; **viii,** Richard Haynes; **x all,** SOHO/ESA and NASA; **1,** Ken O'Donoghue; **2,** Ken O'Donoghue; **3t,** SOHO/ESA and NASA; **3b,** Ken O'Donoghue

Chapter 1
Pages 4–5, Evad Damast; **5r,** Richard Haynes; **6t,** Richard Haynes; **6b,** Eric Lessing/Art Resource, NY; **7t,** Jeff Haynes/AFP/Corbis; **7b,** Paul Sutton/Duomo/Corbis; **8l,** Lawrence Migdale/Photo Researchers, Inc.; **8r,** Ancient Art & Architecture Collection, Ltd.; **9l,** Janet Wishnetsky/Corbis; **9m,** Hazel Hankin/Stock Boston; **9r,** The Granger Collection; **12l,** Paul A. Souders/Corbis; **12r,** Bill Ross/Corbis; **13l,** Tony Stewart/PhotoNewZealand.com; **13r,** Dennis Degnan/Corbis; **15,** Richard Haynes; **16–17,** Paul & Linda Marie Ambrose/Getty Images, Inc.; **20,** Richard Haynes; **21,** E. R. Degginger/Animals Animals/Earth Scenes; **22l,** John Bova/Photo Researchers, Inc.; **22m,** John Bova/Photo Researchers, Inc.; **22r,** John Bova/Photo Researchers, Inc.; **22–23background,** Gerry Ellis/Minden Pictures; **23tl,** John Bova/Photo Researchers, Inc.; **23tml,** John Bova/Photo Researchers, Inc.; **23tmr,** John Bova/Photo Researchers, Inc.; **23tr,** John Bova/Photo Researchers, Inc.; **23b,** Dorling Kindersley; **24,** Digital Vision/Getty Images, Inc.; **25,** G. Antonio Milani/SPL/Photo Researchers, Inc.; **26t,** Bill Bachman/Photo Researchers, Inc.; **26b,** Bill Bachman/Photo Researchers, Inc.; **29,** Richard Haynes; **30t,** Richard Haynes; **30b,** Jay M. Pasachoff; **31all,** NASA; **32t,** John Bova/Photo Researchers, Inc.; **32b,** NASA; **34tl,** Paul Sutton/Duomo/Corbis; **34tr,** Jeff Haynes/AFP/Corbis; **34b,** NASA.

Chapter 2
Pages 38–39, NASA; **39 inset,** NASA; **40t,** Richard Haynes; **40b,** Johnson Space Center/NASA; **41,** Jeff Hunter/Getty Images Inc.; **41inset,** U.S. Civil Air Patrol; **43,** Reto Stockli/GSFC/NASA; **46–47all,** Richard Haynes; **48,** TASS/Sovfoto; **49l,** NASA; **49r,** NASA; **50l,** NASA; **50r,** N. Armstrong/Corbis; **51,** World Perspectives/Getty Images, Inc.; **52,** John Frassanito & Associates; **53,** NASA; **54,** NASA; **55,** NASA; **56l,** JPL/NASA; **56r,** Roger Arno/NASA; **57l,** JPL/NASA; **57r,** David Ducros/Science Photo Library/Photo Researchers, Inc.; **58,** Richard Haynes; **59,** NASA; **60l,** Princess Margaret Rose Orthopaedic Hospital/Science Photo Library/Photo Researchers, Inc.; **60r,** Getty Images, Inc.; **61l,** FRANCK FIFE/AFP/Getty Images, Inc.; **61m,** Smith Sport Optics; **61r,** Pascal Rondeau/Getty Images, Inc.; **62,** NASA/GSFC/Boston University; **63,** Russ Lappa; **65,** Bob Daemmrich/Photo Edit; **66l,** World Perspectives/Getty Images, Inc.; **66r,** NASA.

Chapter 3
Pages 70–71, Detlev Van Ravenswaay/Photo Researchers, Inc.; **71inset,** Richard Haynes; **72,** David Malin/Anglo-Australian Observatory; **73,** The Granger Collection, NY; **74bl,** Science Photo Library/Photo Researchers, Inc.; **74bm,** Photo Researchers, Inc.; **74br,** James A. Sugar/Corbis; **74t,** Bettmann/Corbis; **75l,** Explorer-Keystone-France/Gamma Press USA; **75m,** The Art Archive/Royal Society; **75r,** Corbis Bettmann; **78,** Richard Haynes; **78–79,** SOHO/ESA and NASA; **80,** Dr. Fred Espenak/Science Photo Library/Photo Researchers, Inc.; **81bl,** National Solar Observatory; **81br,** AURA/STScI/NASA; **81t,** SOHO/ESA and NASA; **82,** Ron Sanford/Getty Images, Inc.; **86b,** NASA; **86t,** Julian Baum/Dorling Kindersley; **87b,** NASA; **87tl,** NASA; **87tr,** JPL/NASA; **88,** David Anderson/NASA/Photo Researchers, Inc.; **89b,** Hubble Heritage Team/NASA; **89t,** NASA; **90–91,** JPL/NASA; **91inset,** U.S. Geological Survey; **92b,** Pat Rawlings/NASA; **92–93t,** NASA; **93inset,** Pat Rawlings/NASA; **94,** NASA; **96l,** NASA/SPL/Photo Researchers, Inc.; **96r,** Martin Cropper/Dorling Kindersley; **97b,** David Seal/JPL/CalTech/NASA; **97ml,** JPL/NASA; **97mr,** Corbis; **97tl,** Reuters NewMedia Inc./Corbis; **97tr,** NASA; **98l,** NASA and The Hubble Heritage Team; **98r,** AFP/Corbis; **99b,** Kenneth Seidelmann, U.S. Naval Observatory/NASA; **99t,** Dorling Kindersley/Jet Propulsion Lab; **100l,** Julian Baum/Dorling Kindersley; **100r,** NASA; **101l,** Dorling Kindersley; **101r,** Lynette Cook/Photo Researchers, Inc.; **102,** Richard Haynes; **103,** Richard Haynes; **104t,** Richard Haynes; **104-105,** Jerry Lodriguss /Photo Researchers, Inc.; **105inset,** Dorling Kindersley; **106,** NEAR Project/NLR/JHUAPL/Goddard SVS/NASA; **107,** Frank Zullo /Photo Researchers, Inc.; **108,** Ghislaine Grozaz; **109,** Douglas Faulkner/Photo Researchers, Inc.; **110l,** Calvin J. Hamilton; **110r,** NASA/SPL/Photo Researchers, Inc.; **111,** NASA/Science Photo Library/Photo Researchers, Inc.; **112,** NASA and The Hubble Heritage Team.

Chapter 4
Pages 116–117, Loke Tan; **117r,** Richard Haynes; **118t,** Richard Haynes; **118b,** Florence Museo delle Scienze/AKG London; **120all,** Andy Crawford/Dorling Kindersley; **121l,** VLA/NRAO/Smithsonian Astrophysical Observatory; **121ml,** W. M. Keck Observatory/Smithsonian Astrophysical Observatory; **121mr,** Jeff Hester and Paul Scowen/Smithsonian Astrophysical Observatory; **121r,** Marshall Space Flight Center/NASA; **122l,** Yerkes Observatory Photography; **122r,** Courtesy of the NAIC - Arecibo Observatory, a facility of the NSF; **123t,** NASA; **123bl,** David Nunuk/Science Photo Library/Photo Researchers, Inc.; **123br,** JPL/NASA; **124,** NASA; **125,** Richard Haynes; **126t,** Richard Haynes; **126b,** Dorling Kindersley; **129,** Mark Thiessen/Corbis; **133,** Luke Dodd/Science Photo Library/Photo Researchers, Inc.; **136,** Ariel Skelley/Corbis; **137,** Anglo-Australian Observatory/Royal Observatory Edinburgh; **137inset,** AURA/STScI/NASA; **141,** Frank Zullo/Photo Researchers, Inc.; **142all,** Celestial Image Co./Science Photo Library/Photo Researchers, Inc.; **143t,** David Malin/Anglo-Australian Observatory; **143b,** Celestial Image Co./Science Photo Library/Photo Researchers, Inc.; **144t,** David Malin/Anglo-Australian Observatory; **144m,** David Malin/Anglo-Australian Observatory; **144b,** Royal Observatory, Edinburgh/AATB/Science Photo Library/Photo Researchers, Inc.; **146l,** Dorling Kindersley; **146m,** NASA; **146r,** SOHO/ESA and NASA; **147l,** R. Corradi (Isaac Newton Group) and D. R. Gonçalves (Instituto de Astrofísica de Canarias); **147m,** Bill & Sally Fletcher/Tom Stack & Associates, Inc.; **147r,** Celestial Image Co./Science Photo Library/Photo Researchers, Inc.; **148,** NASA; **152,** American Institute of Physics; **153,** Jean-Paul Kneib/Observatoire Midi-Pyrénées, France/Caltech/ESA/NASA; **154,** Richard Haynes; **156,** NASA.

Pages 158t, NASA; **158b,** JPL/NASA; **159b,** JPL/NASA; **159t,** NASA; **160,** JPL/NASA; **161,** NASA; **162t,** Pat Rawlings/NASA; **162–163b,** NASA/JPL/Cornell; **163t,** Pat Rawlings/NASA; **164,** Tony Freeman/PhotoEdit; **165t,** Russ Lappa; **165m,** Richard Haynes; **165b,** Russ Lappa; **166,** Richard Haynes; **168,** Richard Haynes; **170,** Morton Beebe/Corbis; **171,** Richard Haynes; **173t,** Dorling Kinderlsey; **173b,** Richard Haynes; **175,** Image Shop/Phototake; **178,** Richard Haynes; **185,** Richard Haynes; **188,** NASA; **189,** Reto Stockli/GSFC/NASA; **190t,** G.Antonio Milani/SPL/Photo Researchers, Inc.; **190b,** Royal Observatory, Edinburgh/AATB/Science Photo Library/Photo Researchers, Inc.; **192,** NASA; **193,** Hubble Heritage Team/NASA.